Teaching Oral Communication in Elementary Schools

Teaching Oral Communication in Elementary Schools

Mary Louise Willbrand
Richard D. Rieke

University of Utah

Macmillan Publishing Co., Inc.
New York
Collier Macmillan Publishers
London

Macmillan Publishing Co., Inc.
866 Third Avenue, New York, New York 10022

Collier Macmillan Canada, Inc.

Library of Congress Cataloging in Publication Data

Willbrand, Mary Louise.
    Teaching oral communication in elementary schools.

    Bibliography: p.
    Includes index.
    1. Oral communication—Study and teaching (Elementary)
I. Rieke, Richard D.   II. Title.
LB1572.W47   1983   372.6   82-17220
ISBN 0-02-427750-9

Printing: 1 2 3 4 5 6 7 8   Year: 3 4 5 6 7 8 9 0

Acknowledgments

Permission to reprint "Standards for Effective Oral Communication Programs" granted by the *ASHA* journal and the
American Speech-Language-Hearing Association.

Permission to publish photos granted by Rowland Hall-
St Mark's School, Salt Lake City, Utah

Photos by Craig L. Denton

ISBN   0-02-427750-9

Preface

Oral communication has recently been identified as one of the basic skills that all school children should be taught. Such specification means that oral communication can no longer be a happenstance—an untaught, unplanned but supposedly acquired skill. Direct instruction of oral communication skills in elementary schools has thus far been an enigma. In response to the problem we have written this book to prepare coordinators and teachers in elementary schools to teach the full range of communication behaviors. In contrast to available materials on communication, this book provides a practical guide for immediate implementation of instruction for elementary children. Specifically, this book is designed for courses in university and college training programs as well as preservice and in-service development programs for teachers in the field.

In 1978 Congress passed Public Law 95-561, which confirmed with the force of law the co-equal status of oral communication as a basic skill along with reading, writing, and mathematics. This law specified the improvement of instruction and the development of comprehensive, systematic plans to enable all children to master these basic skills. In this the American Speech-Language-Hearing Association and the Speech Communication Association saw a challenge. They prepared a joint statement on standards for effective programs that reflected the speech-language pathologists' understanding of young children's normal speech and language development and ways of learning as well as the speech communication scholars' knowledge of communication theory. They further acknowledged that preparation of teacher training programs and teaching materials must involve the combined work of the two professions.

As colleagues, we saw that between the two of us we combined the professional backgrounds needed as well as experience in public school teaching and consulting. We decided to prepare a book that would be complete in its coverage of oral communication skills but at the same time practical in providing help to the elementary teacher in the classroom. We determined to meet the following criteria:

1. The book includes all the elements necessary for the working elementary teacher planning to help children learn oral communication: theory, competencies, and detailed exercises. The teacher, of course, will creatively expand these exercises.
2. The book is suitable to use in teaching all children in the elementary school, including "normal," gifted, culturally different, those in resource rooms, or the mentally retarded.

3. The book's approach to the learning of oral communication is such that children will find it fun and exciting and not a source of apprehension or pressure.
4. The book recognizes the importance of the individual student growing and learning in an individual way.
5. The book shows how teachers can integrate the teaching of oral communication with previously established curriculum rather than by the addition of another course. However, it also demonstrates that oral communication must be taught consciously; we know that skills in the various communication situations will not just happen because children know how to talk.
6. The book provides learning goals and objectives at three levels of instruction: beginning, intermediate, and advanced. No grade level designations are given because teachers must be free to adjust the level of instruction to the abilities of their students.
7. The book is structured to provide sequenced instruction of the skills by proceeding through the chapters in order. Skills learned in each chapter are required for learning in the following chapters.
8. The book is based upon exercises that have been field tested in the classroom.
9. Each chapter is written in exactly the same format, proceeding from an introduction to a discussion of concepts, including a conceptional definition, an operational definition, and a discussion of tradition including a historical background, common ways of thinking, current perspectives, and the view of this book. The theory section is followed by general exit competencies and the three levels of specific competencies are followed by exercises. The repetition of format is intended as a practical aid in the use of the book.
10. The book includes a selected bibliography listing both references mentioned in the chapters and additional readings for teacher enrichment.

Early in our work, Evelyn W. Miller of the Pennsylvania Department of Education graciously spent time with us sharing her knowledge and giving advice and materials. For this we are deeply grateful. Later, Elaine Parker, teaching in the Aurora, Illinois schools, tested sections of the book with her students and took the time to write an extensive evaluation with recommendations. We thank her for this important assistance. Toward the end of our project, our students joined with classroom teachers to test various exercises and report the results from Utah schools. We very much appreciate this help. Our colleagues at the University of Utah generously gave of their advice to help us avoid errors and omissions in communication theory. Throughout the project, Marilyn G. Stephenson of our Division of Speech-Language Pathology and Audiology was of enormous importance to us in the many problems of manuscript preparation. She helped beyond usual expectations and our thanks can scarcely communicate our gratitude.

A special appreciation and thank you is reserved for those who helped with the pictures in this book. The children in most of the pictures are from Rowland Hall - St. Mark's School in Salt Lake City. The children, the faculty, and the administration of that school were eager and appreciative supporters of our project as we taught the children and took the pictures. Their support made the picture taking possible. Three of the pictures were taken of people and places in the Salt Lake City area, including LaHacienda, Lisa Olivera delivering a speech, and the sand castle contest at the Great Salt Lake.

The photographer was Craig L. Denton, who contributed more than just clicking the shutter. Craig discussed the chapters with us at length until he understood the philosophy of each chapter. He planned and worked to communicate theory as well as actual behaviors. We think that his visual communication is a valuable asset to this book on oral communication.

Finally, we thank the children who indirectly provided data on learning communication behaviors by enthusiastically participating in our exercises. With their help we can look forward to many, many more children discovering the joy of oral communication.

MLW
RDR

Contents

1

A Philosophy for
Teaching Oral
Communication

OBJECTIVES

At the end of this chapter you should be able to

1. Define literacy so as to make oral communication an integral part.
2. Explain the trivialization of oral communication in the schools.
3. Identify the major components in children's development of speech and language.
4. Explain Public Law 95-561.
5. Identify the central elements in a concept of oral communication.
6. Demonstrate an understanding of the standards for effective oral communication programs.
7. Illustrate how the teaching of oral communication can be integrated with established curricula.
8. Identify and discuss the three steps in overcoming or preventing resistance to communication.
9. Distinguish between communication differences and disorders.

In 1981 The Carnegié Foundation for the Advancement of Teaching urged that all students ". . . from the very first years of formal schooling, learn not only to 'read and write' but also to . . . listen and speak effectively."[1] The foundation made that recommendation because of the perceived need of all citizens as a part of their general education to learn to communicate. They said, "Human beings' use of symbols separates them from all other forms of life. Language gives individuals their identities, makes transactions among people possible, and provides the connecting tissue that binds society together. . . . Language is, and always has been, the glue of our social existence, holding us together, housing us in meaning." The modalities for using language are reading, writing, listening, and speaking: the elements of communication.

The recognition of the importance of human communication is not new. It has been acknowledged for thousands of years. What is noteworthy in the Carnegie statement and others that are being made with increasing frequency is that skill in communication rests not just on traditional definitions of literacy—reading and writing—but on oral communication as well. It would be humorous if it were not so serious to hear people reject notions of literacy that include emphasis upon speaking and listening. It is reading and writing that are the new kids on the block.

---

[1] E. L. Boyer and A. Levine, *A Quest for Common Learning* (Washington, D.C.: The Carnegie Foundation for the Advancement of Teaching, 1981), pp. 36–37.

2

If all those thousands of years of human recognition of the importance of communication were expressed as a 100-meter dash, reading and writing would be little more than the last step. As far back as we can trace civilization, people recognized the importance of speech. More than 2,000 years ago classical writers had expressed systematic theories of communication totally on the basis of an oral society. The oral traditions of various societies and cultures were well established before that time and remain so today. The infatuation with reading and writing is a phenomenon of late December if our history were compressed into a single year.

Look at it another way. If all the communication activity of the typical person for a typical day—all the reading, writing, speaking, and listening—were expressed in terms of getting dressed in the morning, then reading and writing would constitute no greater proportion than that involved in zipping up a jacket. Most of us spend most of our communication day listening or talking. In fact, many people go for days at a time without zipping up their jackets all the way, but they do not go out undressed.

The point of these simple analogies is not to suggest that reading and writing are unimportant or that their place in education should be significantly reduced. Instead, our point is to help us rediscover what people have known for thousands of years: speaking and listening are fundamental to civilized communication and are at least the equals of reading and writing in terms of the attention they should receive in our schools. They have never lost their place of importance in society.

Why did schools come to define literacy as skill in reading and writing alone? It was reasonable that after thousands of years of attention to oral literacy the sudden emergence of print would put a heavy burden on educators to launch a major effort to build skills in reading and writing. That was a job that had to be done and remains so today. But such revolutions often have an unfortunate fallout. In this case it was the trivialization of oral communication. First, it was erroneously concluded that if children could learn to talk they would continue to build oral communication skills more or less on their own. It would be as foolish to conclude that once children learn the basic skills of reading and writing either at home or in the first couple of years in school they can be expected to continue growth without further formal education. This is obviously untrue of reading and writing and it is untrue of skilled oral communication as well.

A second step in the trivialization of oral communication came from the characterization of speech as mere show, bombast, or manipulation. Philosophers described speech as nothing more than the performance of stylized sounds and movements without sense, substance, or ethical constraints. Teachers of speech who adopted the elocutionary methods contributed to this conception. In their hands, it was indeed trivial.

A third element of trivialization was the pedantry of scholars. They believed that people's everyday conversation, or talking together in homes and coffee houses, or making plans in small meetings, or buying and selling, were beneath their attention. They were interested only in great literature. Speech was worthy of their attention only if it were produced during great moments of history by important people doing important things. And then they were interested only if the speech were set down on paper and could be viewed as literature alongside novels and poems. Communication became worthy of study only when it became writing.

Today, language arts textbooks in the elementary schools are only starting to reflect the recognition, which is well established at the college level, that instruction in communication must include the vital oral elements. They acknowledge that speaking and listening are important, but they try to work them in around the basic study of literature by asking students to read stories and then discuss them aloud. This is a start, but it is too little and it is misdirected. This book will present a comprehensive analysis of the teaching of oral communication skills to elementary school children and provide extensive examples of the exercises that can be used in the process.

In this chapter we will talk about the development of oral communication in children and explain our concept of communication, which will demonstrate its importance as a basic skill. We will further present standards for effective programs in teaching oral communication skills, show how the program can be integrated with the established curriculum, explain the phenomenon of resistance to communication, notice differences in communication among various children, present an analysis for the proper referral of children with communication disorders, and explain the uses of this book.

DEVELOPMENT OF ORAL COMMUNICATION

Throughout the centuries little interest was shown in how children talk. Perhaps the axiom "Children should be seen and not heard" explains the lack of attention to children's talk. It is easy to speculate that parents or caretakers have always been thrilled with a child's first words. But somehow as soon as a child starts talking the excitement quickly fades. The evidence is clear that no scholarly attention was directed toward the way children speak or toward training in speaking for children until very recent times.

In the 1920s speech pathology began to emerge as a field. It soon became apparent that if one were to treat children who had problems, then knowledge about the speech of normal children had to be sought out. Early studies concentrated on the emergence of human sounds from birth to one year through the birth cry, babbling, and cooing. Then investigators turned to speech sound production. It was found that children's articulatory skills improve with age and that they use certain speech sounds appropriately with a predictable sequence specified for acquisition from three years to seven or eight years of age. By the time a child was between seven and eight years old he could be expected to use all the sounds of a language appropriately. During this same time fluency and voice production of children was investigated. It became apparent that children are normally quite disfluent when they talk until about six years, and that amount of disfluency peaked at four years. Some children (notably those with cleft palates) had hypernasality problems, so normal nasality and voice production were investigated.

In 1957, a linguist, N. Chomsky, wrote a book that revolutionized the field of theoretical linguistics and influenced the study of language development in children.[2] He proposed that language is composed of a finite set of rules that generate the infinite number of sentences of a language. This gave researchers a useful tool (rules) to use to study children's language development. Chomsky revised his initial theory, and other linguists proposed changes in his theory as well as new and different theories. The new theories were also rule-based, although different rules were used. Psycholinguists, those researchers devoted to the study of children's language development, emerged from the areas of speech/language pathology, linguistics, psychology, and sociology.

Children's language is now viewed as a system of rules restricted to child language. In other words, child language is not just aborted adult language. Child language has its own set of rules, and children develop language in stages until they ultimately use adult rules. This study of child language began with syntactic rules, then phonological rules, and some descriptions of semantic rules. Although studies continue in children's language development and many years of continued research are needed before all aspects of language acquisition can be specified, it is now evident that language acquisition continues to ten years and beyond.

In the last few years psycholinguists have begun researching pragmatic development in children. That is language in social situations. This refers to social in the broadest sense, meaning in communication. Finally, we are beginning a study of linguistic and communicative strategies during communication. It is interesting to observe that the study of children's communication began by parsimonious division of various elements and has finally arrived at the encompassing act of communication. This separation of elements has parallels in the science field. E. P. Odum[3] commented that scientists could investigate hydrogen and oxygen as separate elements, but until water itself was studied, water would not be understood.

The comparison to communication is obvious. A past president of the Ameri-

---

[2] N. Chomsky, *Snytactic Structures* (The Netherlands: Mouton and Co., 1957).

[3] E. P. Odum, *Ecology: The Link Between the Natural and the Social Sciences* (New York: Holt, Rinehart and Winston, 1975).

can Speech-Language-Hearing Association, N. S. Rees, in her presidential address explained the state of the art:

> The message is clear: if we are to understand human communication in its normal and disordered versions, we will have to study not only acoustic signals, distinctive features, phonemes, and morphemes; not only filtered speech, masking competing messages, and cloze procedure; not only syntax, semantics and pragmatics, not only nasality, hoarseness, and disfluency; but human communication.[4]

A few studies in children's communication development are beginning to appear. At this stage, most studies are reporting initial investigations. A recent survey of communication development studies is presented by B. S. Wood.[5]

It might be predictable that programs or plans for teaching children would follow the pattern of developmental studies, and that is just what has happened. Programs to teach skills and to remediate problems were developed for articulation, for fluency, and for voice. Mechanical aids and programs for the hearing impaired were developed. Programs for language, primarily in syntax, were put into use. And now we see the need for teaching children communication skills.

CONCEPTS OF ORAL COMMUNICATION IN ELEMENTARY SCHOOLS

Thus far we have turned to the Carnegie Foundation for the expression of a fundamental principle that human use of symbols is central to our identity and existence, and we have examined the data on how children develop their use of symbols, which has ultimately led to the need for work in communication as a whole. Now we can move to an explanation of the focus of this book: teaching oral communication.

We have laid a foundation for the claim that oral communication is one of the basic skills society has an obligation to provide its children. We can turn to the federal government for a formal reiteration of that claim. A new Title II of the Elementary and Secondary Education Act of 1965 was passed, effective November 1, 1978 as Public Law 95-561 (20 USC 2881). The purpose is expressed in Section 201, ". . . to assist Federal, State, and local educational agencies to coordinate the utilization of all available resources for elementary and secondary education to improve instruction so that all children are able to master the basic skills of reading, mathematics, and effective communication, both written and

---

[4]N. S. Rees, "Breaking out of the Centrifuge," *Asha* (1979), **21,** 12: 994.

[5]B. S. Wood, *Children and Communication,* 2nd ed. (Englewood Cliffs, N.J.: Prentice-Hall, Inc., 1981).

oral." Undoubtedly, there is room for improvement in the teaching of mathematics, reading, and writing. But Congress' addition of speaking and listening to the traditional three R's did two significant things: (1) it acknowledged oral communication as a co-equal partner among the basic skills in a formal way that had not been done for years, and (2) it confronted educators with the tremendous problem of generating teaching materials for the elementary schools in speaking and listening where there had been no serious development of such materials for an equally long time.

In recent decades serious instruction in speech communication has been concentrated at the college level, with gradually increasing attention at the secondary level. Virtually all attention to oral communication at the elementary level and most of it in secondary schools has been performance-based activities heavily influenced by the elocutionary principles that have remained almost unchanged since the eighteenth century. Briefly, the elocutionists believed that all speech situations were governed by rules of voice, gesture, expression, melody pattern, and movement. They believed that to learn to speak one simply needed to be taught the "proper" behaviors and then practice them. The content of the speech was controlled either by having students recite poems, plays, essays, stories, and orations, or by having someone from a "content" field such as history help students prepare their debates. What oral communication one is likely to find today in the elementary schools is most likely unplanned, or if recently planned, is likely to be some version of previous secondary models. Too much of the instruction in secondary schools is oriented around contests and festivals aimed at the rehearsal of stylized patterns of speech.

It has been at the universities that theory and instruction in speech communication has moved beyond the essentially elocutionary or sophistic patterns of the past. Within this century, even within the past 50 years or so, concepts of oral communication have been based upon descriptive studies of what people *do* when they communicate rather than based upon what people *should* do in order to follow the prescriptions of ill-founded theories.

With the mandates of reason and law, teachers and administrators in the elementary schools should have dedicated themselves to providing instruction in oral communication skills. Why, then, have schools not done so? We suggest five reasons. First, some are concerned with cost. In fact, the costs are minimal since regular classroom teachers with training and initial supervision can do the instruction. Second, many people are ignorant of the law or choose to ignore it. The law, of course, will not go away because it's being ignored. At the same time, it is the teachers who care about developing the skills not because they fear the law but because they are excited about the needs of children and what skill in oral communication can do for the children. Teachers will not let the need be unmet. Third, a few schools have indeed made tentative steps toward establishing programs in oral communication but they fall short of completion because of incomplete coverage of communication or the failure or inability to set out

7

specific competencies. These limited attempts need to be recognized as tentative steps and be developed further. Fourth, some districts claim they have programs but what they are truly doing is reporting on clinical speech programs or assistance from the high school speech teachers. It must be recognized that neither of these is providing a communication skills program for elementary children. Fifth, and most pervasive, schools have not built programs in oral communication because of the lack of teacher training and suitable materials. At this time teachers are not trained and materials are unavailable. This book should remove these roadblocks. Used in the university teacher training programs, it will send graduates into the schools with the knowledge necessary to instruct students in oral communication. Used by the classroom teacher, this book provides specific competency statements and specific exercises designed to yield those competencies which can be put to use immediately.

In recent years, a number of conceptions of communication have been advanced and discussed. An outcome of this work is that no single sentence or paragraph definition of communication can be stated to which all specialists will agree. In fact, most would be uncomfortable in trying to make such a simple definition. Instead, most observers would prefer some comments on the important points of view that are currently held. That is what we shall do throughout this book.

Communication is a pervasive phenomenon worthy of study. Our scholarly interest in communication is not limited to instances of great literature or oratory. Ordinary people going about their ordinary daily business within all social situations employ communication, and they need instruction in the skills involved. No communication is so unimportant as to be beneath our consideration. The skills addressed in this book are applicable to all people in any of their communication activities.

"You're not supposed to talk nasty!"
"I didn't talk nasty."
"Did too."
"Did not."
"Well, when you said that word you made it sound nasty."
"If it's not nasty I can't make it nasty by saying it nasty."
"Can too."

There are no formulas or lists of procedures that will guide people to effective communication in any situation. We have discovered that sensitivity to the factors involved in various kinds of communication combined with experience in participating in them will help individuals respond appropriately to the many different communication needs they face daily. Accordingly, in this book we will take time to talk about the concepts and characteristics associated with various forms of communication, we will identify competencies associated with participation in communication situations, and we will provide exercises designed to generate those competencies. We will not provide lists of rules and techniques to be learned to guarantee effectiveness in every situation. They do not exist.

Communication involves human transactions. Although the word *communication* has been used in connection with electronic circuitry such as that involved in telephone systems or computers "talking" to one another; although communication has been examined in connection with the activities of other beings such as bees, dolphins, or chimpanzees; and although communication has been studied in terms of neurophysiological systems within beings, we must ultimately face the fact that human communication rests on people relating to each other.

Communication is not simply setting up a circuit. Communication is not merely making a transmission as in uttering or writing a word. Communication is not totally a function of what people say to each other. Communication is a process of people combining their beliefs, attitudes, values, perceptions, intentions, ideas, information, within an ongoing series of situations. There is no necessary beginning or end. There is no established sender and receiver. There are people relating to one another.

"Does it hurt?"
"Unhuh."
"You got tears in your eyes."
"No I don't."
"Oh, Georgie! There's blood on your knee."
"Mommy! I fell down."

Thus, communication behaviors are processual. Many variables are involved, such as past experience, self-perception, perception of others in relation to self, the context in which people come together—who they are, the time of day, the kind of weather, the clothes worn, physical appearance. Time involved in communication is continuous. There is a parable that says we cannot step into the same river twice; it's always flowing; we are always changing. It is impossible to say precisely when any communication began or ended. So, communication involves *continuous change.* Who you are, what you say, how you will respond to others are always changing, sometimes only a little and sometimes significantly. One who understands the processual nature of communication will not be surprised to extend a cheery good morning to the same person on two consecutive days and receive two remarkably different replies. If on the first day the person has just left a happy and successful class and on the second day has just been up all night with the flu, the process-sensitive communicator will understand and respond appropriately.

Communication involves the *use of symbols.* Notice that we did not say "words." Many more things than words act as symbols. A symbol is anything that people have agreed to let stand for or represent something else. If we could not symbolize, communication would be dreadfully difficult. To communicate "orange" I would have to carry one around with me. Symbols can also be gestures, facial expressions, vocal inflections, time spacing of sounds, sequences of sounds, or marks on paper. Symbols are symbols because people agree to let them be such. We work out the meaning of symbols by transactions among people, usually employing other symbols. Dictionaries and grammar books report some of the conventions of the symbolic process, but we must look to people transacting to understand symbols in use. So in this book we will discourage the drilling of students on "correct" usage because "correct" is only a report of some people's conventions. We will encourage instead a concentration upon people transacting.

The classroom teacher needs to remember that above all the sharing of a message is the main concern rather than correctness of expression. As times have changed, the trend in the study of communication is toward description rather than prescription. The importance of the message communicated over the "properness" has been explained by J. Lair:

And that's the problem with the terrible fear we bring to talking and writing. That fear screws up all the things we say. We worry about correctness. There ain't no such thing. This language is a living thing and the way you and I use it is the way she is.

Bergen Evans, the great linguist, says that we don't hold up a mouse and ask if it's a correct mouse. Same with any word and any use. When you and I are ready to use a word, it means we've heard it enough so that it's the best word to use. Granted, the English teachers won't catch up with us for fifty years, but that's their problem. By the time they adopt what you and I are saying today, we will be a long ways down the road. . . .

But because of a fear the English teachers of the country have tenderly bestowed on us, we're scared stiff of our damn language. We don't have any confidence in our ability to use the tongue. We actually use the language like masters, but we don't see that and know that and understand that. And this is a big problem in communicating with each other.[6]

An eminent speech pathologist, W. Johnson, spoke similarly in the dedication page of a book:

Listen to the child well, to what he is saying, and almost saying, and not saying at all. He has something he wants to tell you, something that has meaning for him, that is important to him. He is not just being verbally frisky.

Respect him as a speaker. Listen to him enough to hear him out. It is wonderful for him as a growing person to feel that he is being heard, that others

[6]J. Lair, *I Ain't Much, Baby—But I'm All I've Got* (New York: Doubleday & Company, Inc., 1972), pp. 66–67.

care about what he is saying. Assume he's doing the best he can and that it is more important for him to want to talk to you than to sound correct.[7]

These are some of the important concepts about communication that have emerged within the recent past. One additional word is needed. The communication scholars who have generated concepts have dealt with adults. They have not typically examined the particular needs and abilities of children. To address the demands of the present day, to bring the teaching of oral communication skills into the elementary level, it has been necessary to combine the talents of specialists in adult communication with those of specialists in the communication behavior of children. The authors of this book represent such a combination. And the standards for effective oral communication programs in elementary schools, listed in the following section, represent the combined efforts of speech communication specialists within the Speech Communication Association and of speech and language specialists within the American Speech-Language-Hearing Association.

STANDARDS FOR EFFECTIVE PROGRAMS

The following statement prepared by these two national professional associations provides an excellent statement of overall standards.

Standards For Effective Oral Communication Programs
Prepared by American Speech-Language-Hearing Association and Speech Communication Association

Adequate oral communication frequently determines an individual's educational, social and vocational success. Yet, American education has typically neglected formal instruction in the basic skills of speaking and listening. It is important that state and local education agencies implement the most effective oral communication programs possible.

The following standards for oral communication were developed by representatives of the Speech Communication Association and the American Speech-Language-Hearing Association.

If effective oral communication programs are going to be developed, all components of the recommended standards must be considered. Implementation of these standards will facilitate development of adequate and appropriate oral communication necessary for educational, social and vocational success.

Definition
Oral Communication: the process of interacting through heard and spoken messages in a variety of situations. Effective oral communication is a learned

[7]W. Johnson, and D. Moeller (Eds.) *Speech Handicapped School Children,* 3rd ed. (New York: Harper & Row, Publishers, 1967).

behavior, involving the following processes:

1. Speaking in a variety of educational and social situations: Speaking involves, but is not limited to, arranging and producing messages through the use of voice, articulation, vocabulary, syntax and non-verbal cues (e.g., gesture, facial expression, vocal cues) appropriate to the speaker and listeners.
2. Listening in a variety of educational and social situations: Listening involves, but is not limited to, hearing, perceiving, discriminating, interpreting, synthesizing, evaluating, organizing and remembering information from verbal and non-verbal messages.

Basic Assumptions

1. Oral communication behaviors of students can be improved through direct instruction.
2. Oral communication instruction emphasizes the interactive nature of speaking and listening.
3. Oral communication instruction addresses the everyday communication needs of students and includes emphasis on the classroom as a practical communication environment.
4. There is a wide range of communication competence among speakers of the same language.
5. Communication competence is not dependent upon use of a particular form of language.
6. A primary goal of oral communication instruction is to increase the students' repertoire and use of effective speaking and listening behavior.
7. Oral communication programs provide instruction based on a coordinated developmental continuum of skills, pre-school through adult.
8. Oral communication skills can be enhanced by using parents, supportive personnel, and appropriate instructional technology.

An Effective Communication Program Has the Following Characteristics:
Teaching/Learning

1. The oral communication program is based on current theory and research in speech and language development, psycholinguistics, rhetorical and communication theory, communication disorders, speech science, and related fields of study.
2. Oral communication instruction is a clearly identifiable part of the curriculum.
3. Oral communication instruction is systematically related to reading and writing instruction and to instruction in the various content areas.
4. The relevant academic, personal and social experiences of students provide core subject matter for the oral communication program.
5. Oral communication instruction provides a wide range of speaking and listening experience, in order to develop effective communication skills appropriate to:
   a. a range of situations: e.g., informal to formal, interpersonal to mass communication.
   b. a range of purposes: e.g., informing, learning, persuading, evaluating messages, facilitating social interaction, sharing feelings, imaginative and creative expression.
   c. a range of audiences: e.g., classmates, teachers, peers, employers, family, community.

     d. a range of communication forms: e.g., conversation, group discussion, interview, drama, debate, public speaking, oral interpretation.

     e. a range of speaking styles: impromptu, extemporaneous, and reading from manuscript.

6. The oral communication program provides class time for systematic instruction in oral communication skills. e.g., critical listening, selecting, arranging and presenting messages, giving and receiving constructive feedback, non-verbal communication, etc.

7. The oral communication program includes development of adequate and appropriate language, articulation, voice, fluency and listening skills necessary for success in educational, career and social situations through regular classroom instruction, co-curricular activities, and speech-language pathology and audiology services.

8. Oral communication program instruction encourages and provides appropriate opportunities for the reticent student (e.g., one who is excessively fearful in speaking situations), to participate more effectively in oral communication.

Support

1. Oral communication instruction is provided by individuals adequately trained in oral communication and/or communication disorders, as evidenced by appropriate certification.

2. Individuals responsible for oral communication instruction receive continuing education on theories, research and instruction relevant to communication.

3. Individuals responsible for oral communication instruction participate actively in conventions, meetings, publications, and other activities of communication professionals.

4. The oral communication program includes a system for training classroom teachers to identify and refer students who do not have adequate listening and speaking skills, or are reticent, to those qualified individuals who can best meet the needs of the student through further assessment and/or instruction.

5. Teachers in all curriculum areas receive information on appropriate methods for: a) using oral communication to facilitate instruction, and b) using the subject matter to improve students' oral communication skills.

6. Parent and community groups are informed about and provided with appropriate materials for effective involvement in the oral communication program.

7. The oral communication program is facilitated by availability and use of appropriate instructional materials, equipment and facilities.

Assessment and Evaluation

1. The oral communication program is based on a school-wide assessment of the speaking and listening needs of students.

2. Speaking and listening needs of students will be determined by qualified personnel utilizing appropriate evaluation tools for the skills to be assessed, and educational levels of students being assessed.

3. Evaluation of student progress in oral communication is based upon a variety of data including observations, self-evaluations, listeners' responses to messages, and formal tests.

13

4. Evaluation of students' oral communication encourages, rather than discourages, students' desires to communicate by emphasizing those behaviors which students can improve, thus enhancing their ability to do so.
5. Evaluation of the total oral communication program is based on achievement of acceptable levels of oral communication skill determined by continuous monitoring of student progress in speaking and listening, use of standardized and criterion-referenced tests, audience-based rating scales, and other appropriate instruments.

Integration in the Curriculum

Because oral communication is the cement that binds society together and is the medium through which we learn and share our knowledge with others, it is possible to build skill in oral communication while studying other subjects. Unlike some special subjects that necessitate bringing a new teacher into the classroom in order to teach children, communication can be taught by the regular classroom teacher as a part of the regular daily activities. As long as teaching of communication skills is not lost in the concentration on teaching other subjects, such as mathematics, reading, social studies, and science, there is value in combining experience in communication with the teaching of other parts of the curriculum.

People learning to communicate need to have something to talk about. It is difficult enough for college-age students in a speech communication course to develop topics for group discussions, public speeches, debates, and the like. It would be even more difficult for elementary children to do so. The answer, of course, is that among the topics they talk about are the other subjects they are trying to learn. Skill in communication is enhanced by being learned through transactions on the vital issues of other subjects, just as the learning of those subjects will be enhanced by the growing communication skills of the students.

To be sure, classroom teachers will have to develop their own abilities to teach oral communication skills. It is not true, as some would assert, that any adult who knows how to talk can teach children how to communicate. As you read this book you will understand that teaching oral communication requires special understanding and skill. In most school districts there may already be a specialist in speech pathology who has a background in speech communication (this is not necessarily so, and speech pathologists are now working to see that they do have this background). If so, the speech pathologist will be able to assist teachers in establishing plans. At least, the speech pathologist will have a thorough understanding of children and their normal and disordered communication behaviors.

Possibly the school counselor will be of some help in working up plans for teaching interpersonal communication. Training in counseling relies heavily on understanding certain communication situations. As we will explain in Chapter 4, "Person-to-Person Communication," much of modern theory in person-to-person communication comes from the experiences of people trained to help

14

others work out their personal and social problems. However, the counselor will not be trained in communication generally and thus will not be of much help in working with other skills.

In addition, communication education specialists are available and can be added to the staff to help develop programs and assist classroom teachers. Such additions would be valuable, particularly if the specialists have knowledge of children.

Remember that we said that learning of other subjects is enhanced as children improve in communication. Direct instruction of oral communication is necessary just as direct instruction of other subjects is necessary. There is a genuine reciprocity in teaching oral communication: children learn to communicate and their communication facilitates their learning of all subjects. Spending the day in class working problems, reading assignments and completing pages in the workbook, writing answers to questions posed by the teacher, and taking quizzes and exams produces learning, but there is so much more that could be learned. Understanding of mathematics can be more meaningful and useful if students explain problems to each other aloud, if they use the math to work out group decisions, if they produce evidence in their speeches and decision making that is based on arithmetical calculations. Appreciation of social studies is enhanced if children can re-live experiences from the past by performing historical literatures, or if they experience for themselves through discussion and debate some of the critical decisions of the past: should we leave our homes and venture into the unknown to find new opportunity; should we separate from the mother country through revolution; should we try to live with the Indians or drive them away; how can we grow enough food to last the winter; is slavery ever justified. Children must learn to *function* in society and they cannot be fully taught through books and written exercises. Children can do so much more by interviewing people who are now involved in society, by presenting prepared speeches on social problems, by debating current issues, by participating in work groups to accomplish social tasks, by learning to interact with people of various backgrounds and cultures. Of course, our literary heritage must be heard and experienced to be fully understood. This means discussions of and the oral performance of literatures. These are examples. Classes in art, music, physical education, reading, writing, as well as science are all enhanced by oral communication. A central concept of this book is that integration of oral communication instruction with the current curriculum is not just possible, but that it is crucial.

The exercises provided with each chapter in this book are designed to illustrate how the oral communication competencies can be built while working with other subjects in the curriculum. For each skill we have suggested exercises for integration with several of the typical subjects. The classroom teacher will quickly see how this is done and be able to devise even more exercises to accompany all the subjects in the curriculum. With imagination, there is virtually no subject that cannot be taught while working on oral communication skills.

15

In the course of writing this book and teaching a class on the basis of it at the college level, we have had the benefit of a number of classroom teachers trying out our exercises with their students. They have worked with children in regular classrooms and in such special education classrooms as those for the educable mentally retarded and the trainable mentally retarded. The reports from these field tests have been consistent: (1) children were able to do the exercises and enjoyed the experience; (2) teachers readily saw how to develop more exercises; (3) teachers report that oral communication is easily incorporated within present academic subject areas and both teacher and children appreciated the novel approach; and (4) teachers report that oral communication exercises also provide a valuable break in the usual routine. That last point deserves some elaboration. Any experienced teacher knows that children grow restless from time to time. It may be restlessness induced by long periods of quiet work or listening to the teacher, or it may be restlessness that comes from continued physical activity on the playground. In both cases—we have a report from a physical education teacher as well as others—the children found the communication exercises to be an enjoyable break in routine.

Resistance to Communication

Those who work with the teaching of communication continually encounter people who avoid communication to varying degrees, ranging from a reticence or shyness to an immobilizing dread. Some people have a tendency to avoid any communication situation, whereas others have specific fears related to certain speech behaviors such as public speaking or meeting a stranger. These responses have been variously labeled stage fright, communication anxiety, communication apprehension, speech reticence, or people are called dysfunctional communicators. There is general agreement that no matter what the label, a person is being described who has the expectation that the potential loss from communicating outweighs the anticipated gain. People tend to avoid any situation in which the expected loss exceeds the potential gain.

There has been considerable discussion of the phenomenon of resistance to communication in recent research literature.[8] Much of the work has been directed toward constructing tests and inventories to discover people with some form of resistance to communication, and we will not discuss that research. Of more interest here are the theories of why this occurs and what teachers can do about it.

J. McCroskey and V. Richmond[9] suggest five types of what they call low verbalizers: (1) the skill deficient; (2) the social introvert; (3) the socially alienated;

[8] See *Communication Education* (1980), **29**, 2: 95–111.

[9] J. McCroskey and V. Richmond, *The Quiet Ones: Shyness and Communication Apprehension* (Dubuque, Iowa: Gorsuch Scarisbrick Publishers, 1980).

(4) the ethnically/culturally divergent; and (5) the communication apprehensive. They further suggest that at this time there is no clear method for helping the social introvert and the socially alienated. They believe that there are ways to help the others.

It must be understood that anyone engaging in communication is likely to experience some physiological changes, typically characterized by increased heart rate and its consequences, such as shortness of breath, increased perspiration, and some trembling of the limbs. This is quite ordinary and is associated with the need for alertness and concentration necessary to do something important. As such, it is important and helpful to the communicator. It only becomes a problem, say the researchers, when the communicator notices these physiological manifestations and *interprets them as fear.* Notice it is not fear that *causes* the physiological changes; rather fear and physiology interact with one another through a process of interpretation. Whether or not a person interprets the behaviors as fear and whether or not the person accordingly develops an aversion to communication are functions of the kind of learning and experiences one has had in the past.

What then can be done to encourage children to grow up with a positive approach to communication? We offer these adaptations of three recommended approaches. First, children need to learn the skills of oral communication so they will be neither skill deficient nor apprehensive toward communication situations. Second, they need to develop positive mental attitudes about communication. For example, they need to learn that in communication it is neither reasonable nor probable that everyone who listens will agree or even like the speaker. Nor will others be particularly concerned that a person has not said or done everything as planned. Nor are others likely to be interested in hurting or frightening the speaker. The more children engage in a wide variety of communication experiences, the more they come to see that they are very much like everyone else and that communicating is quite an ordinary and unthreatening process. In this way they will develop positive mental attitudes. Finally, children need to learn to deal with the expected physiological responses to communication. When they observe their increased heartbeat, they will know that it will increase their capacity to do a task and does not signal fear. They can learn through experience to keep the physiological responses within a manageable range. If they seem to be getting too excited, they will learn to relax, think of something pleasant and peaceful, take a few deep breaths, and go right ahead. Most of the best performers report that they always feel the physiological responses before a performance. If they did not, they would worry that they were not taking it seriously. But they do not interpret the responses as fear and they do not allow themselves to become immobilized and unable to perform. They use the excitement to do a better job.

Perhaps the most important point we can make here is that resistance to communication is not innate. There is no reason to expect young children to have such a reaction. If they begin to learn oral communication skills from the earliest age, if they are surrounded by supportive teachers and peers, if they are allowed to see how rewarding it is to be a part of a communicating society, they should never develop resistance to communication. If, on the other hand, they fail to learn the skills, if they are surrounded by critical and correcting teachers and peers, if they never see how much fun it is to communicate, they will become those shy and apprehensive college students who require so much special attention. The time to begin the work is before fear appears. The time to begin the work is at the elementary level.

Communication Differences

In teaching oral communication skills, nearly every classroom teacher will need to know what to do with a child whose culture–specific communication behavior results in different communication. In the past it might have been assumed that problems such as this would be restricted to United States border towns or to large cities. However, with the increased mobility of families within the United States and current influxes of people from other countries, a variety of communication methods might be expected in almost any school. And the chance is high that any teacher can expect to have at least one child who has learned a different type of communication.

Despite the fact that America was founded by a polyglot of people from a variety of cultures, standard American English quickly became a widely used communication system. In the process, those who did not use standard American English became obvious. The people this encompasses are from broad and varied backgrounds.

The most obvious group of children who will demonstrate culture–specific communication are those who speak a different language or primarily use a different language. This group includes children who have just come from another country and those children whose families continue to function in a culturally segmented portion of the population. The groups most apparent are those speaking Spanish, native Americans from reservations, and, most recently, those using the various Oriental languages, although any language may be involved. The federal government has spent considerable effort in encouraging and providing funding for bilingual education programs. No doubt the best beginning for an education in our schools is a bilingual program. All schools do not have such programs and the children are forced into a different language and communication system immediately.

Other differences in communication may not be so immediately or obviously apparent. By the middle 1960s the view emerged that children who had been considered disadvantaged, deficient, or substandard in their use of language should be regarded as different language users. This movement was headed by sociolinguists who began describing the language as equally rich, structured, and accepted within a given language community, although such a language might be different from the white, middle-class language of the American school system.

The research in Black English (Ebonics) contributed considerable evidence to support the position that different is not deficient. Researchers in Black English have described syntactic and phonological rules that make the language different. Furthermore, differences in social expectations, nonverbal symbols, problem solving, and interaction patterns result in different communication strategies. Although having black skin does not necessarily mean using Black English, the problems of communication between children using Black English and teachers using Standard English have been repeatedly documented.

Other differences exist across cultural groups in the United States. Dialectal variations present considerable differences. The dialect among Appalachians has been investigated, with differences in phonology and vocabulary reported. The phonological and stress pattern differences as well as vocabulary have been described for northern, midland, and southern regions. And each of these broad regions is comprised of groups of subdialects. Children who are natives of any of these regions may be expected to demonstrate differences in communication if they move to a new region. Often the differences cause no problem, but at times the differences can make a child unaccepted or the brunt of cruel jokes.

Another group of children that might be expected to demonstrate communication differences are poverty children. These children have not had the same social or language experiences as middle-class children. The parents typically present different models for reasoning, control, quest for knowledge, and achievement standards. Different responses to requests as well as less variety in syntactic alternatives have been documented. These children are culturally different.

This discussion presents a brief summary of the types of communication differences the classroom teacher might expect to encounter. A detailed description and references to specific research are provided by M. J. Mecham and M. L. Willbrand.[10]

Children with communication differences all need to be taught basic oral communication skills. It is important for the teacher to remember that usually (some children have disorders as well as differences) the child's method of communication was appropriate within the specific community in which he or she learned to communicate. Just because the majority of the children in a classroom use another communication system does not make any method a point for being wrong or unacceptable. The lessons in this book are designed for development of communication skills and for an encouraging and accepting atmosphere. Thus, these children are expected to participate with the class and to be accepted as they develop their communication skills. Although Chapter 12 is

---

[10]M. J. Mecham and M. L. Willbrand, *Language Disorders in Children* (Springfield, IL: Charles C Thomas, Publisher 1979), Chaps. 1 and 2.

devoted to intercultural communication, it permeates every chapter and should not be restricted to one set of lessons. The majority of teachers using this book will be using standard American English. Without defending whether this is as it should be, it is a fact that education in the United States is based on standard American English. Any such child who plans to live in the United States and who wants to achieve will need to learn standard American English in addition to another language. However, these lessons are so designed that teachers in bilingual programs, whether the program is Spanish, Black English, languages of native Americans, or others, may use the lesson in that language as well. For those teaching in standard American English, if an effort is made to accept and understand differences, the children will gradually learn the method of the communication in the community in which they are now functioning.

If the child with a language difference is concerned or if his listeners have trouble communicating with him, then a referral to a speech clinician should be considered. Most speech clinicians are prepared to assume part of the responsibility in helping a child learn standard American English. However, a critical question for the speech clinician will be whether the person wants to learn standard English as a second language. Some are definite about maintaining only one language, dialect, or subdialect. In summary, if the child's language was acceptable in his own language community, then he is displaying a language difference. If a child does not function within the norms of any language community, then he has a disorder.

Communication Disorders

Another group of children who may cause concern for the classroom teacher are those children with communication disorders. Conservative estimates indicate that about 7 per cent of the school-age population are considered communicatively handicapped. These children with communication disorders may be found any and everywhere in a school system from preschool through high school, from the accelerated to the mentally retarded student, and from regular to special education classrooms. Communication disorders are no respector of intelligence, educational status, social class, or physical appearance. Although certain groups of children with other disabilities may have a larger percentage of communicatively handicapped children among them, a word of warning seems necessary. Children with communicative handicaps, particularly those with language problems, may be misplaced educationally, because the very tests used to determine school placement (IQ tests and achievement tests) usually depend heavily on language performance. Additionally, judgmental mistakes may be made such as assuming that poor oral performance indicates other problems or, conversely, that if a child is an excellent student, the difference you hear in his oral performance couldn't really be there or couldn't make a difference.

How may the classroom teacher identify the student with a communication

20

disorder? A language, speech, or hearing problem may be considered a disorder when the oral performance of an individual: (1) interferes with communication, (2) is so different from that of his peers that it draws attention to itself, (3) concerns the listener, or (4) concerns the speaker. Although all of these criteria may not be present, they function individually or together as a general guideline.

Teachers may have in their classrooms children who have language, articulation, fluency, voice, or hearing disorders. The classroom teacher need not be concerned with diagnosing or treating communication disorders. That is the responsibility of the speech clinician or audiologist in the school. The classroom teacher needs to recognize any problem in oral communication and to refer the person with that problem to the speech clinician or audiologist. The teacher should not be concerned about overreferral. The speech clinicians or audiologists do not make fun of unnecessary referrals; they appreciate the observant teacher. So if a question arises, refer.

In addition to special diagnostic or therapeutic attention, the children all need to develop oral communication skills in the classroom. The lessons in this book have been designed for every child to participate. Those children with communication disorders need this training every bit as much and usually more than "normal" children. The competency levels proposed in the book allow the teacher to adjust the competency being developed to the capabilities of the student, regardless of school placement. A few students will present specific concerns in adapting the lessons for them, and the speech and hearing clinician will assist the teacher in planning those adjustments.

Some teachers may be in areas that have no speech or hearing clinician in the school. In such cases the classroom teacher who desires referral sources may write to the American Speech-Language-Hearing Association, 10801 Rockville Pike, Rockville, Maryland 20852. The teacher may request an American Speech-Language-Hearing Association directory, which must be purchased. Or the teacher may ask for the appropriate state listing from the "Guide to Clinical Services in Speech-Language Pathology-Audiology." A copy of the state listing will be sent free of charge and will indicate state resource people, clinics in the state, and individuals primarily engaged in private practice. The obvious difference in the two is that the directory lists individuals and the guide lists clinics and centers.

Many states now require a state license for professionals desiring to see individuals on a private basis. The number of states requiring licensure will probably increase. A list of licensed professionals may be obtained from the individual state licensing boards.

Some teachers may need to deal with children who have or have had communication disorders and have been in special classes but are now being mainstreamed. These children, just like those with communication disorders who have remained in regular classrooms, need the oral communication skills. They can participate with the other children. The teacher can adjust the competency level for those

21

children with his understanding of the child and with help from the previous special teacher and the child's Individualized Education Program (IEP). Discussions of children who are being mainstreamed are provided through useful case studies in *American Education.*[11] If nondisabled children have difficulty understanding the mainstreamed handicapped child, a film, *Feeling Free*, funded by the Office of Education and broadcast by PBS stations, is available. It has been widely acclaimed as a help for adults and children in understanding handicaps and in seeing the child with a handicap as a person who is more like other children than different from other children.

In the classroom, if the concentration remains on what is communicated rather than on how, on the messages rather than the correctness of each sentence, word, or sound, the atmosphere is a healthy one. As the teacher and the children accept themselves and each other and truly want to communicate, oral communication skills can be learned by all (except for the few who remain nonverbal, and they will be in special institutions).

HOW TO USE THIS BOOK

This book provides a competency-based program as a guide to teaching oral communication skills in the elementary classroom. The classroom teacher will teach oral communication skills as an integral part of all other academic subjects. In many elementary schools, the speech clinician, in addition to treating differences and disorders of communication, will be a key person in planning, in coordinating, and giving demonstration or model lessons in the program for developing normal communication skills. In some schools a communication person may also participate, but that is more expected at secondary levels. This book is planned as a guide to all professionals involved in oral communication skills programs at elementary levels.

Chapters 2 through 12 are sequenced for instruction both across the chapters and within the chapters. The theory and activities are planned so a child may gradually progress through the areas in sequence. Thus, level one activities should progress from listening to nonverbal to person-to-person, and so on through the book. The intention is that beginning level competencies and activities should be taught across all the communication areas before any intermediate level competencies are begun. Then all intermediate level competencies should be met before any advanced level competencies are begun. The teacher who tries to begin with later chapters should anticipate problems. The children will not be prepared for the demands placed on them. Asking too much too soon is likely to induce failure or fear or both.

Within each section, beginning level, intermediate level, and advanced level

---

[11] *American Education,* 1978, **14**, 9: 13–38.

competencies are provided. No specific grade level is specified deliberately so that teachers may proceed through the levels for the skills to be developed, depending on the ability of the children in the classroom.

Specific classroom lessons are provided in each topic for each level. The activities match the competencies. The activities merely provide suggestions for the teacher and are not intended to be all-inclusive. The teacher should use the activities as a springboard to create other activities to use until the child can be evaluated on the basis of the competency.

The general competencies provide general guides and the level competencies provide specific goals. The activities are suggestions for working toward those goals. It will take a number of activities to meet a competency. All competencies are called "exit" competencies to indicate the desired skill performance at the end of a unit necessary before moving on to the next higher level.

This book provides a guide to those developing programs and to those implementing programs in oral communication skills at the elementary level. Each teacher involved will need to adjust the activities to meet the needs of the group as well as those of individual children. Teaching and learning oral communication skills are enjoyable and make a vital contribution to the knowledge of individuals who must function in the world of human communication.

Nonverbal
Communication

OBJECTIVES

At the end of this chapter you should be able to

1. Identify nonverbal elements and explain their role in the total communication process.
2. Define the operational categories of nonverbal communication.
3. Contrast the prescriptive approaches with current descriptive analyses of nonverbal communication.
4. Understand typical nonverbal gestures and messages within our culture.
5. Discuss idiosyncratic aspects of nonverbal communication.
6. Discuss how the general and specific level competencies are designed to yield, by the time of exit, an elementary mastery of nonverbal communication as currently conceived.
7. Explain how the general exit competencies represent broad goals that accompany each specific level competency.
8. Match each exercise to the general exit competency or competencies and the specific level exit competency or competencies that the exercise addresses.
9. Explain why the successful completion of one exercise does not fulfill the objectives of the competencies.
10. Design additional exercises for the fulfillment of the stated competencies.

It was the first day of classes. The smell of autumn was in the air and the children were looking fresh in their clean clothes and holding their new pencils proudly. The teacher stepped in front of the class and began talking. At once she knew she would enjoy the boy in the third row because he would nod his head sharply in agreement with virtually every comment she made. What a bright young man, she thought. He listens and responds. It was only a short time later that her illusion was destroyed as she observed the same boy continuing to nod his head even when no one was speaking. He obviously had a tick and moved his head that way all the time.

The strange thing about the story, though, is that even after she knew the child's head shakes were involuntary she continued to feel a sense of reinforcement when he would nod his head after a particularly important statement. Sometimes when the class was acting lethargic she would focus her attention on the boy in the third row just to get some kind of response.

It is not surprising that the elementary teacher frequently felt a lack of nonverbal response from the class. Children in school typically do not demonstrate the skill of providing feedback as members of a group through facial expressions, head movements, and body postures, which adults use frequently. However, by the time they enter school, children have already been using nonverbal communication for most of their lives.

Making contact with others through smiling, touching, making noise, and moving the body is the most primitive form of communication. If there is communication between adults and infants during the child's first months, it is done through nonverbal means. Studies over many years show a steady development in children's use of sound, movement, and touching as a means of learning about themselves, their environment, and the people around them. By the time they begin to use words, children have already spent some time practicing what will come to be the nonverbal elements in their communication skills.

THE CONCEPT

There is something inherently contradictory in trying to explain the concept of nonverbal communication using words alone. We could do a better job if the communication were oral rather than printed.

Most important to understanding the concept of nonverbal communication is realizing that it is, to the best of our knowledge, only a *part* of a total communication system, and not a separate system existing as an alternative to the use of words. Look at it this way: this printed page is perhaps the nearest thing to a pure use of verbal communication, and yet it does not operate without nonverbal elements that contribute to the total meaning communicated. The size and shape of the type, the way the words and sentences are arranged on the page, the frequency and spacing of paragraphs, the amount of blank space left on the page, the quality of the paper, the use of pictorial and graphic illustrations, and the characteristics of the binding all help the development of meaning in the reader. In this sense, it is impossible to communicate by verbal means alone.

As we have just suggested, this is even more true in oral communication. Studies tell us that we draw meaning from the physical characteristics of the speaker, her facial expression, location of her body in relation to those with whom she is communicating, her voice, gestures, pauses, rapidity of speech, and any sounds or noises she makes that are not words. Again, it is not possible to speak by verbal means alone. And again, the nonverbal aspects of the speech contribute to the meanings others generate from what is said.

On the other hand, it is not so easy to say that it is impossible to communicate by nonverbal means alone. The question is still being debated by experts and no definite answer can be given. On some points, however, there is some agreement.

If nonverbal cues formed a medium of communication separate from the use of words, it would be possible to write a grammar for them. That is, in language we can identify some rules, such as the combination of a noun phrase and a verb phrase makes a sentence. We have a set of syntactic and semantic rules for a language. To date, at least, no such grammar of nonverbal cues has been written.

There are times, it seems, when a nonverbal behavior such as a gesture, a visual expression, or a vocal tone has become a symbol in itself as an alternative to a word. But understanding of such a symbol is very much a function of the context in which it occurs. Many people like to believe that their dog, for example, can communicate with them. The dog wags his tail and we say he is telling us he is happy. But whether he is happy, hungry, excited, uncertain, or bored will probably be supplied by the people and context involved in the "communication."

Or, consider the wave as an example. We lift an open hand with the palm out and move it from side to side, and it seems to be generally understood in our culture as an indication of a friendly greeting or farewell. Again, the context determines the meaning, but it is not difficult to tell whether someone is saying "hello" or "goodbye" with a wave. But one cold winter night a group of people left a meeting and got into their cars to drive home. As the next to last car to leave drove out of the parking lot, the driver of the last car lifted his hand, palm out, and moved it from side to side. The passing driver waved his hand in return and drove on. The next morning, the driver of the last car stormed into his friend's office and asked indignantly why the other had not stopped when he waved. It seems as if his car would not start in the cold weather and he had been trying to stop the other car to get help. So, there was a definite ambiguity even in a widely recognized noverbal gesture. The intention of the communicator becomes an important factor. But, there can be ambiguity in words, too.

Even where nonverbal cues may function without the accompaniment of words, meaning must be available within the culture of the speaker and listener if communication is to occur. It is most difficult to say whether meaning can evolve without the presence of an inner language—a set of concepts learned with which to interpret all symbols, both verbal and nonverbal. The way the human being processes information may ultimately reveal the intimate connections among verbal and nonverbal elements of communication.

Conceptually, then, nonverbal communication calls attention to a body of behaviors within a total communication process that generally cannot be accounted for by the grammar of our spoken or written language.

It is easier to explain nonverbal communication *operationally*. The various categories of nonverbal communication are explained by M. L. Knapp.[1] A first general category is that of body motion, which includes such behaviors as movements of the body, arms, hands, legs, feet, all gestures, facial expressions, postures assumed, and activity of the eyes. Within this category are included a

---

[1] M. L. Knapp, *Nonverbal Communication in Human Interaction* (New York: Holt, Rinehart and Winston, 1978), Chap. 1.

number of subordinate elements. "Emblems" are behaviors which have a relatively direct verbal translation. Examples would be a wave of the hand to say hello or holding a finger to the lips to indicate the need for silence. Emblems are not necessarily the same across cultures although the search for universals continues. However, use of emblems is universal in the sense that some communications are typically expressed nonverbally. Some examples found in research are "yes," "no," social status indicated by level and position in a gathering, and the communication of gender. But the emblems to express these concepts may vary from culture to culture. In fact, it is quite dangerous to assume that an emblem in your culture will communicate the same concept in another culture. People have found that raising the eyebrows in the friendly acknowledgment of another's presence may be taken as a crude sexual invitation in Japan. Putting the thumb and first finger together to form an "O" while raising the other fingers may communicate "everything's okay" in North America, but it may again communicate a crude sexual suggestion in South America.

"Illustrators" are another subcategory of body movements that are used to illustrate or add meaning to words. Here a person may point to the object being discussed or bring a fist down sharply on a table to emphasize a point. To hold up one finger as you say, "My first point is . . . ." employs an illustrator to increase the strength of the verbal organization.

"Affect displays" help us communicate our feelings. Happy faces and sad faces, drooping head or shoulders may tell others about your feelings even when you are not aware of them.

People use "regulators" to help control the interaction process: who gets to speak, how long one can hold the floor, and how someone else gets to talk. Children learn in school to raise their hands if they want to speak. They pump their hands up and down frantically to communicate an urgent desire to speak. The teacher learns to look directly into the eyes of the student he wishes to talk and to avoid eye contact with those who will not get the floor. An authoritarian algebra teacher loved to play games with students by looking into the eyes of one student while posing a question and then calling out the name of another student on the other side of the room for the answer. He knew we were reading his nonverbal regulator as promising to put the other person on the spot, relaxing our attention accordingly, and then finding someone else called upon. It kept us on our toes but injected considerable tension into the classroom.

People learned that in our society it is difficult to say to persons visiting in your office or home that you want them to leave. But it can be done nonverbally with a regulator such as standing up and taking a step toward the door.

Another major category of nonverbal behavior involves physical characteristics. Some of them, such as the size and shape of the body, may be relatively outside our control, but they communicate nevertheless. We spend a good deal of time in dress, grooming, cosmetics, and personal hygiene to help communicate the meaning we have in mind. The European who appeared at a business conference in the United States dressed magnificently in expensive clothes, beautifully groomed, but reeking of body odor failed to appreciate the meaning Americans attach to some smells. The middle-aged man who went to a disco wearing a suit and tie did not realize what that physical characteristic communicated to others. We have included what some call artifacts in this category.

Touching, as a category, includes hitting, pushing, stroking, or just lightly placing a hand or fingers on another person. Shaking hands and embracing while touching cheeks and perhaps "kissing the air" are common forms of touching communication in the United States. We have some significant meanings attached to touching in our culture. Who is touching, who is being touched, and what part of the body is touched may communicate widely different meanings. Duration of touching may also change meaning: a brief handshake quickly released may communicate a different meaning from one in which a person's hand is held warmly for several seconds. Touching between sexes may communicate either close personal feeling to enhance words spoken or it may suggest sexual attraction.

Physical location and orientation among people communicating may influence the meaning generated. How close or how far away we situate ourselves for communication, whether we stand or sit or change position, whether we face the other person directly, at an angle, or turn our back all may have something to do with the totality of communication. Seating arrangements in formal situations may make considerable difference in the type of communication that results. A round table rather than a rectangular one may change the way interpersonal status emerges, or the way interaction occurs. A classroom with chairs fixed in rows as in a theater may yield a different communication situation from one in which chairs can be moved into small groups, a large circle, or some other arrangement.

A final category of nonverbal communication deals with the use of the voice other than to form actual words. Some call it *paralanguage*. We need to distinguish *prosodic* signals from paralanguage. *Prosodic signals* are pitch pattern, stress pattern, and use of pauses and timing to affect the meaning of sentences. They are regarded as essentially parts of the verbal utterance. *Paralanguage*, on the other hand, includes use of tone of voice to communicate emotions, or personality expressed by voice quality and manner of speech. Paralanguage also includes vocalizations such as laughing, crying, sighing, yawning, clearing the throat, groaning, screaming, raising or lowering the pitch or loudness of voice, and inserting such sounds as "uh-huh," "um" or "ah" into a conservation. Extended silence may also be included in paralanguage. If someone addresses a comment to you and you allow several seconds to pass without replying, the chances are the person will next say something to indicate awareness of the silence as having meaning.

A caution must be made on two points. First, as we will explain in the following section's discussion of the tradition of nonverbal communication, there has been—and in some cases still exists—a tendency to want to *prescribe* certain behaviors as the correct ones. For example, many believe there is a *correct* way to pronounce words, a correct way to move the mouth, lips, and tongue while talking, a correct way to use the voice in terms of so-called proper quality, pitch, and intensity. People have been told to use "round, pear-shaped tones," and to speak smoothly without "ahs" interrupting or without running words together too rapidly.

There is no research support for these assumptions of correctness. As long as voice, articulation, and fluency are within normal limits—that is, not diagnosed as pathological by a clinical specialist—no teaching of correctness for certain patterns is justified. In our exercises no provision is made for the teacher to select one pattern over another as being correct.

A second caution must be made on the subject of the need for direct instruction of nonverbal communication. We are stressing throughout this book that oral communication skills do not develop on their own or incidentally. They require direct and planned instruction by the teacher. This must be made especially clear with regard to nonverbal communication. While we reject the elocutionary prescriptions of the past, we do not suggest that children should be left without instruction in nonverbal communication. The rest of this chapter details how we think this should be done.

THE TRADITION

Classical studies of rhetoric included interest in the nonverbal elements involved in presenting a public speech. They were concentrated on gestures, facial expressions, movements, voice, pronunciation, and articulation. Early in the Christian era, the classical commitment to the close integration of verbal and nonverbal elements gave way to a fixation upon form rather than substance. Speakers were virtually actors who were proficient in all the nonverbal behaviors with little regard for the content of their message.

By the eighteenth century, the elocutionary movement was established because of a wide dissatisfaction with ministers who were poor speakers, because there was a desire to standardize spoken English, interest in techniques to improve social status through speech lessons (as Shaw portrayed in his play about Dr. Henry Higgins and Eliza Doolittle), and a general interest in pleasing delivery. Using what they claimed were scientific methods to discover what were the "natural" elements in nonverbal communication, writers charted in elaborate detail the postures and facial expressions judged to express various emotions. They listed every conceivable gesture of the arms, hands, and fingers, provided directions for articulation, pronunciation, accent, pause, pitch, vocal quality, and intensity. They created phonetic alphabets and built notation systems to record melody and rhythm for speech.

31

Although elocutionists believed their prescriptions about nonverbal communication were natural rather than artificial, they based their definition of "natural" on the presumption that scientific study of the speech of all people revealed laws of expression. That is, if one felt a certain emotion, there was a law governing the nonverbal expression of that emotion. This led to enormous lists of the minute details required in the natural expression of feelings and ideas. These excesses of prescription caused speech training to fall into disrepute. The training was removed from established schools and colleges and found its way into private schools of elocution and in private elocution lessons in the teacher's home. This continues in some places today.

Common Ways of Thinking about nonverbal communication are mostly influenced by work done in the last 40 years. The prescriptions of the elocutionists are totally rejected in favor of systematic efforts to describe without value judgments the nonverbal elements in communication. They lead to studies aimed at understanding rather than practice aimed at proficiency. In addition, there is recognition that the excessive concentration on nonverbal laws of the elocutionists led to excessive focus on verbal behaviors in communication. We now seek a balanced emphasis on the total process of communication with the recognition that nonverbal cues are at least as important as verbal ones, and, if measured in terms of quantity, we see that of all the human message systems, the clear majority are nonverbal.

Current Perspectives include notice of the importance of nonverbal cues in various communication situations. In the arts, in the diagnosis and therapy of those who are emotionally disturbed, in our social and cultural ceremonies and rituals, in intercultural communication, in work with the blind and deaf, in persuasive campaigns in the mass media, in classroom teaching, and in courtship behavior, nonverbal cues seem to play an unusually important role. However, frequently unrecognized is the importance of nonverbal communication in ordinary conversation. Obviously, teaching of communication skills to elementary school children must involve work with nonverbal cues.

The View of this Book begins with the position that nonverbal cues form a part of the total communication process in both producing and comprehending messages, and thus they should not be separated from the verbal aspects. However, we recognize that there are still some nonverbal communications that are independent of the verbal and further acknowledge the need to isolate nonverbal behaviors, at least initially for learning purposes. We support the continuing search for universal rules and language-specific rules of nonverbal messages. It seems as if certain nonverbal behaviors communicate a dependable message *within a culture*, and students should have a broad range in interpreting them.

32

But they should also learn to recognize the idiosyncratic aspects of nonverbal behaviors.

Finally, while the search continues for accurate interpretation of nonverbal cues, there remains a strong likelihood of misinterpretation because the people communicating may hold different presuppositions. Students need to learn to use verbal messages to validate their nonverbal interpretations. For example, there may be a conflict between verbal and nonverbal messages. If a person communicates agreement verbally but employs nonverbal cues of disagreement, adults tend to believe the nonverbal message whereas children may be more faithful to the verbal. Or there may be a conflict between two nonverbal cues as in the case of the parent who smiles but uses a negative intonation of the voice. The child must learn to check for the meaning intended. And there may simply be a misunderstanding of some nonverbal behavior as in the teacher believing that the student who falls asleep in class is uninterested or bored. The student may be taking a medication that induces drowsiness. Our view holds that children should be sensitized to all these and other problems in nonverbal communication.

Nonverbal behavior is one part of the total communication process. Everyone needs to understand it in order to fully communicate. Our exercises provide opportunities in successful communication that are less tension-producing for students who have oral communication problems. Thus, just as nonverbal communication is first in the development of human communication, we recommend beginning teaching communication skills with nonverbal behaviors.

COMPETENCIES TO BE DEVELOPED

We advance two *general exit competencies* for skills in nonverbal communication.

The students should be able to

1. Perceive nonverbal behavior and recognize it as part of the total communication process.
2. Express themselves nonverbally.

We have said that concentration on learning language that is strengthened by school experiences tends to put emphasis upon the verbal aspects of communication. A major goal, then, of work in nonverbal communication is to establish in students' consciousness the full range of cues they use in communicating.

They will become skilled in recognizing the typical meanings attached to various nonverbal cues within their culture. They may also be alerted to the fact that cultural agreements underlie these meanings and therefore be able to respond more effectively to those of cultures other than their own. Instead of becoming nervous in the presence of the strange nonverbal behavior of people from other cultures, or instead of feeling inclined to ridicule them, students skilled in nonverbal communication will be more inclined to analyze the behaviors and generate more useful understanding. We will discuss this more fully in Chapter 12, "Intercultural Communication."

Working with the first general exit competency will sensitize students to the multiple nonverbal cues, individual as well as culture-bound, that everyone uses. They will become aware that total meaning is a function of more than words alone. As they grow in their skills, students will become increasingly able to talk about the understanding they have generated from a communication experience and describe rather well the role nonverbal cues have played in the formation of that meaning.

At the advanced level, students will become sensitive to situations in which verbal and nonverbal messages are in conflict. Or they will be able to deal with situations in which the nonverbal cues present conflicting messages. Rather than respond to one message over another, they will be able to use various communication skills to verify the intended message, thus resulting in more responsive interpretations of total communication.

As students increase sensitivity to the use of nonverbal behavior as part of the total communication process of others, they will work with the second general exit competency of expressing themselves nonverbally. First they will become aware that they will, necessarily, be engaging in nonverbal communication a great deal of the time, whether they realize it or not. Then, they will become more proficient in using the nonverbal cues to enhance rather than detract from their intended meaning. Finally, they will increase their repertoire of nonverbal cues so as to have greater choice in the ways they use them in communication. So when we say that the second general competency is to be able to express themselves nonverbally, we mean that they will be exercising more conscious choice among a wider range of alternatives.

Beginning Exit Competencies include the following:

1. Ability to communicate with and understand typical nonverbal gestures, without simultaneous verbal communication.
2. Ability to communicate basic feelings through facial expression.
3. Ability to communicate by touch or gesture the referent of a sentence.

The first beginning exit competency works with children using and understanding typical nonverbal gestures such as the following listed by B. Wood:[2]

[2] B. Wood, *Children and Communication*, 2nd ed. (Englewood Cliffs, NJ: Prentice-Hall, Inc., 1981).

1. Go away.	8. Shape: for example round or
2. Come here.	square.
3. Yes.	9. I don't know.
4. No.	10. Goodbye.
5. Be quiet.	11. Hi.
6. How many?	12. Raised hand for attention.
7. How big?	

The caution that must accompany this list is that it may be biased toward middle-class nonverbal communication. There is evidence that not all children are adept at using and interpreting these standard gestures, but because this is an aspect of nonverbal communication that shows marked improvement after one year of school, it is a good place to begin. Children should experience quick success here, and that will get them moving in the nonverbal exercises to follow. They will instantly be aware of how much they can communicate nonverbally without any words.

Reflecting facial expressions of others is a behavior found in infants, and young children gradually develop the ability to show their own feelings through such expressions. Because this is such a basic way of communicating feelings, the second beginning competency works with facial expressions. Although children will have probably learned some of society's inhibitions about showing feelings by the time they reach school, this is still a nonverbal skill that should be easy to work with. Essentially, our goal here is to make students aware of the feelings they are communicating with their faces. We begin by having children respond facially to words about feelings. In this way they will increase their sensitivity to what they do with their faces to express feelings. With this increased sensitivity, they can then move into understanding the ways in which the particular context will influence the feeling communicated by facial expression. When they smile at other people, they will notice variations in response. They will find themselves using the face as a means of communicating their relevant response to the context. The outcome should be to see that social inhibitions against expressing feelings are offset by the need for full disclosure and the freedom to use nonverbal means to do it. And the children should be aware of how they are, in fact, using their faces to tell others what they are feeling.

Finally, at the beginning level, students start the process of integrating verbal and nonverbal means of communication. A basic way of doing this is to let nonverbal cues enhance the meaning of a spoken sentence. Evidence in communication research supports the notion that emphasis and thus recall and understanding are increased by the use of nonverbal cues. Watch the TV commercials and notice how often the speaker not only talks about a product, but at the same time points to it or touches it. On giveaway shows, while the announcer is describing a prize to be won, someone else is shown standing beside the prize

35

pointing, touching, and even caressing it to increase the communication of value and desirability. In many situations, when the purpose is to describe and explain an object, holding up the object—as television speakers do with products—increases the meaning and importance communicated. This is also quite common in any instructional situation.

Students will thus learn two lessons. First, they will begin the process of integrating verbal and nonverbal elements in their communication. Second, they will learn an important skill in using nonverbal means to give greater meaning to their words.

Intermediate Exit Competencies are these:

1. Nonverbal demonstration of the actions of things in the environment.
2. Ability to communicate a message without words.
3. Ability to identify the contribution of verbal and nonverbal elements when the messages are not in conflict.
4. Ability to combine verbal and nonverbal elements in a single message.

The first intermediate exit competency is aimed at sharpening the students' awareness of the ways in which their environment is filled with actions and sounds that have meaning for them. Some communication theorists have argued that the environment produces persuasive messages for us through nonverbal means. They have suggested that we are constantly being actors within a scene and performing our roles in response to much that goes on around us: the actions of birds and animals, the movement of machinery, the sounds of whistles, trains, cars, music, the frantic actions within a city, the quiet movements in the country, or the rhythmic waves of the ocean. In this competency, children will free themsleves of inhibitions as they practice these widely varied "messages" from the environment and try to duplicate them. At the same time, they will broaden their own repertoire of ways of expressing themselves nonverbally.

This will lead to proficiency in the second intermediate exit competency as students try to communicate a full message without using words. First, they will need to do much observation of people and objects around them. They will need to notice how people communicate without words. Then, they will have a chance to try out their newly learned means of conveying to others their meaning through movement, gesture, sound, and expression. They will include ways of using the voice that do not involve words: shouts, screams, whistles, sighs, clearing the throat, clucking the tongue. They may try such things as the television commercial for a fried chicken franchise in which a women said, "I can describe this chicken in two words: umm, ummm!" They will be able to try their hand at the use of the more widely understood emblems that are employed in communication among people who do not share a language.

By this point, students should be ready to do some total communication analysis in the sense of noticing the contribution of both verbal and nonverbal elements as they combine consistently to produce a message, as suggested in the third intermediate exit competency. This is a designed to sharpen children's perceptive abilities. By performing some exercises in which the verbal elements are eliminated, they will become increasingly aware of the substantial role played by nonverbal behavior in general communication. They will become aware that both verbal and nonverbal elements are most meaningful when combined. They will become more effective observers and thus more effective communicators. The skills developed here will become more obviously valuable when we move to the study of listening, discussed in Chapter 3.

Finally, at the intermediate level, students will begin to develop their own proficiency in the combined use of verbal and nonverbal methods of communicating a single message. We begin here in simple communication exercises to restore some of the spontaneous nonverbal activities children have been using for some years but which have become less common because of the inhibiting effects of a more formal social situation. It is important to start early to build the children's confidence in the combination of nonverbal behaviors with their spoken presentations as a foundation for the skills to come.

Advanced Exit Competencies include the following:

1. Ability to pantomime everyday behaviors.
2. Ability to identify emotions communicated by others.
3. Ability to communicate different meanings with the same sentence.
4. Ability to recognize and deal productively with conflicting verbal and nonverbal messages.

With the background of the first two levels of competency, students should be ready to continue their progress into the advanced level. They will first increase their skill in performing nonverbal behaviors by doing some pantomime. To perform pantomime, students will have had to become rather acute observers of people's behaviors. Pantomime requires extreme sensitivity to minute details in all the movements, expressions, and gestures that accompany ordinary behaviors. For students to perform pantomime is to become skilled in using their own bodies as means of communication. Doing pantomime will build upon previous skill levels in freeing children from inhibitions against full nonverbal expressiveness.

Becoming careful observers of others involves improving upon the ability to understand the emotions communicated nonverbally. In the discussion of the tradition of nonverbal communication, we noticed that the elocutionists worked with stereotypical ways to communicate emotions on the theory that there was a law governing each one. Modern research tells us this is not a sound assumption. People cannot interpret with certainty the emotion being communicated nonverbally. Another assumption by some people would lead us to believe that only weak people express emotions. Counselors are helping us learn that we all express emotions and that suppression in one place means emotions erupt in another. Children can become more sensitive to the fact that emotions are presented through nonverbal cues, perhaps more frequently and more validly than through words. In this competency, students will sharpen their ability to make sense of nonverbal behaviors that express emotions.

The third advanced exit competency addresses the ways in which we give meaning to verbal utterances through nonverbal accompaniment. In some languages, particularly Chinese, words take second place to the melodic patterns of the voice in speaking them. But English is not so different as one might expect. The use of inflections, pauses, facial expressions, intensity of voice, gestures, and bodily activity can make significant differences in the meaning communicated. We know individuals who make friendly suggestions sound like orders through a habit of speaking with a stern, precise, and forceful manner. We know others who would like to communicate strength and certainty but who cannot through a habit of speaking in soft, mousy tones, often with head turned down and use of few gestures. Students practicing for this competency will learn the various ways meaning can be changed or enhanced through nonverbal cues.

Finally, students must work with the problem of conflicting messages communicated because of an inconsistency between words and nonverbal cues. Remember that children have particular difficulty in such situations. At least, they tend to operate differently from adults. Adults usually follow the meaning communicated nonverbally in the presence of a conflict with the words uttered. Children demonstrate problems in understanding conflicting messages. We cannot say which medium is more accurate as a rule, but we can work with children in reacting to conflicting messages. By dealing productively with conflicts, we are suggesting that children first must be aware of the conflict and second they must continue interaction with the other person in an effort to resolve the conflict. This may involve using words: "You're telling me that you feel fine, but you look as if you aren't well. Please tell me how you really feel." In a drama, a mother said to her child, "I'm mad at you," and the child responded, "You don't look mad." Given that response, the mother paused, and then agreed, "I guess I'm not really so mad as I thought." That child dealt productively with a conflict.

Sample Exercises for Nonverbal Communication

Three levels of elementary instruction are suggested through sample lessons. The teacher needs to be aware of the stated nonverbal competencies that are the goals for each level as well as the general competencies that apply to all levels.

To review, nonverbal communication is part of the total communication of a message and as such the nonverbal element usually serves to augment, to con-

38

firm, or to contradict the verbal message. Also, certain nonverbal messages may be delivered without verbal accompaniment in that they convey a "standard" meaning, at least within a given culture. In addition, some nonverbal emblems have enough universality that we can use nonverbal symbols to communicate even when we can not or do not use the oral language across cultures as well as within cultures.

At each competency level, exercises have been designed to separate nonverbal from verbal communication. This has been done for two purposes: to call attention to the nonverbal aspect of communication so it can be raised to a conscious level in communicating, and to help children learn to transmit and interpret standard gestures, movements, and expressions. The teacher should be aware that typical or standard gestures are culture-bound and that all children are not from American middle-class backgrounds.

Likewise, at each level of instruction exercises have been planned to combine verbal and nonverbal communication. This is intentional because in most everyday communication both verbal and nonverbal messages are sent and received simultaneously. Recognizing and comprehending both channels of communication require experience.

When possible, the nonverbal exercises have been suggested to incorporate with other academic subjects. However, many of the exercises will require a time just for that purpose. Children enjoy nonverbal lessons, and these may provide a needed relaxation period. In addition, nonverbal communication provides a successful communication experience for children who have problems in verbal communication. Thus, it becomes an important adjunct to the curriculum.

BEGINNING LEVEL EXERCISES

1. Children identify body parts by gesture. This is designed to be a group activity in which the response to a verbal cue is to touch a body part. Depending on the ability of the children in a class, this activity may take any of several forms. On the most simple level the teacher may say, "show me your nose," "show me your hair," and so on with the children responding. A more advanced version is to play "Simon Says" with the teacher or another child giving the cue. Still another variation is to use the familiar songs, "Head and Shoulders, Knees and Toes" or "Put Your Finger In the Air." In order for the lesson to be meaningful the teacher should explain that we often point to things we talk about. The lesson may accompany a lesson in self-awareness, body identification, or music if songs are used.

2. Each child responds to yes/no questions by shaking her head in affirmation or negation. The teacher explains that we often answer people with gestures and without words. Then the teacher asks each child a question and she responds with head movement only. Such questions may be general: "Is this your book?" Or the question may be adapted to any subject. For example, a series of yes/

39

no questions can be asked about a reading story: "Did Tom go home?" or "Is Jane the name of the girl?" or "Did Spot spill the milk?" This can also be used with an art project: "Did we use glue?" or "Did you draw a circle?" "Is this shape round?" or "Is this color blue?"

3. Children respond to a word cue for a common gesture. In this exercise the teacher gives the word for a typical gesture and the students as a group use the gesture. Frequently employed gestures have been identified as *yes, no, go away, come here, be quiet, how big,* shapes (round or square), *I don't know, good-bye, hi,* and raised hand for attention. The teacher may expand this list by looking for common ones in the school culture, such as *stop* by the school patrol or raised hand of the principal for *quiet,* and so on.

4. Each child comes to the front of the room and transmits a message, using one of the standard gestures. This exercise builds on the previous lesson because now a single child uses the gesture in front of a group and the classmates all respond with the message they have interpreted. Of course, children will learn that *hello* and *goodbye* have similar gestures and one cannot tell the difference without knowing the situation. This also expands the exercise. In some groups, it may be necessary for the teacher to whisper the verbal cue to the child presenting the gesture in order to keep the nonverbal emblems within the common knowledge of the group.

5. The students sit in a circle and respond with a facial expression to a word the teacher uses. This lesson is designed to call specific attention to the expression of emotion. The teacher should say words such as *sad, happy, pouting, angry, surprise, fear, delicious, bad,* and so on. It is important for students to sit in a circle so they can observe each other. The group may respond at the same time and the exercise might be repeated with one child responding and then choosing the next child to respond.

6. Each child is given an assignment to smile at three people outside of the classroom and see what the people do in response. The next day children name the people they smiled at and tell what the people did. The teacher may give suggestions such as, "try smiling at a baby, mother, daddy, a friend, a policeman, the checker in the grocery store," and so on. The purpose of this lesson is to call attention to the expression of emotions in the actual environment. Thus, it is important to discuss how the others responded. For example, a smile may not beget another smile. The teacher may need to help explain the responses of others.

7. Each child communicates nonverbally the meaning of a word written on the board. This exercise provides the opportunity to use the whole body in addition to a hand movement, a facial expression, or a nonverbal sound. The assignment provides an interesting variation for the introduction of the week's spelling words. As the teacher writes the spelling words on the board one at a time, she does not say them but instead asks children in turn to show what the word is.

8. Each child responds to a sentence by nonverbally pointing to or touching the referent of the sentence. The children may act out a sentence. However, the sentence should be about something they can see or hear at the time or about a common occurrence. The teacher gives sentences one at a time and each child has a turn to respond. The sentences may be nonemotional such as: "That is my book," "The children are on the playground," "Be quiet," or "Let's go." Or the sentences may be about feelings: "I'm sleepy," "I hurt my finger," "That's a loud noise," or "Don't do that."

9. Each child verbally says a sentence and simultaneously nonverbally indicates the referent. This lesson is a natural accompaniment to an arithmetic lesson. For example, if the arithmetic lesson is addition, each child in turn can give a problem and the answer while pointing to written numbers or to objects. Thus, "two plus three equals five," is both spoken and indicated.

10. The students in the class have a nonverbal time. This assignment presents a creative use of the traditional "quiet time." However, instead of telling the children to put their heads down and be quiet, the teacher tells the children not to talk but to communicate whatever they wish by gesture. Of course, this lesson becomes most useful just before lunch or at the end of the day. The teacher also participates by nonverbally communicating that a student may erase the board, or a student may water the plants, or everyone should go get their coats. It is important to insist on no sounds and on not leaving seats unless signaled (by the teacher or another student if so allowed). The rules must be carefully explained in advance. By so doing the teacher can creatively direct into a nonverbal experience the children's needs for movement as well as his and the children's needs for quiet.

INTERMEDIATE LEVEL EXERCISES

1. Students are given the name of an animal and then they show the movement and the sounds that animal makes. Students should be in a large enough space so they have freedom to move. Depending on the abilities of the class, this assignment may be used with the entire class at one time or with small groups taking turns. This lesson could be improved if it were preceded by a trip to the zoo, a filmstrip of exotic animals, or a trip to a farm. Then students can watch movements carefully with the intent to copy them later. Of course, commonly observed animals such as cats or dogs can be added to the repertoire. The important factor is to provide both observation experience and demonstration experience.

2. Students in the class act as an inanimate object moving under some outside force. Suggestions for this activity are to ask students to be a tree in the wind, a flower in the rain, a whistling tea kettle, a revolving door, or a bouncing ball. These are similar to the previous exercises in that they may be performed by the entire class or by small groups. One exercise that requires a small group working

together, with each child doing a different action, is to simulate a machine that has many moving parts. This is a slight variation of the inanimate object movement because it requires observing others so one can fit in or be different.

3. Each child transmits a nonverbal message that he has observed a person in the environment using. The teacher asks the student to spend a day or two observing people at school, at home, or in the town, and to notice a nonverbal communication that is used. The message should include gestures as well as sounds: a whistle, scream, sigh, or yell. Each child demonstrates such a person and the class guesses who the person is. For example: a police officer directing traffic, a person signaling a dog or a horse to come (no words), a baby crying, a child rubbing her eyes, someone who has cut a finger, and so on.

4. Small groups act as Indians and Pilgrims, communicating different messages. The teacher points out that the Indians and Pilgrims did not use the same verbal language, but they still communicated. The groups show various Indian and Pilgrim scenes, for example: Indians greeting Pilgrims when they landed, Pilgrims indicating they want to be friends, Indians showing Pilgrims corn and how to plant it, Pilgrims inviting the Indians to Thanksgiving dinner, and so on until a series of Indian-Pilgrim scenes has been performed and every child has been part of the lesson. This is, of course, designed to accompany a history lesson.

5. Each child becomes one person or animal in a story just read and the story is acted out nonverbally. This assignment works into reading groups. It may be used after the story is first read silently as a novel method of checking comprehension. It can also be used after reading the story aloud as a less advanced assignment.

6. The children watch a TV program with no sound turned on. This should be done as a group, with the teacher helping the children discuss the nonverbal components of communication. The teacher may want to use a live TV program, if he is lucky enough to have one on the air at the appropriate time; or he may find it is better to videotape a program and then replay it, being careful to observe copyright laws. The purpose is to make the students aware of the contribution of the nonverbal elements to verbal communication. The children should discuss facial expressions, gestures, and body action. Have the students see how much of a message they can interpret with no sound, but also point out that communication is most effective when both verbal and nonverbal comments are combined.

7. The students watch persons gathered together and discuss the nonverbal and verbal components of the communication. A school assembly is a natural occurring event to observe. For instance, they can watch the principal introducing the program, the persons participate in the program, and the audience respond (smiling, clapping, restless, whispering). Students should be given the assignment before the assembly. Discussion occurs after the assembly.

8. The class as a group uses nonverbal emblems to accompany verbal symbols

in a song. Pete Seeger's album "Birds, Beasts, Bugs and Little Fishes"[3] provides an excellent example of such songs. This lesson is designed to accompany music.

9. Each child explains verbally and nonverbally to a small group how to do a game or activity. This assignment works well in an activity center in the room where students go when work is finished. It also works in an open-class school where students rotate in activity choices. In either situation both the student and the teacher need to be aware in advance of the activity the student will demonstrate. The teacher needs to keep a list of children participating in order to be certain each child has the opportunity to do so, probably over a period of weeks.

10. Each child tells the entire class how to do something, using both verbal and nonverbal symbols. The teacher may need to keep a list of opportunities and assign them one at a time to students until everyone has an opportunity. Explanations should involve practical things that will naturally require nonverbal as well as verbal messages, such as how to run the tape recorder or filmstrip projector, how to plant seeds, showing seeds in various stages of growth, mixing paints to achieve different colors, or cleaning the erasers. With a little imagination, the teacher can think of assignments throughout a week in a number of different classes.

ADVANCED LEVEL EXERCISES

1. Small groups pantomime the everyday behaviors of a group of people. The teacher might list a number of options on slips of paper, and each group of students draws one slip. They have time to plan their performance before they present it to classmates. Have class members decide what the group was doing. The options presented by the teacher should include common experiences of children. Among the options might be students in school, children in line at a drinking fountain, playing baseball, playing dodge ball, jumping rope, people in an elevator, people waiting for a bus, people skiing, a family at dinner, and so on.

2. Each child pantomimes a common behavior of hers. The teacher should suggest a number of possibilities from which each student chooses. Possible choices are getting a drink of water, putting on an item of clothing, wrapping a present, setting a table, picking up a baby, petting a kitten, milking a cow, gathering eggs, and so on. The students should be given this assignment a day in advance. The purpose is to carefully analyze the nonverbal actions in the selected behavior and then to be able to repeat the actions without the object present. Pantomimes are to be performed individually in front of the class. Classmates may guess what the behavior is.

[3] Pete Seeger, "Birds, Beasts, Bugs and Little Fishes" (New York: Folkways Records and Service Corp., 1958), distributed by Folkways/Scholastic Records, Englewood Cliffs, NJ.

3. Each child acts out a description of a walk. This lesson is designed to be preceded by a creative writing assignment in English studies. For the assignment, each student writes a paragraph describing a walk he took, for example: down a busy city sidewalk, up a mountain, through fields and pastures, across the barnyard, or through the halls at school. After the paragraph is written, each student in turn takes that walk nonverbally. The students should read the paragraph aloud first and then follow with the walk so classmates can watch the walk with anticipation.

4. Each student watches a program or film and describes nonverbal displays of emotion. A good program for this home assignment is the TV series "Little House on the Prairie" because every episode includes a variety of emotions. If the teacher prefers, a film shown in the classroom might be used. The purpose is to ask students to make a list of the type of emotions and the display of those emotions. The next day the students discusss their observations.

5. Each student goes on a one-day scavenger hunt to find people who show emotions verbally and nonverbally. In this lesson, the teacher gives each student a list of emotions to search for and beside each word are three columns, "verbal," "nonverbal," and "who." The lists might include someone who is happy, sad, scared, hurt, angry, tired, in a hurry, worried, nervous, and so on. Students who return with a complete list that they can explain win the game.

6. Students describe the meanings of some sentences that are said differently. The teacher says sentences such as, "John don't stop," "Would you like to go," "I'm really upset," and "This is important." He says each sentence three times changing inflection, pause, or tone to give different meanings to the same sentence. After each sentence the students discuss the meaning.

7. Each child gives a sentence at least twice and changes the meaning of the sentence. The teacher might decide to deliver the sentence first in a neutral way or to write each sentence. Sentences for students might include any of those in the previous lesson or might include additional ones that are particularly meaningful to children such as, "I think I'm gonna throw up," "That was good," "That hurts," "You're being bad," or "I'm gonna tell on you."

8. Students discuss a group of messages that present conflicting verbal and nonverbal information. This exercise is probably best prepared by a videotape of the teacher or someone else who practices and is skilled at giving conflicting messages. For example, the person might smile but say, "I don't like your behavior," or frown but say, "I understand," or act angry but say "Let me do that for you." The teacher may do this live but it should be prepared in advance. Students then describe what the verbal and nonverbal behaviors communicated.

9. Each student delivers a conflicting verbal and nonverbal message to the class. This assignment coordinates well with a writing assignment in English. The student writes what is said and describes the verbal message and then writes a description of the feelings that are in conflict. After the teacher checks the writing assignment to be certain a conflicting message is sent, the student does

both verbal and nonverbal components for the group. Among choices to give students are: tell someone to do something you don't intend to do; talk politely but be angry; tell a friend something is good to eat but it's awful; or say you're not hurt when you really are. The class discusses the conflicting messages sent.

10. Each student gives a response to a conflicting message. This is an expansion of the previous assignment in that two persons role play. One person delivers the conflicting message (students repeat those given before or plan new ones), and the other person responds. The teacher should precede this lesson with a discussion that centers around the need to recognize the conflict and to respond in such a manner to resolve which message the speaker meant to send. A creative response to someone who wants you to do something might be, "you don't act like you want to do that" or "I don't think that's a good idea." A creative response to someone who acts angry might be to ask, "Are you mad at me?" or "Are you angry about something?" A creative response to someone who says he is not hurt might be, "Let's get some help" or "You need a bandage." The important point is to give the students experience in practicing the art of clearing up conflicting messages.

3

Listening

OBJECTIVES

At the end of this chapter you should be able to

1. Explain the difference between hearing and listening.
2. Discuss the effects of novel stimuli on listening behavior.
3. Discuss the effects of contexts, sound sequencing, and cognitive operations on listening.
4. Discuss realistic expectations of active listening.
5. Describe some possible behaviors associated with active listening.
6. Explain the joint responsibilities of speaker and listener in affecting listening behavior.
7. Discuss how the general and specific level competencies are designed to yield, by the time of exit, an elementary mastery of listening as currently conceived.
8. Explain how the general exit competencies represent broad goals that accompany each specific level competency.
9. Match each exercise to the general exit competency or competencies and the specific level exit competency or competencies that the exercise addresses.
10. Explain why the successful completion of one exercise does not fulfill the objectives of the competencies.
11. Design additional exercises for the fulfillment of the stated competencies.

Listening is an integral part of all communication behavior, and there is some danger in talking about it as if it were a separate process. Current views of communication tend to talk about systems in which people interact to build mutual understanding without identifying some as talkers and others as listeners. To spend too much time looking only at the listening functions runs the risk of distorting our perception of the communication process. The same problem has been observed in approaches to communication that focus only on speakers.

Just as we saw value in pausing to examine nonverbal communication as a separate entity before moving it into its place as one element in a broader system of sharing meaning, so we see a similar value in looking specifically at listening. There are several reasons for doing this.

A first reason is the need to alert children to the importance of listening in their lives. It is estimated that adults spend almost half their communication time (that involving reading, writing, speaking, or listening) acting as listeners. Elementary school children are said to spend more than 50 percent of their time in school listening. By the time the students reach college they will spend almost

48

70 percent of their school time listening. If these figures are even moderately accurate, some notice of listening behavior seems warranted.

A second reason to spend some time talking about listening comes from some popular misconceptions about the process. Over the past few hundred years, during the rising importance of printed communication, we have developed an educational bias in favor of the teaching of reading and writing. This, of course, ignores the several thousand years preceding that time when oral communication occupied an eminent place in education. People naively assumed that everyone learned to speak and listen as a natural part of growing up. Reading and writing were perceived as the activities that call for serious educational treatment. Today, the naiveté has been exposed as specialists recognize the equal need for educational attention to all communication skills: reading, writing, speaking, and listening. Although communication theorists see these as all parts of a process of communication, there is some value in calling attention to them individually.

Finally, writers on communication rarely consider the particular problems of teaching young children. Those who spend most of their time studying and teaching adults miss some of the unique needs of elementary-age children. The value of helping children develop their understanding and skill in listening early in their lives is a most potent reason for examining listening.

THE CONCEPT

Obviously, listening begins with the assumption of normal hearing ability. Any problems at that level should lead to an examination by a specialist. In normal functioning, sound waves activate the hearing mechanism. Neural activity carries sound through the brain, into the cerebral cortex, and by the processes of perception and discrimination into a linguistic process in which the listener recognizes words and sentences communicated by the sound waves. But this by no means is the total process of listening.

Audiologists have observed the hearing process through physiological measurements that include but are not limited to evoked potentials.[1] Their measurements show that a person may be hearing and understanding sounds buy may vary widely in the extent to which one gives them full attention within the higher mental processes. At the start of a hearing experience, one may use full cognitive abilities to consider the material. Soon, however, if expectations are that more of the same will be forthcoming, cognitive activity will be reduced and the information will have less total impact. If some novelty occurs, as in a change of sound, if some unexpected information is presented, or if some new

[1] G. A. McCandless and D. E. Rose, Evoked Cortical Responses to Stimulus Change, *Journal of Speech and Hearing Research* (1970), 13 (3), 624–634.

valuable information is anticipated, a sudden surge of brain wave activity will take place. This would seem to predict what McCandless calls "bursts of learning." For that short time in which the full cognitive facilities are engaged by the hearing experience, more robust communication takes place.

An example is the experienced police officer who drives for hours with the radio turned down low—almost to the point of being inaudible. The policeman may converse with a companion, observe what is going on in the street, and to the untrained observer it would appear impossible to receive any information from the radio. But when the dispatcher mentions that particular car's number and goes on to direct police to the scene of a crime, they actively listen. Announcement of the call number triggers alert attention. They have, in a manner of speaking, been listening to the radio all along, but they have not bothered to do more than recognize that it is routine involving someone else. When the familiar signal is heard, the full cognitive channels open up and a different kind of listening takes place.

Of course, it is not just the mention of the special identification number that would trigger the burst of listening. If, during the routine of police calls, the dispatcher were to say in the same monotonous voice, "Bunny rabbits like carrots, but spiders don't care for them," it is predictable that a similar burst of listening would be stimulated as the police tried to figure out what is going on in the dispatch office. By the same token, if every call on the radio were to begin with the special identification number of that one police car, the officers would soon close down some of their cognitive processing.

Contexts in which sounds occur influence greatly the meanings attached to them. In one study reported by the Bell Telephone Laboratories,[2] a group of people heard the same sound wave representing a word that sounded different when the word was used in three different sentences. Depending on the sentence, the same sound wave was interpreted as either "bit," "bet," or "bat." Those who speak several languages fluently, say the Bell Labs, sometimes hear distinct words or phrases as having been spoken in one language only to realize later that another language was used. When airline passengers listen in on the calls from the tower to the pilot, they usually find them difficult to understand. Not only is the talk unfamiliar to them but the static seems to drive out all sensible words. But pilots, knowing the context, understand completely.

Knowledge of sounds and the sound sequencing of a language is also a determinant of the kind of listening to be expected. We select from total sounds communicated the distinct meaning units heard. When listening to people speak an unfamiliar language, it usually seems as if they speak much more rapidly than we expect. They seem to produce an almost continuous flow of

---

[2] See P. Denes and E. Pinson, *The Speech Chain* (Bell Telephone Laboratories, 1963).

sound rather than separate words. But when we know the language, that seemingly senseless flow becomes clearly discernible meaning.

We can characterize listening *conceptually* as "the selective process of attending to, hearing, understanding, and remembering aural symbols."[3] The concept of listening includes a series of cognitive operations, according to Barker, which include attention, sound isolation, language recognition, primary meaning assignment, which includes interpretation, evaluation, and information retention. Listening also includes affective processes that can be characterized as seeing a purpose or value in listening to satisfy personal intrinsic motives, to appreciate the listening experience whether it is a concert or a lecture.

We have already noted that attending—paying attention—operates at various levels. A basic or primary attention is the type given by the police officers during routine calls and by the rest of us as we are perceiving sounds and selecting information from them at a low level of cognitive processing. We are likely to notice in particular those sounds that are novel, intense, or changing. All of us learn to note particular signals in the environment: a clock chimes the hours, a siren goes off in the distance, music stops at the end of the tape, the washing machine goes off and we know the cycle is ended. A higher form of attention occurs, usually triggered by one change that allows a burst of listening such as a siren immediately behind us, or a clock which chimes 20 times. Then we select great amounts of information from the sounds and process them more carefully.

Important to understanding the concept of listening is the fact that none of us attends at the highest level all or even most of the time. Even continued intense communication, as in a continuous flow of loud sound or striking ideas, will rather quickly be habituated or moved down to the lower level of cognition. To tell children to pay attention all the time is to fail to understand human capabilities. Just because children are slouched down in their chairs and looking around the room doesn't mean they are necessarily failing to listen. They are listening at the most common level, just as the police officers listen to their radio. When something novel, intense, or changing occurs, the children will be ready for a burst of listening. One study of college students found that at any given time during a lecture only about 12 percent were actively listening. The others were thinking about something else and listening to the lecture at a minimal level. Although further study of listening skills might improve that figure, it is not suggested that listening training could create an entire classroom of constant active listeners.

This approach to the concept of listening, therefore, puts a good deal of the responsibility on the communicator. The classroom teacher or any other speaker must see that novel, intense, or changing elements occur in the communication

---

[3] See L. Barker, *Listening Behavior* (Englewood Cliffs, NJ: Prentice-Hall, Inc., 1971), p. 17.

to trigger students or other listeners to open up for a burst of learning. Study under our concept of listening will help people make full use of their bursts, and even help them increase the frequency of bursts, but a major responsibility for listening effectiveness falls on the communicator.

Operationally, listening can be characterized by indicating a series of behaviors which are recommended for those who are active listeners. Recall from Chapter 1 that an operational definition is one that derives the meaning of a concept from specific operations and that in this book we will frequently report operations that are associated with optimal performance of the particular communication skill being discussed. Often, as is true with listening, these operations may include suggestions for effective behavior that have not been derived from descriptive research.

Presuming an individual has decided to be an active listener in a communication situation, the following operations are performed:

1. Before listening, one can anticipate what is expected from the communication.
2. During communication, one may listen for ideas which go beyond the expectations or stereotypes.
3. The listener might consciously identify his or her role in the communication.
4. One should focus as much attention as possible on the communicator and reduce as much as possible concentration on private thoughts or other distractions.
5. The listener can focus attention on what the speaker is saying rather than on the manner of speaking, dress, or random behaviors.
6. The listener can review the role the communicator is assuming and what his purpose is in speaking.
7. The listener might review from time to time how he or she relates to the speaker.
8. The listener might search out the speaker's main ideas.
9. One can think about how the speaker sees the world.
10. The listener can reflect upon how she and the speaker are alike and different, and how someone like the speaker can be different in some ways and still be a reasonable person worth listening to.
11. At selected points, the listener can help herself experience a burst of listening by shifting position, leaning forward, jotting down a note, or saying to herself, "This is different. This is important."
12. The listener can notice how material from the speaker relates to her own needs and interests and how the material can be of value to her.
13. Listeners should use note taking selectively. Trying to write down everything said may be less useful than noticing main points; outlining to observe

the relation of main points to supporting points may sometimes be helpful and not so helpful at other times.

14. The listener can notice points in the communication which include words or phrases that trigger a series of private thoughts. Sometimes these thoughts are more useful than what the speaker says next: sometimes they merely distract. The listener should consciously decide whether private thinking is useful at any point.

15. The listener might think about what the speaker has said in making his ideas believable and worthwhile and what the speaker has not said that may be important in deciding on the value of the communication.

16. An active listener carefully notices the extent to which she is really thinking about what she will say when the speaker has finished his turn and has thereby failed to listen carefully to what he is saying. She will selectively hold off developing her ideas for future communication when she wants to listen.

17. The listener provides responses to the speaker from time to time that communicate nonverbally understanding, confusion, agreement, or concern.

18. Finally, before starting her own contribution to the communication, the careful listener first tries to communicate in her own words what she understands the speaker to have said.

This is an exhaustive list of operations gathered from many writers, and it reflects the absence of a central unifying theory. Not all are appropriate to all communication situations. Listeners play many roles, such as friend, counselor, learner, advocate, judge, consumer, or interested bystander. To be an active listener in any of these roles may call on only a few of these operations. Some will call for more than others. And, or course, no one will be a full-time active listener.

THE TRADITION

Writers on listening seek to establish a tradition for the subject by quoting pithy sayings of ancient commentators. For example, they note that the ancient Egyptian Vizier, Ptahhotpe, wrote that "Hearing is good and speaking is good, but he who hears is a possessor of benefits," about 5,000 years ago. They quote the Greek historian Plutarch as saying, "Know how to listen and you will profit even from those who talk badly," and they observe that the ancient philosopher Epictetus said, "Nature has given to men one tongue but two ears, that we may hear from others twice as much as we speak."

Additionally, a listening tradition is tied to the fact that rhetoricians were interested in theories of memory more than 2,000 years ago. But the rhetoricians were approaching the subject from the perspective of the Orator who needed to memorize a speech for delivery. So the fact is that listening as we are talking about it here has a relatively brief tradition. It has been within the past 50 years or so that writers have seriously addressed the subject.

The Common Ways of Thinking about listening center on concern that people listen poorly even though they spend a great deal of their time doing so. The concern is magnified by the fact that virtually no formal instruction in listening is available in the schools or colleges. The bulk of material written about listening tends to be rhetorical in the effort to convince more people to support the teaching of listening. The other common way of thinking about listening is the preparation of lists of do's or don'ts for the effective listener. Our operational definition of the concept reports the essence of such lists. These lists form the basis of workshops and short courses taught to business and professsional people. It is with such audiences that listening has been most popular. It seems as if people who have spent some time in the world of work have more clearly seen the problems that arise from their poor listening habits, and they are willing to pay substantial sums to teachers who promise to improve their listening skills.

The Current Perspectives reveal two schools of thought, separate and unequal. The larger school perceives that teaching and research aimed at listening per se violates a unified theory of communication in which the speaking and listening processes are inseparable. They also condemn the field as being too prescriptive and lacking a serious research foundation. This group is made up of most contemporary scholars in speech communication.

The second, smaller group also consists of speech communication people for the most part who take the opposite stand. They believe that listening deserves attention from teachers and scholars and they have formed the International Listening Association to promote their position. They claim that with more research, which they are encouraging, the importance of teaching in listening skills will be established.

The View of This Book is that both positions have merit and that we should reflect the best work of each. Thus, we take the position that listening must ultimately be viewed as inherently a part of a broader process of communication. To that end, the chapters that follow will discuss communication skills from that broad perspective, and we expect that students will actively participate as both speakers and listeners. We recognize the prescriptive nature of current materials on listening and caution the reader against placing more reliance upon the ideas presented than is warranted by the thin research foundation.

We are particularly anxious to alert the teacher to the fact that there seem to be several levels of listening/learning. The individual on his own initiative will selectively attend to stimuli on the basis of his internal states. Still, we offter this chapter on the grounds that there seem to be values to be gained, particularly in work with elementary children, from development of listening skills as such. That will be our focus.

We will also take the view, consistent with the majority of speech communication scholars, that much of the responsibility of listening rests with the communicator to provide the novel, the intense, and the changing elements so as to make possible the bursts of learning discussed earlier. We also take issue with the implication by some advocates of listening that one can become a full-time active listener if only he will study the subject and make the effort. This is not supported by serious research. In our view, lower, less cognitively robust listening will continue to be the most common and, in many situations, the most appropriate behavior.

COMPETENCIES TO BE DEVELOPED

Three *General Exit Competencies* encompass the skills to be developed in listening.

The child should have the ability to

1. Demonstrate awareness of listening opportunities and selectively attend.
2. Use listening as a factor in both recalling ideas and thinking.
3. Integrate listening behavior into the total communication process.

Recognizing that active listening occurs only occasionally, the first general exit competency asks the student to be able to identify those opportunities for such listening and take full advantage of them. A child will be more conscious of self in recognizing mental and physical states that promote or retard active listening. He will consider his own needs in relation to the communication present to determine those instances in which active listening is not only possible but worthwhile. Having made those decisions, the child will be able to engage in the kind of listening deemed appropriate.

When active listening is chosen, the second general exit competency becomes appropriate. The child will be able to use the listening to enhance both recall and thinking. Short-term memory has been identified as that most valuable in oral communication. Within this general competency children will work first for immediate recall of small amounts of information and move toward the ability to recall greater amounts of information for longer periods of time. At all levels, independent thinking by the children will be encouraged.

Finally, the third general exit competency calls for the student to integrate listening behavior into the total communication process. Here a child will reveal the ability to listen and respond in all forms of communication, most of which call for a transaction in which two or more people talk together, hear and understand what others have said, and demonstrate that by appropriate responses as full communication participants. Just as it is troublesome when someone hogs the conversation, never letting others speak, and instead engages in a social monolog, it is troublesome when someone's sole communication role is that of listener. It is just as problematic to have two or more people doing what is called a duolog. That is, people apparently talk together, but each is actually intent upon telling his story without really interacting with the others to build a joint meaning or understanding. Of course, listening as a member of a formal audience will be considered. Integration of listening into the total communication process is the goal of this competency.

Beginning Exit Competencies include the ability to

1. Perceive and discriminate among sounds in the environment.
2. Perceive and discriminate among sounds in words.
3. Listen to and follow directions.
4. Use listening to generate answers to questions.

Even in the so-called quiet country there are multiple sounds in the environment: birds, animals, tractors, cars on the highway, wind in the trees, an airplane overhead. In the city, there are even more sounds. Early learning in listening calls for perception and discrimination among these sounds in the search for meaning. A common example is that of the mother who can tell by the sounds or their absence what her children are doing. This is not a skill inherently possessed by mothers. Anyone who bothers to listen and learn could do the same thing. The farmer who can tell by the sound of the wind what is likely to happen to the weather is similarly not unique but merely skilled. The first beginning exit competency aims at sensitizing children to the sounds around them and the potential meaning they offer.

Similarly, children have a need to focus their skills in perception and discrimination to the sounds in words. Because language is the basis for communication and because sound is the medium for oral communication, it is necessary to learn word sounds just as ultimately children will learn to recognize written language. Young children need to discriminate among speech sounds first, and then the teacher can identify those sounds as being represented by a letter or several letters. Phonics is one of the several methods that can be combined to identify words in reading. Thus, discrimination among oral language sounds is excellent preparatin for aonther type of communication: reading.

Listening to and following directions is a particular point of contention be-

56

tween adults and children. Adults regularly claim that children simply do not pay attention. They call children lazy listeners. To be sure, children need work in developing listening skills, and this competency addresses the particular one of following directions. But this work needs to be done with the understanding that children always sitting up straight and looking directly at the teacher or parent is not going to happen. It is the responsibility of the communicator to present the directions in a novel, intense, or changing way so as to encourage an opening of cognitive processing in the children. Furthermore, when children ask that the directions be repeated, they are acting as responsible listeners rather than exhibiting laziness. We know a teacher who refuses to repeat directions and announces instead, "LTFD" or "LL," which she has explained stand for "Listen To and Follow Directions," and "Lazy Listener." So when children are trying to check their understanding and work at listening, she is chastising them for missing the directions in the first place. We realize that some children take advantage of the right to ask for repetitions, but those instances can be dealt with inside a context of respecting the need for a restatement. We suspect that the "LTFD" teacher is actually a lazy communicator.

The final beginning competency calls for children to be able to listen to what others say in order to answer specific questions. This brings together the personal need for seeking information with the skill of using active listening to satisfy that need. It is a skill that will be built upon in later communication behavior.

Intermediate Exit Competencies call for children to develop the ability to

1. Demonstrate the use of memory and attention in recalling communications.
2. Listen for details in order to respond appropriately on the basis of those details.

At the intermediate level, the first objective is to expand the children's ability in terms of the quantity of material that can be recalled. This will be observed in two ways: the children will be able to demonstrate memory through verbal behavior, and they will demonstrate their skill through actions based upon communication. Because at this level memory sequences are longer and because actions will be required, there will also be some expansion of the duration of recall.

The second intermediate exit competency begins the gradual movement toward the development of critical listening by sensitizing children to the importance of listening for details. There will be two kinds of listening involved here: they will be introduced to the process of selecting main ideas in a communication, and they will begin the process of noticing the details in a communication with sufficient fullness to be able to report details, use details, and act upon them. As a part of this work, children will begin to notice confusing aspects of another's communication. Typically, children resist evaluating any kind of adult speech. Therefore, we have asked teachers to modify the syntax of sentences so that children will not be afraid to notice such details. We are not intending through this competency to teach children to adopt the habit of correcting the speech of their peers or of adults. This is simply a method of helping children learn to listen for details.

Advanced Exit Competencies involve the ability to

1. Use listening abilities in a variety of enriching experiences.
2. Use critical listening to distinguish the relative importance and merit of elements of a communication.
3. Use listening with others in order to understand and report information.

Listening serves us in situations other than those calling for information gathering. Full appreciation of much of the experiences available within our culture comes from being able to listen fully and build understanding and satisfaction. What a barren life it would be if we experienced only those things already familiar to us. Part of growing is being exposed to the new and different: new foods, new locations, new ideas, new art, new music, new dance. Without learning to use listening in a variety of experiences, children would grow up with ears closed to many of the finest aspects of culture. Learning instead to use listening widely to experience the world will yield adults who are both more cultured and more able to grow culturally. This means that children should begin such adventures in listening as early as possible.

Critical listening is a vital skill to many communication situations, but one that requires careful learning for effective use. Essentially, critical listening calls for analysis of others' communications: what did they say, how did they support or prove their points, how did they identify main ideas and relate them one to another, how did they structure their comments, how did they express the ideas, what is their perspective, what were they trying to accomplish by communicating, what did they not say?

Two points of caution need to be made about critical listening. First, "critical" does not mean negative. To be *critical* is to be *analytical*; it is not to be destructive. This concept is discussed more fully in Chapter 8, "Reasoning." Second, critical listening requires analysis without becoming so involved in that process that what the speaker is saying becomes lost. If the listener is not careful, much will be lost while analysis is going on.

Critical listening should permit the child to build unusual understanding of what others have said. It should be a creative and constructive act contributing to the total communication experience.

This, of course, leads to the final advanced competency, which calls for children to use their skills in listening to communicate effectively with others.

By this point, they should have learned that listening is truly not a distinct behavior. It is, rather, an important element in all communication. They will see that communicators are simultaneously listeners and talkers—working together to build shared meaning. While talking, the students should be "listening" to others in the sense of constantly being aware of who the others are, what they believe, how they will understand what is being said, what they will likely say to themselves or others during the communication. Even in more formal lecture or public speaking situations, members of the audience are very much on the mind of the speaker, just as audience members should be actively listening with a view toward how they will use what they hear in their own talk. Listening skill will soon be integrated into all other communication experiences.

Sample Exercises for Listening

The suggested exercises that follow provide examples of types of listening lessons at three levels of elementary instruction. The lessons are designed to teach skills that meet the general exit competencies as well as the exit competencies at each level.

Listening is both an active and a passive process done by an individual who brings his own background of experience, knowledge, and interest to the communication situation. The individual will select what she attends to on the basis of both background and current needs. Outside of novelty of stimuli, the speaker has little control over what the listener listens to. It is not difficult to realize that a person neither wants to nor can actively attend to all auditory stimuli. In addition, passive listening can be just what is intended or is needed in some cases. Nevertheless, moments of learning probably occur in conjunction with attention at the time of surges in brain waves. Thus, teaching active listening is meant to enhance learning as well as communication skills.

Beacuse children spend more than half of their time in a classroom listening, the need for attention to listening early in the school year is apparent. Listening is an inherent part of communication and thus is part of every skill in this book. The lessons for listening in this chapter are designed to train listening in a broad scope, with being aware, recalling, thinking, and integrating listening with communication as the focus. These lessons in active listening are an introduction to the listening that must be incorporated into the other skills. They are isolated here in the same manner that nonverbal communication was isolated— to call attention and to enhance skill acquisition. The active listening lessons are offered not because active listening will occur all day or even the half of the day a child is supposedly listening, but because moments of active listening are crucial to both communication and to learning. Some of the listening lessons must stand by themselves, whereas others are designed to accompany other academic subjects. Considering the effect of developed listening skills on successful functioning in school, the time spent in these lessons is easily justified.

In addition to the following exercises, teachers may find several commercially prepared audiotapes useful. For example: *Let's Listen* (for grades Kindergarten-3) and *Adventures in Listening* (for grades 4-6) by Coronet Publishers, 65 East South Water Street, Chicago, Illinois, might be included for varieties of sounds. Although teachers usually have better lessons when the teacher takes a few ideas from outside sources and then generates his own lessons appropriate to the class, teachers who desire more prepared lessons in listening might use *Listening Games* by G. Wagner, M. Hoiser, and M. Blackman (Darien, CT: Teachers Publishing Corporation, 1970).

BEGINNING LEVEL EXERCISES

1. The teacher draws sets of ears on the board (suggestions: a rabbit's, an elephant's, a cat's, and a person's ears) and asks the children what animals these are attached to, what they are, and what the ears are used for. This is, of course, designed as a task to initiate a discussion of listening.

2. The children identify environmental sounds by use of auditory perception and discrimination. Have the students put their heads down, and be certain their eyes are covered. The teacher asks students to raise their hands as soon as they can tell what sounds they've heard and what they represent. Children answer one at a time but heads stay down. Initially, allow children to identify naturally occurring sounds such as other children on the playground, traffic in the street, a siren, a dog barking, shuffling feet, and so on. Then, the teacher should create additional sounds such as dropping a pencil, crushing paper, pouring water, shuffling cards, sweeping with a broom, and so on. This listening activity is a creative use of the traditional quiet time and can be used productively to quiet children when they are restless or near the end of the day.

3. Each child locates sounds by listening. Select one child to leave the room. This child is mother cat. Then select three children in various locations of the room to be kittens. All children in the room cover their mouths. When mother cat returns, she utters a "meow" and the three selected children answer with "meow" until she can find them. As soon as mother cat has found her children, have her select someone to be the next mother. Change animals as needed; for example, ducks, chickens, pigs, and dogs are good choices. In addition, increase the number of children to be found as soon as the students gain proficiency.

4. The students clap when they hear a word with a certain sound. For example, the students are studying the /s/ sound (do not say the name of the letter, "es"; use the sound /s/). The teacher instructs students: "Clap when you hear a word with the /s/ sound." So the teacher says a series of words each with the same pitch and intensity; for example: snake (clap), sky (clap), book, sweet (clap), jump, torn, sister (clap), sad (clap), and so on.

Lessons presented here are given with different sounds to demonstrate variety, but any lesson can be used with any sound. As with any sound lesson, only one sound should be taught at a time, and the most effective method is to use

60

different activities for the same sound on consecutive days so that one sound is learned before another is begun. After a number of sounds have been learned, they can be combined and compared.

5. The students participate in answering puzzles for words that have a certain sound. In this activity it is good to start with a repeated catch phrase for each riddle that contains the sound you are working on. For example: Crazy, Crazy Key, Whatever Can This Be.

It is something that begins and ends with /k/ and we have it for a birthday party. (cake)

Crazy, Crazy Key, Whatever Can This Be.

It is something that begins with a /k/ and we put it on a birthday cake. (candles)

Crazy, Crazy Key, Whatever Can This Be.

It is something that begins with a /k/ and is an animal that gives us milk. (cow)

Crazy, Crazy Key, Whatever Can This Be.

It is something that begins with a /k/ and says meow. (cat)

Crazy, Crazy Key, Whatever Can This Be.

It is a word that begins with a /k/ and is a time of year when Santa comes. (Christmas)

Crazy, Crazy Key, Whatever Can This Be.

It is a thing that begins with a /k/ and is used to open a door. (key)

These are examples of riddles for the /k/ sound. The teacher may make up all of them or let the students make up others after the game is begun. Remember to teach only one sound at a time. Note that the teacher always uses the sound /k/ and does not say the name of the letter — "kay" or "see." Also note that this is not spelling or reading (although it is excellent training for both), so no attention is called to the different spelling. This is listening. Later the teacher can point out that the sound /k/ is sometimes spelled with a k, a c, a ch, or a q.

6. Students dictate a story to the teacher that has words with /l/ in it. The teacher is well advised to name in advance the central character of the story so that the name has the sound in it. Each reading group might tell a different story centered around the same sound. Then the teacher can read aloud all the stories to the group, emphasizing sounds. In storytelling, the teacher should remember that some sounds (/s/, /z/, /r/, /l/, and /th/) are difficult for normal young children to produce correctly. Thus, she should not correct faulty production. Instead, if a sound is not said appropriately (such as the /th/ instead of the /s/ that young children and children without front teeth will doubtlessly use), she should merely repeat the word or sentence using the sound appropriately.

To demonstrate a type of story children can write, we are including a story for the /l/ sound written by students when one of the authors was a classroom teacher.

LEO THE LION

Once in a jungle there lived a baby lion named Leo. He was afraid of everything. His mother tried to teach him that he was the king of the jungle. He was afraid of any little creature moving through the leaves. Every time someone came close to him he would run away.

One day Papa Lion said, "You must learn to be king of the jungle. You must learn not to be afraid of things. When someone comes close to you, growl loudly at them." Leo tried to growl, but he never could do it.

One day a leprechaun came skipping along. The leprechaun saw Leo lying by his mother and father and crying. The leprechaun said, "Do not feel so bad. I will help you."

The leprechaun told Leo to try to scare the rhinoceros. He took Leo by a lake on the way to Mister Rhinoceros's house. Leo looked in the lake at himself and tried to roar. But he saw how fierce he looked, and he ran away. Then slowly he crept back. He looked in the lake at himself again and was so frightened he roared. Just then Mister Rhinoceros came walking by. He tried to butt Leo into the lake, but Leo roared so loudly the rhinoceros ran.

That is how Leo the Lion found out he was the king of the jungle. Everyone was so proud of him they had a celebration that night in the jungle. (As told to Dr. Willbrand by M. Burnham, K. Bennett, and K. Allen, Columbia, Missouri.)

7. Students follow directions given by the teacher for body movements. As a group all students participate but to make a game students may be asked to drop out when they miss. An interesting variation is to use this also to teach right and left orientation. For example, the teacher says, "Raise your right hand. Wiggle your fingers on your left hand. Close your right eye. Tap your right foot. Shake your right arm. Bend your left knee," and so on.

8. Students follow directions by reproducing on paper what the teacher describes. In arithmetic this may mean writing down dictated numbers in problems. In art the teacher might direct students to draw a red circle, a blue square, a green line, and so on. Time should be given after the teacher utters each symbol. Memory sequencing is not required until students are more sophisticated listeners.

9. Students get ready to leave the room in order by listening to descriptions that fit them. The teacher may say, "The person with a red-and-white sweater may get her coat. Everyone whose name has a /d/ sound in it may get ready. People with black hair may go. People with a ring on their finger may get ready," and so on until every child has had a chance to listen and respond. The teacher must be innovative and use descriptions appropriate to the children as well as to other desired learning. The description should change every time and not follow a predictable pattern such as all colors in order to maintain maximum attention.

10. The students guess the answer to a description of an animate or inanimate object. The teacher says, "I'm thinking of something that is big and has a trunk." If one sentence cue doesn't work, another must be given. The teacher has a box containing pictures. As soon as a child gets the answer, the child draws a picture out of the box and then describes it to the class as a puzzle, such as "I'm thinking about something that is in the kitchen and cooks food."

INTERMEDIATE LEVEL EXERCISES

1. Each child should have repeated opportunities to play *Simon*, an electronic game by Milton Bradley. This commercial game provides excellent training in auditory discrimination and memory for nonverbal sounds. It can be challenging to mid-elementary children and remains so through adult years. This task is designed for an activity center in the classroom that children use independently. It has advantages in that the game of discrimination and memory is self-monitoring and can be used by one to four children.

2. Children pass along a sentence or two from one person to another by whispering to each other in turn. This game has various names and is frequently called "gossip" to indicate that communication passed along verbally often does not end with the same message as at the start. The leader starts the message. It is whispered from person to person around a circle, and the last person tells what the message was. Then original and final messages are compared. The message may be anything, but a clever teacher may want to use it to call attention to current information. For example, the sentence could be, "Friday, we get out of school at noon," or "Chaunukah (Hanukah) is a Jewish festival that lasts eight days and is called the feast of lights," or "We need cucumbers in order to make pickles tomorrow."

3. Each child repeats series of digits from memory. The teacher may want to use repetition of random digits as intelligence tests do. But at least part, if not the whole lesson, should be learning meaningful sequences. For example, have one child say his address and another repeat it. Then ask who can repeat two addresses, three, and so on. The winner is the one who can repeat the largest number accurately. After addresses, use memory for telephone numbers which usually have more digits than do addresses.

4. Children perform a series of tasks in exact duplication of a command given. The command may be for the entire class, such as "touch the table, the floor, your head, and your nose," or practical such as "take out one sheet of paper, put it on your desk, and then get one of the paints from the back of the room." Teachers give classes series of orders all the time, but the purpose of this lesson is to be certain the actions follow the exact sequence of the command. All orders should have a series of three or more actions. In addition, each child should have to demonstrate the skill individually. Children who have problems with this type of memory are frequently not noticed in a group action. The

63

individual participation may take place at the end of each day. For example: "Mary, will you put the scrap paper in the wastebasket, clean the erasers, and wash the board" or another day, "Tom, please clean up the table at the back, water the plants, and lower the blinds."

5. Children repeat words used by others and continuously add to the series. This can be a game. The first child says, "I'm going on a trip and I'm taking a suitcase," The next child says, "I'm going on a trip and I'm taking a suitcase and a hat." The game continues with each child repeating those items of the previous children, and adding a new one. This game can be adjusted to several classes. In health, "I like to eat . . . ." can be used, or in science, "Liquids are things such as . . . . " can be used.

6. Each child listens to a sentence that is modified and changes it to an appropriate form. This lesson is designed to coordinate with English and to call attention to syntactic structure. The teacher should organize a series of sentences around one structure at a time. Examples of this follow.

Prepositions: I'll put the ice cream under the refrigerator.
                  Tom watches TV from his favorite chair in back of the set.
Pronouns: Mary and me are going to the store.
                  Them are the ones I wanted.
Verbs: I winned the game.
                  He gots lots of records.

These sentences are planned for structures children modify and can be used to increase their competence. The teacher gives a sentence to each child in turn as in a spelling bee, only this is a sentence bee. Then in similar fashion each child changes the structure to include the appropriate form or she misses and sits down.

7. Children identify the important elements—who, what, where, when, how or why—of a story they have read. This lesson is designed to accompany reading. After a group reads a story, have each child draw a card that has *who, what, where, when, how,* or *why* on it. Then he has to answer the question.

8. Children review a story that the teacher has read aloud. This assignment has two goals: retelling a story and thinking about the problems and solutions. All children like to be read to. The teacher may select a book such as *Hans Anderson: His Classic Fairy Tales* (translated by E. Haugaard, London: Victor Gollancz Limited, 1976). After a story is read, have one or two children retell the story. Then have the class discuss the problems and the outcome, and suggest that they talk about what else could have happened or whether the solution was good or not.

9. One child reproduces something explained by another. The children should be separated visually by a flannel board or some other divider. One student has a project in front of him (a block tower or building, an abstract

design, a puzzle) that he verbally instructs the other to reproduce step by step. It is important that no visual observation or physical contact between the two is possible. This must be done by listening, asking questions, and so on. This activity is designed for a work center in the room that the children may use independently.

10. Children answer a test that is given orally. Of course, this may be used with any class. In order to make the listening important, it should be a real test that is graded. Teachers should be reminded that if a listener so requests, a question or problem should be repeated.

ADVANCED LEVEL EXERCISES

1. The class as a group attends a public performance, the purpose of which is to enjoy listening. A symphony, a soloist, guitar or banjo music, a play, an opera, a musical, a lecture at the zoo or the planetarium are all possibilities. Obviously, the larger the city, the broader the choices. However, if a live performance is not possible, then the teacher may choose any one of a number of programs of this type broadcast by the Public Broadcasting System (PBS) or tapes or records. Afterwards, students describe what they listened to and make some value judgment about whether it was enjoyed or not, and why. The purpose here is to encourage appreciative listening.

2. Each child attends a program other that those the whole class attended. He gives a description of what he has heard along with his impressions of it. The teacher should prepare a list of options in advance, using live programs, PBS programs, and audio recorded programs as possibilities. A student should select from the list or add his own with prior approval of the teacher. Broadening cultural and listening experiences can be part of any academic subject that the experience fits from fine arts to the humanities to science.

3. The class listens to people from different cultures performing on a common topic. An excellent class for this is music, and a good time of year is Christmas. Records are readily available with songs from white Americans, black Americans, Hawaiians, Japanese, Mexicans, and so on. At the same time of year, Chanukah songs are appropriate. Children enjoy this, and intercultural appreciation is developed.

4. Each member of the class is assigned the name of a person and discovers who they are by asking questions. In this lesson the name of a person is written on a paper that is pinned to the back of each student. The names are prepared by the teacher and may be general such as TV personalities or recording artists; or may be linked to an academic subject, for example, famous people in history, authors in English, singers in music, and so on. The object is that the student can only discover who she is by asking classmates (who can, of course, read her tag) any question except, "Who am I?" The game continues until every listener can figure out just who she is. In this manner, speakers try to communicate as

65

much as possible in a one-sentence answer to each question. But as many questions are asked as are necessary to arrive at an answer.

5. Each student participates in jointly telling a story. The leader starts a story with a few sentences and then, in turn, each person adds to the story. The rules of the activity are that each person must add to the story as it has been told thus far and only the last person may end the story.

6. The class listens to several guest speakers give informative talks, and each student writes down the main idea and supporting ideas or evidence for each speaker. The notes on main ideas and supporting material must be discussed orally or checked in written form at a later time to ascertain whether each student can do the task. The teacher is well advised to ask students in advance to inquire if their parents would be available for such a talk and what the topic would be. For example, we know parents who can talk about the hearing of dinosaurs, how to put out a fire, breeding horses, rotating crops, children's language, childhood diseases, and so on. Students might select which *topics* (do not make it a contest of people) they would like to hear about after parents have returned their suggestions.

7. Each student introduces two people to each other using both names and descriptive sentences. This is an excellent way to teach introduction, but the main concentration is on the listeners (those introduced). The two students who are introduced assume the role of the person described and as listeners they must respond accordingly for a brief exchange. For example: "Mother, this is Jane. She and I are taking dance together. Jane, this is my mother, Dr. Jones, who is a professor at the university." Then Jane and Dr. Jones must call each other by name and add some statement relevant to the information given. The important point is to listen to both name and information and be able to use it in a following communication.

8. Each student participates in privately telling a member of a group a message that must be received accurately. This is a variation of the gossip game. The class is divided into four or five teams. Each team has one person who is given a message, and that message must be given to each person one at a time until the last person repeats it aloud. Accuracy of the message is the goal. Thus, each listener may ask to have it repeated or ask a specific question. Of course, the message is whispered from person to person. The first team to have the exact message repeated by the last person wins. This can be a clever method to teach important facts in any subject. For example, in history, one statement might be, "Abraham Lincoln was the President when the slaves were freed." Another might be, "Atlanta was destroyed by fire during the Civil War," and so on. As many facts as there are groups in the class can be reviewed at one time.

9. Each member of the class participates on a team to solve a problem. This assignment is designed for math class and is a variation of math contests. The class is divided into four or five teams. Each team is given a problem orally. They may ask for it to be repeated and take notes or whatever is necessary. As a team

the members arrive at an answer. As soon as the teacher begins giving the problem to a group, time is noted. The team that supplies the correct answer in the shortest time wins.

10. Each student participates in a word game in which popular opinions are the basis for priority selections. This game is a variation of the television program "Family Feud." The first step of this game is to ask the class a series of questions to which there is no definite answer. This can be created around any academic subject. For instance, in science, "What place has good weather?" or "Name a place with mountains," or "Name something that lives in water," or "What makes plants grow?" and so on. After the written answers to at least ten sets of questions are collected, someone (the teacher or an aide) tallies the answers so that the top five answers are obtained. The next day the class is divided into teams. Each team is asked a series of the same questions aloud. They must arrive at a team answer. For presenting answers that coincide with the top five answers, they get five points (for top), four points (for next), and so on. No points are given for an answer not in the top five. The team with the most points wins. Listening, thinking, and reporting are involved in every step of the activity.

4

Person-to-Person
Communication

OBJECTIVES

At the end of this chapter you should be able to

1. Identify the transactional features of person-to-person-communication.
2. Explain why person-to-person communication does not allow a linear causal analysis.
3. Characterize person to person communication situations.
4. Describe the effect of context and background of experience on person-to-person communications.
5. Distinguish two types of interpersonal communication: personal and impersonal.
6. Explain the change in perspectives that led to consideration of interpersonal communication among ordinary people in unplanned discourse.
7. Discuss how the general and specific level competencies are designed to yield, by the time of exit, an elementary mastery of person-to-person communication as currently conceived.
8. Explain how the general exit competencies represent broad goals that accompany each specific level competency.
9. Match each exercise to the general exit competency or competencies and the specific level exit competency or competencies that the exercise addresses.
10. Explain why the successful completion of one exercise does not fulfill the objectives of the competencies.
11. Design additional exercises for the fulfillment of the stated competencies.

"Billy, say hello to Grandma and tell her how glad we are that she has come to pay us a visit."

"Hello, Grandma. We're glad you've come to see us but we hope you don't stay as long as you did last time 'cause Daddy really got tired of having you around."

"Billy! Hush! That's just not true. We want Grandma to stay as long as she wants."

"But that's what Daddy said this morning!"

Children have a lot to learn about person-to-person communication, but they have a basic inclination to communicate their thoughts and feelings honestly. If they are hurt, they cry. If they are happy, they laugh. If they do not like some food, they will say so no matter who the cook was.

Learning ways to communicate with people honestly and with fullness and still do so with sensitivity to the other people and to communication situations is the object of this chapter. We will address the issue that communication situations range from the most personal to less personal to the relatively impersonal, and notice that person-to-person communication deals with situations along that continuum. Some of the communication we will include will be the relatively impersonal use of interviewing to gain information. The fact that even in this case the communication occurs in a face-to-face interaction, with the chance to build even a temporary relationship, makes it part of the study of person-to-person communication.

When Mommy told Billy to hush, she was starting a socialization process that often does more than alert children to be sensitive to others' feelings. It tends to create a sense of secretiveness that may carry into adulthood in the form of an inability to be open and self-disclosing. We will try to help children maintain their natural ability to be open in the face of this socialization while still helping them learn to understand the consequences of their communication.

Some might believe that interpersonal communication may be too inconsequential to warrant serious study. We suggest to the contrary that person-to-person communication is a skill that requires careful instruction and will not necessarily flourish on its own; we suggest, in fact, that our failure to develop skills in person-to-person communication may be directly related to some of the significant personal and social problems that plague contemporary society.

THE CONCEPT

To be understanding of person-to-person communication it is first necessary to distinguish it from other communication situations. Most significant is the presence of mutual communication or a transaction. In many communication situations, such as public speaking, it is not likely that people will communicate with each other simultaneously. People in the audience usually remain silent and listen to what the speaker has to say. Of course, their nonverbal behaviors may provide some feedback to the speaker, but even that is not always reliable.

Person-to-person communication is different. Here people are talking in a face-to-face situation which allows them to speak freely, sometimes not allowing one person to finish a sentence before the other starts one of his own. If something is unclear, the other person can say so and let the first speaker restate it to make it more clear. If one person does not fully understand the values and interests of the other, she can ask for some talk about the subject before going on to make a point. So person-to-person communication *operates as a transaction*: people are in a constant process of mutual influence.

In many communication situations guesses must be made about how the audience will respond to messages. The advertiser, the politician, and the educator must generalize about their audiences in framing their messages.

71

Again, person-to-person communication is different. Because of the transactional nature of the situation, I do not need to predict the other person's response by what I know about her cultural or social group memberships. I can base my predictions about someone on the personal reports he makes about his own psychological state. By talking back and forth, we learn each other's beliefs, attitudes, values, intentions, motives, needs, and so forth.

Look at another distinguishing feature of person-to-person communication. Some communication situations permit a linear, causal conception of the process (although we will show problems with that conception for all communication in the chapters that follow). Think, for example, of a public speech. It is easy to think of it as a series of points in time along a time line with each point influencing the next. A speaker has an idea he wants to communicate to an audience. The idea is framed into a message, it is sent through a channel (in this case direct speech) within a context in which there may be elements of distraction that may reduce the effectiveness of the communication (called noise) such as a bad public address system, coughing and shuffling within the audience, distracting thoughts in the minds of audience members, ambiguities of words, or unclear concepts, and the audience members act as receivers of the message in that they must hear and understand what is said. Finally, the message has some effect on the audience. Time 1 is the thought, time 2 is the message, time 3 is the actual broadcasting of the message, and time 4 is the act of receiving the message. Actions in an early time are seen as the causes of actions in later times, and so on. This is a causal, linear notion of communication.

Person-to-person communication does not follow such a model. It is not useful to think of person-to-person communication as linear or directly causal. Rather, we must think of people as both sources of messages and receivers of messages simultaneously. There is a constant mutual causality: what I communicate is influenced by what you say, and what you communicate is influenced by what I say. Instead of looking at the process as a series of causes and effects occurring in time, it is necessary to understand that in the face-to-face interaction, the process is more an ongoing system of interrelated parts, each influencing and being influenced by the others. It is common to make an analogy to the heating systems in homes. The temperature in the home influences the thermometer in the thermomstat, which influences the switch on the furnace, which influences the heating elements, which influence the temperature in the home, which in turn influences the thermostat, and so on in an endless process of mutual causality. It is less important to think of where it all started and what the series of causes was than it is to look at the status of the system's functioning overall. The same is so with person-to-person communication.

So, *conceptually*, person-to-person communication involves those instances in which people predict others' communication outcomes on the basis of psychological analysis rather than cultural or sociological analysis within a transactional system of communication. These concepts are discussed at length by G. Miller and M. Steinberg.[1]

Operationally, we can characterize person-to-person communication by examining situations in which it occurs, the elements it typically involves, and the characteristics it usually displays. These will not be absolute operations because there is much variation from situation to situation.

Situations in which person-to-person communication occurs include those instances in which a *transaction* is possible. Two or three people (group communication, which is similar in most ways, is discussed in Chapter 5) communicate in a context that allows full and free communication by all involved. These people fall somewhere along a continuum ranging from total strangers at one end to those with whom we have the most intimate and enduring relationships at the other. Along the continuum will be those people with whom we have no familiarity, casual acquaintances, colleagues, fellow students, teachers, closer acquaintances, friends, best friends, lovers, and so on. Person-to-person communication may involve casual chats, passing the time of day, business talk, informal interviews, formal interviews, telephone conversations, solving problems, helping one another, counseling, supporting, or loving.

Elements typically involved in person-to-person communication include its process nature, presence of source-receivers, communicating and understanding messages with the competence necessary to fulfill the needs and desires of the situation, within a certain context and field of experience. The process elements refer to the transactional system discussed previously. All the elements are in an ongoing process of constant mutual influence. Who you are, what you are wearing, how you and I feel, what we have done together in the past, what we plan to do together in the future, how we feel about each other, what our needs and purposes are, where we are communicating, the time of day, what you and I expect of each other, what you and I know of our psychological states, where we come from socially, professionally, culturally, linguistically, all operate in constant mutual interaction.

The presence of source-receivers calls attention to the fact that in person-to-person communication there is no clear definition of who is speaker and who is listener. We are simultaneously sources and receivers of communication. Even while I am speaking, you are communicating nonverbally and by means of my knowledge of who you are and our past relationships. My choice of words, phrases, concepts, and subjects is influenced by you and your continuing communication just as yours are influenced by mine.

[1]G. Miller and M. Steinberg, *Between People* (Chicago: Science Research Associates, Inc., 1975), Chap. 1.

Communication competence includes both the linguistic competence necessary to use language appropriately and to accomplish the pragmatics of language, and the competence of communication needed to fulfill our objectives. Some elements of communication competence are developed in full in the chapters that follow. For example, decision making, reasoning, persuasion, creative performance, and intercultural communication are forms of communicative competence. We have already discussed nonverbal communication and listening which should also be included in the list.

Context and field of experience are important elements in person-to-person communication. Where we communicate makes a difference. We can laugh and shout at a ball game, but we whisper in churches and libraries. It seems easier to talk intimately in a quiet place where there are no other people. Who we are in relationship to each other also contributes. We can self-disclose more easily with close friends than with parents or teachers. Relative status makes a difference. A student in high school who had just come out of the shower after a physical education class found it easy to stand around joking with other students while wearing no clothes. But when the principal came in to talk to the student, it became awkward for him to carry on a serious conversation with the principal while standing naked in the locker room. Similarly, the psychological factors present make a difference in person-to-person communication. Family members share more common understanding and thus are able to use a different kind of talk than with relative strangers. A child may come home full of the details of what happened in school today: an alarm went off, fire trucks came, everyone marched outside, no fire was found. When a neighbor drops over and parents suggest the story be shared, it comes out quite differently. There may be reluctance to tell it at all. When it comes out, there may be a single sentence statement, "Fire trucks came to school." The presence of the neighbor changes the communication environment from close interpersonal family talk to communication with a person outside the family group. Research does not allow an explanation of precisely what happens in this change or if children are aware of their changes in communication behavior, but observation confirms that it happens commonly. Close friends engage in more mutual self-disclosure than do those who are only casually acquainted. When a child first goes to school each year, the teacher may be an unknown quantity, and conversation with her may be difficult. Later, after learning more about her, some changes will take place, either warmer or colder communication, depending upon what the child now understands about her psychologically. Even the time of day plays a role. Some of us are cheery and bright early in the morning whereas others take a long time to wake up. The eager person in the morning may have trouble talking with those who move more slowly. General Douglas MacArthur was reported to have delayed important decisions until 5 P.M. when his staff was tired and ready to go home. They tended to be much more willing to agree at that time.

To engage in any form of communication there must be some sharing of experiences. Unless the fields of experience of those engaged in person-to-person communication overlap, there will be problems. A friend of ours was a soldier captured by the Japanese during World War II and forced to engage in the infamous Bataan Death March. He was one of the few who survived. Now, when he tries to tell of that experience he finds it difficult to explain it to those of us who know the war only as history and have no common experiences that help us relate to such torture.

Finally, we can operationally define person-to-person communication by noticing some of its distinguishing characteristics. As we have already suggested, in a person-to-person situation we base our understanding of others on what we know of them personally rather than by what we would generalize about them on the basis of their membership in certain groups and cultures. For example, those who have some racial prejudices often find themselves holding to ethnic generalizations such as the belief that black people are lazy, but they easily recognize that a friend, who happens to be black, is certainly not lazy. Their communication with the friend can be personal even as they employ these impersonal prejudices in relation to other blacks whom they do not know well. This idea will be developed more fully in Chapter 12, "Intercultural Communication."

A second characteristic is similar to the first: in person-to-person communication we can predict others' reactions even in advance of talking with them on the basis of personal knowledge. After years of living with family members, we can explain their reaction to certain communications in advance and adjust accordingly. We know, for example, what subjects are going to be difficult for some people to talk about. We know that some people hate to talk business on the phone while others prefer it.

A third characteristic of person-to-person communication calls attention to the fact that some interaction is conducted within certain social norms and is thus impersonal, whereas personal communication operates on the basis of rules people have established for themselves. When two people have just been introduced, they tend to be more formal and polite and they talk of general subjects. Later, as they become better acquainted, their formality may drop away and the subjects may become more intimate. At first, they may address each other as Ms. Smith and Mr. Brown according to socially established norms, and later call each other "Skeets" and "Buck" on the basis of their interpersonally created norms. Students and teachers operate on carefully established norms of formality for the most part. But sometimes a close interpersonal relationship is built between a teacher and student which allows them to set up their own way of communicating, at least outside the classroom. The TV series "Little House on the Prairie" shows a big sister who becomes the schoolteacher. Her brothers have trouble learning to call her Miss Wilder and interact with her as the teacher according to formal norms because they have such a close person-to-person relationship already established with her. They manage to do this in school, but at home the personal norms quickly come back into use.

A more detailed discussion of the characteristics and definitions of interpersonal communication can be found in J. DeVito.[2] Much of our discussion is based upon his work.

THE TRADITION

Studies in speech communication have not traditionally examined person-to-person communication. As we shall see in Chapter 5, research into group communication, which is a forerunner of work in interpersonal communication, began only about 50 years ago. Studies of two- and three-person interaction in face-to-face situations have been done only within the past 20 years or so. Traditional perspectives and research methodologies explain why this interest has been recent. In the past, communication scholars were interested in what they thought to be the important instances of communication that took place among important people doing important things: government leaders, business persons, lawyers, religious speakers, and the like. They thought then that ordinary talk about ordinary topics by ordinary people was hardly worth serious research. Furthermore, research methodologies were based either on the critical examination of the texts of important communications such as speeches, judicial opinions, or literature, or they were based on linear, causal, experimental studies of the effects of communication on selected listeners. Thus, the research procedures were not appropriate to studies of person-to-person communication.

The disdain of person-to-person communication began to dissipate in the face of increasing reports from professionals who worked with people experiencing personal or emotional problems. It was reported repeatedly that a significant factor underlying troubles in marriages, personal relationships, working situations, and general human functioning was difficulty with communication. It became apparent that we did not know much about ways in which people use and misuse person-to-person communication in their daily lives. Research was called for, and now the perspectives and methodologies are changing to allow that work to be done. It remains today in an early stage of development.

Thus, *common ways of thinking* about interpersonal communication have undergone a significant change in recent times. Moving from a position of presuming that when people learn to talk they should be able to go about their daily lives interacting with other people without formal training, we have

---

[2] J. DeVito, *The Interpersonal Communication Book* (New York: Harper & Row, Publishers, 1980).

arrived at a point of suspecting that a lack of person-to-person communication skills may be at the heart of some of our most troublesome human problems. There is a new body of folklore that tends to interpret any interpersonal problem as the result of a breakdown in communication.

Current Perspectives acknowledge that research does not exist as yet to support such broad generalization regarding the significance of communication in interpersonal problems. On the other hand, research that does exist certainly does not diminish the importance of interpersonal communication. On the contrary, with each new study we become more convinced of the need for research on interpersonal communication, and we become aware of the importance of an ability among people to be able to talk about their ways of communicating with each other, that is, to do *metacommunication*. Scholars are also learning the importance of building our understanding of how people get things done with communication in ordinary, unplanned situations. That is, we must study the *pragmatics of language*; how does it happen that when one person says, "I'm cold," another person understands that to be an indirect request to shut the window; or when one person says on the phone, "Is Amy there?" the other knows that it is not an inquiry as to Amy's whereabouts but a request to speak to her. We have also come to realize that the context of communication is critical to understanding the meaning people share. More understanding is emerging yearly.

The View of this Book is that skill and experience in person-to-person communication is deeply significant to all people and should occupy an important place in our teaching. Although the research that is going on will surely modify some of our generalizations about the process, we believe that the extensive experience of those in the helping professions—psychology, psychiatry, social work, counseling—combined with the theory and research available from communication scholars provides a sufficient basis for teaching. Moreover, we take the position that skill in person-to-person communication is fundamental to the development of all other skills to be discussed in this book. For example, the ability to talk to other people in an interview situation and learn from them will form the basis of research called for in our chapters on public speaking, group communication, reasoning, decision making, persuasion, mass communication, and intercultural communication. Listening and nonverbal communication are integral to person-to-person communication, and the combined skills will be important in all other skills we will discuss. We do not accept the idea that ordinary talk among ordinary people is less important to society than important talk by important people. Instead, we suspect that person-to-person communication may be the most important of all.

COMPETENCIES TO BE DEVELOPED

Three *General Exit Competencies* suggest the ability to

1. *Communicate* your objectives to another person.
2. Express self-perspectives in a manner that indicates a self-definition.
3. Interact with others so as to indicate an appreciation and respect for their self-definition.

We have put "communicate" in italics in the first general exit competency to stress that communication means the other person *understands* what it is you have on your mind and can *take appropriate action* in response. Of course, people will not always choose to do as we wish them to do, but if we communicate, they at least know what it is we wish. This general competency relates to the pragmatic aspects of language in social interaction. That is, we can use language to get our business done,whatever it may be. It may be as simple as obtaining the salt at the dinner table, asking a friend to go to the movies, or learning the price of a candy bar before trying to make a purchase. It may be as complex as securing an appointment to interview the chief of police, or interviewing a manager of a radio station to learn why they broadcast the programs they do, or getting your physician to come and talk to the class.

The second general exit competency addresses the skill to communicate one's self-perspectives so that others can understand *your self-definition*. We cannot say whether a self-definition precedes the communication of it, or if the process of communication of self-perspectives serves to build the self-definition. We suspect that they are reciprocals, or interdependent. In this skill, then, concentration is on the expression of self-perspectives. Through such expression and the resultant interaction with others, self-definition will grow, and thus the expression will become more complete. The major task is learning to do the *self-expression*. So many people reach adulthood without the ability to self-disclose. They cannot communicate their feelings, they cannot reveal their most personal thoughts, they cannot tell others about themselves—who they are and where they are coming from, to use the colloquial expressions.

Research tells us not only do people suffer from this inability to reveal their own self-definition but their inability to do this kind of communication also hampers their ability to develop their self-definition to their own satisfaction. Research also tells us that when one engages in such self-expression, the response from others is typically not negative or judgmental. It is, instead, a response which provides self-disclosure in return. The teacher will need to be sensitive as self-disclosure is generated in the classroom. Some parents and educators oppose requiring self-disclosure. It is possible that some children will carry disclosure further than is appropriate to the situation. We suggest that self-disclosure not be required. It should, instead, be encouraged within a permissive atmosphere. We suggest further that the teacher exercise judgment to divert the communication if self-disclosure seems to be going beyond levels appropriate to the classroom.

This brings us to the third general exit competency: the skill to interact with others so as to indicate an appreciation and respect for their self-definition. Person-to-person communication that addresses some of our most intimate and revealing thoughts seems necessarily based upon a transaction with others. We need other people with whom to talk in order to sort out our own thoughts, feelings, problems, or concerns. But others will not be available for this kind of transaction if it is not mutual, if we are unable to listen and interact with them with understanding, appreciation, and respect for their self-definition. The ability to be *supportive to others* in communication is difficult but important. It requires active participation rather than just listening, although good listening is a critical element. Supportive transactions are characterized by responding so as to tell the other person you have heard and understand. It calls for encouragement to continue the transaction. It discourages judgmental or critical responses as well as leaping to an immediate or pat solution to a problem or concern. Primarily, it calls for a transaction partner who can participate in the communication in such a way as to allow the other person to work out a self-definition and thus solve problems and satisfy concerns.

People spend a great deal of money these days to pay for counselors of one sort or another simply to play the role of supportive person-to-person communicators. As we have said, much of what we know about person-to-person communication comes from the theories and case studies of such counselors. Developing these skills early in life might reduce the need to seek out professionals later.

Beginning Exit Competencies include the ability to

1. Talk about yourself.
2. Talk about someone else as that person has reported to you.
3. Receive messages and deliver them to others accurately.

At the beginning level simple first steps at self-disclosure can be made. Each child will have some things that are common to many others, and it will be rewarding to communicate them and discover the extent to which others are similar. Of course, each of us has some characteristics that are individual, and it will be rewarding to learn how easy it is to communicate that to other people who are interested and not critical. Here practice is on learning the skill of revealing yourself. At the same time, there will be practice on talking to someone else and telling others what you have learned. This will increase sensitivity to what people are disclosing: if the child knows there will be an opportunity to pass on information gained in person-to-person talk, he will listen carefully and formulate ways of restating it. He will also know that he will be reporting that information in the presence of the person who originally provided it, so there will be concentration upon trying to report accurately and without editorial comment.

Obviously, the objective of these first two beginning exit competencies is to establish skills at personal transactions. The experiences should be as *positive* as possible. That is to say, the teacher should discourage laughter and ridicule of what someone has revealed. It should be established that telling others about yourself is an ordinary and pleasant experience. The teacher should also encourage students to pay attention to understanding what someone has told them. In listening exercises, the children will have played the gossip game and they will know the extent to which distortion can occur in passing along information. Now, they will see how important it is to see that distortion is held to a minimum as they report what they have learned from others.

The beginning level also provides an opportunity for preliminary development of the ability to receive and deliver messages accurately. Writers of comic strips get a good deal of humor out of the tendency of many adults to fail as messengers. Stereotypes of men as taking a telephone message and then either forgetting altogether to pass it along, or passing it on in such general form as to make the message useless are common, and they may reveal some sex differences that our culture allows or even encourages. Anyway, it is not funny in real life. Functioning on the job or in families or other close groups so as to be unreliable as a simple messenger can have serious consequences. This is a skill that can be easily learned and will be useful in many situations.

Intermediate Exit Competencies ask students to be able to

1. Talk about things that are positive and negative to you as a person.
2. Demonstrate the ability to seek information from other people.
3. Talk about things that are positive and negative to other people.
4. Specify some elements of friendship important to you.

At the beginning level, students started the process of telling about themselves in terms of relatively simple information. Now, at the intermediate level, they can move to the more challenging task of communicating feelings. To tell about things that are positive and negative requires first a recognition of your own feelings, and, as we have said, many people reach adulthood without being able to recognize their feelings, much less communicate them. Talking about things that are positive and negative will bring to the surface the fact that for many aspects of life we have not only information but feeling. We know, for example, all about school—rooms, books, chalkboards, teachers, playgrounds—and we will most likely have a feeling about all aspects of school. Experience in reporting those feelings on a simple plus-minus basis will develop a more general skill of recognizing and communicating feelings.

Some first steps toward skill in interviewing can be started at the intermediate level by giving opportunity to seek information from other people. We know of a child, for example, who could study bus routes and travel around the city quite well, but she refused to ask the bus driver for information she did not have. As a result, she made a number of unnecessary false moves. Others may search around a store for long periods of time simply because they are unwilling to ask a clerk for the location of an item. Still others hate to use the telephone for information seeking and therefore waste a good deal of time looking on their own. The telephone company tells us to let our fingers do the walking in the yellow pages, but it is our ability to communicate for information seeking that does the work.

A reasonable development of the ability to tell about our own feelings is the skill to talk to other people about their feelings. This is just a growth of the necessary person-to-person transactions we will face throughout our lives. Just asking, "How do you feel?" will probably obtain a surface response, "Okay." The skill lies in the ability to continue the transaction until the other person feels comfortable with reporting feelings. It may be necessary to do some self-disclosure in order to demonstrate a sincere invitation to listen to the other person's feelings. It may be necessary to ask some specific questions in a non-threatening way. In general, learning of other's feelings requires a supportive approach to person-to-person communication.

Finally, students at the intermediate level can begin to bring to the surface and communicate their feelings about friendship. Psychologists such as J. Lair tell us that understanding friendship is a particularly important factor in our lives.[3] We have many people with whom we interact daily; we have some people we call friend. But many adults have never developed the skill of talking about the meaning of friendship, and that affects their personal functioning negatively. Early development of the skill of talking about friendship can reduce this problem.

Advanced Exit Competencies embrace the abilities to

1. Talk about the ways you respect or appreciate yourself as a person and the ways you do not.
2. Communicate supportiveness of another person.
3. Demonstrate interviewing skills.

Person-to-person communication operates best among people who have a thorough and realistic understanding of themselves and have the ability to share

[3] J. Lair, *I Ain't Well—But I Sure Am Better* (Garden City, N.Y.: Doubleday & Company, Inc., 1975).

that understanding with others. Most counselors, and certainly psychiatrists, must undergo extensive counseling on their own before trying to counsel others. Unless they have developed this understanding of themselves, unless they know their strengths and weaknesses and learn to accept themselves without regret or guilt, they will be of little help to others. So, an important skill in person-to-person communication is to develop this balanced and realistic self-understanding to the point that it can be openly communicated. The act of making ourselves public by communicating to others our sense of ourselves is a skill important to the development of genuine self-understanding and to participating in person-to-person communication.

It should be reinforcing to children to discover that others have characteristics they do not appreciate. Sometimes that discovery will be helpful as another student is concerned with the same thing you are. At other times, it will be informative to see someone dissatisfied with a characteristic that seems perfectly fine to you. Such discoveries will make it easier to practice the open communication of self.

Just as important is the skill in communicating things about yourself with which you are satisfied. Children learn early and many carry into adulthood that it is immodest to talk about ways in which you feel positive about yourself. This is probably a function of never learning the skill of communicating self-satisfaction without boasting or making others feel diminished. Professional athletes, who are interviewed on television frequently, often have this ability. They can say to the millions of listeners that they were pleased with the way in which they played defense, for example, and easily go on to point out that their offense left something to be desired. It is possible to communicate these judgments without offending listeners.

Communicating supportiveness to another person is a tremendously important skill. We have already worked with the children in previous competencies to develop skills in talking with others about their feelings. Now we address the skill in engaging in a supportive transaction. As before, this may be as simple as helping someone learn a school lesson, or it may be as complex as helping a person figure out why he has no friends. In either case, supportiveness is manifest in communicating interest and caring and a willingness to continue the transaction until the person feels better about the task or problem. It does not necessarily involve solving the problem for the person. In fact, that may often evidence a lack of supportiveness. Parents, for example, often have the choice of taking the time to help a child work out a problem for herself or saying with impatience, "Here, let me do it for you." The latter choice often leaves the child feeling put down, not helped or supported. Supportiveness will often involve feeding back to the person what he has said, presenting it in a new light, showing a willingness to listen without judgment, offering alternatives for him to consider, and ultimately letting him make the choice or find the solution.

Finally, at the advanced level, students can demonstrate skills in interviewing. As we have said, this skill will come into play in many of the research assignments connected with other communication skills. To communicate to reason, persuade, speak in public, make decisions, or generally be socially active requires the ability to interview. The object of an interview is to learn what someone else has to say relevant to your questions. It is not just to confirm your own preconceptions. Many interviewers learn precisely what they expect to learn because they do not enter the exchange with an open and inquiring mind. Many fail to learn some of the important details because they do not show the patience to continue the question-answer relationship long enough. Many do not learn what they might have learned because their manner of communicating puts the other person off. Many fail to take full advantage of the interview because they do not do a good job of paying attention to what is said so that the information can be retained and used later. Scholars in person-to-person communication are learning more and more about the importance of interviewing skills. Children can develop them.

Sample Exercises for
Person-to-Person Communication

The general exit competencies as well as the competencies for each level of elementary school provide guidelines for the expected outcomes of these exercises. In the following exercises the teacher needs to be careful that acceptance of and appreciation for each individual is stressed. There is not a better way to encourage such attitudes and behavior than by the teacher's own example. Children do not possess an innate belief that they are unacceptable or weird, or an innate predisposition to be inhibited about expressing one's ideas or feelings. In fact, the exact opposite is true of normal language of young children. The teacher's job is to combat children's learning negative responses from others who teach them.

The essence of person-to-person communication is understanding and communicating one's self along with accepting another's communication of self. Obviously, this is difficult, because psychiatrists' and psychologists' offices are full of children and adults who must work on these bases. Perhaps early encouragement of natural inclination and discouragement of societal teaching may help prevent feelings and communications that are detrimental to personal health and well-being. These are difficult concepts to promote in children but are more difficult to teach the older the learner becomes.

A much easier part of person-to-person communication is that which is impersonal. Learning to communicate from person-to-person in order to accomplish life's business is necessary but can be conducted on a superficial contact level. The following exercises are designed to provide input data for the child to process on personal, relational, and impersonal person-to-person interactions.

BEGINNING LEVEL EXERCISES

1. Each child tells about herself and her family. Students should feel as if this is a quiet conversation, not a public performance. So the classmates should sit in a circle on the floor and talk about themselves one at a time. The teacher should have each child bring a box or a sack with a photograph of herself and her name. So a child begins "This is my box. And this is my picture. I am . . . . or I have . . . ."

2. Each child draws a picture that shows something about each person in the class on the basis of previous talks. For example, it may be a picture of a boy to indicate a brother, a dog or a cat for a pet, and so on. As soon as a picture is drawn it is placed in the appropriate person's sack. This is a project for art class that may take a number of days to complete. At the bottom each artist signs his name. When the project is finished, the artist explains the picture, and the subject indicates whether it is really something about him. Pictures that are not true are taken from the sack.

3. Each child matches things about other people to the people. The teacher prints or writes (depending on style of writing taught), each student's name on a dittoed list. Each child in the class is given one picture from among those in the sacks. The teacher says, "You have a picture about a person. That picture may tell something about other people too. Look at the list of names of everyone. Circle every name that fits the picture." Sacks should still be visable in case a student needs to match a name on the list with a name and picture on the sack. As soon as children have selected names, the picture is posted on the board. Each student comes to the board and prints or writes the names of all the people she has circled on the list. Children may need to carry the list to the board so the names can be copied. Then each child tells the class in sentences what he or she has decided. For example, "This is a dog. Jimmy has a dog. Sally has a dog. Tom has a dog, and Martha has a dog." This lesson is designed to combine with writing class. If the class is accelerated, students may be able to write sentences instead of just the names.

4. Each child selects a color and uses crayon or paint to color what color they are today. Of course, this lesson is preceded by a discussion that colors can indicate feelings. Then each child tells why he has selected a color. For instance, "I am yellow today because I am happy," or "I think I am red. I am excited today." This can combine well with an art class.

5. Each child names three things she has liked to do. The sentence should be, "I . . . . and I liked that." The purpose of this lesson is to tell about something of personal importance and to concentrate on past tense verbs. So the lesson combines with grammar. At this level children will predictably have difficulty with most irregular past tense forms and may need help.

6. Each child describes how another person feels in a riddle. Each child asks another student how he feels today. Then they make up a riddle with two parts:

how the person feels and some other description. For example, "I am thinking of a person in this class who feels happy and has blue shoes. Who is it?" If the class cannot guess, the person the riddle describes identifies himself and then tells his own riddle. If someone has an appropriate answer, it becomes the answerer's turn. The teacher might allow limited guesses.

7. Each child tells about something another child has that is important to him. Children draw names. They talk to the person whose name they draw in order to be able to describe something important to that person. For example, "Tommy has something that is tiny and soft and furry with long ears. What is it?" or "Amy has something that is wooden, turns around, and plays music. What is it?" This lesson helps children appreciate others and also works on expanding descriptive phrases in the grammar. More than one descriptive phrase should be required so language can be expanded.

8. Each child takes a telephone message. Divide the class into dyads. Each pair uses a toy phone and has a conversation. The teacher plays mother. The child answering the phone tells mother what is said and then returns with any message. The mother should always give a message or ask a question. Some examples follow.

    Child: "Mother, Grandma wants to talk to you."
  Mother: "Tell Grandma I'm busy and I'll call back."
    Child: "Mom, telephone."
  Mother: "Find out who it is."
    Child: "Jane wants me to come over."
  Mother: "Ask Jane if her mother is there."

This is a good opportunity to work on ways to answer the phone, to say good-bye before one hangs up the receiver, as well as message delivery.

9. Each child takes a turn at being the message carrier for the day. This assignment may take a month to complete, but the teacher should keep a list of message carriers so that each child has a day. The teacher needs to be certain there is a message to be taken, but in the course of a school day this is normal routine. The message should be verbal and it may be delivered to the secretary, to the principal, to another teacher, to a student, to the janitor, or any person at school as long as it is a real message.

10. Each child actually uses the telephone to call for information. Each child thinks of something he wants to know. Perhaps it is whether mother will pick him up after school, when the library is open, what movie is playing, how much it costs to go skating, how many cows Mr. Jones has, where is cub scout meeting, what is the time, and so on. This lesson naturally combines with arithmetic, because after each child thinks of his question, the teacher would dictate the telephone numbers. The numbers will be written and then matched in order to dial. The phone call should then be made. If the teacher doesn't have a phone, special

permission can be obtained to use a school phone. Finally, each child should tell the class the answer to his question that he learned on the phone.

INTERMEDIATE LEVEL EXERCISES

1. The class members join in making lists of things that make them happy and things that make them sad. Because happy and sad are personal feelings, each child should suggest an item for each list, even if it is a repetition. At the end the teacher might notice how many things students feel in common, although personal opinion, not mass opinion, is the object.

2. Each child gives one sentence in which she tells something she likes and does not like. This is an excellent lesson to combine with grammar. The teacher may call this a "but" session. Each student says likes and dislikes in a sentence conjoined with "but." Children tend to connect most sentences with "and" and this is an excellent opportunity to work on "but" as a conjoiner. So the sentences might be, "I like candy but I don't like cake," or "I like sun but I don't like rain," or "I like to play baseball but not football."

3. Each child indicates words she likes and doesn't like on the spelling list. Each student is given the list or copies the spelling list. After each word the child marks a plus (+) to indicate like and a minus (−) to indicate dislike. The words may indicate things (nouns) or actions (verbs) the person has feelings about. However, some words in a spelling list such as *there* and *their* would have to be rated for different reasons—ease in writing, difficulty in spelling, unimportant, boring, and so on. It will be fun to hear why a plus or minus was selected and this offers an excellent review of the spelling words.

4. Each child tells someplace he wants to go to another student and together they locate this place on a map or globe. Children should draw numbers or matching straws to divide into dyads. Each child in the dyad tells the other a place and together they locate both places. After all pairs have finished, they show the class the places. Classmates try to guess which person in the dyad selected that place. This lesson combines well with state, national, or international social studies or geography.

5. Each child is a good fairy who asks one or more classmates what their three wishes are. The teacher should decide how the fairy chooses the wishes (every child should be fairy and wisher). As soon as wishes are gathered, the fairy writes a paragraph story to tell about who the wisher is and what the wishes are. This lesson helps give meaning to a writing lesson.

6. Each child draws a map of how another gets home from school. This assignment demands dyad interaction again. Children should be assigned to someone not in their immediate neighborhood. They talk to each other to find out how they go home. Then they draw a map of the other child's route. Even if a school bus or a car pool is involved, a map can be drawn. The details will con-

sider the space the child walks. Any transportation can be indicated by a drawing of the vehicle and a line. This lesson is designed for a variation of art class.

7. Each child seeks everyday information from people in the community by role playing. The teacher and children can set up the classroom as a pretend city (their own). Stores, buses, street corners can be labeled. As soon as the city is prepared, children take turns being business people and children. The ones playing children ask prices or buy items in the store, ask the bus driver if this bus goes to a certain place, ask the policeman for help, and so on. This lesson combines practical lessons in communication with social studies.

8. Each child names foods he enjoys and doesn't enjoy. The classmates sit in a circle and, one at a time, share their personal likes. For instance, "I like steak but I don't like liver" or "I eat meat but I don't eat vegetables." After each child has had a turn, the person who can retell the most personal information gets a prize (perhaps an apple). This activity coordinates with health class.

9. Each child answers a question inventory. The teacher prepares a common inventory that is dittoed to provide a copy for each child. Examples of questions to be included follow.

I like people who . . . .

People make me angry who . . . .

The best thing about school is . . . .

The worst thing about school is . . . .

I wish teachers would . . . .

When I'm with small children I . . . .

When I'm with grown-ups I . . . .

Each child talks to another classmate to get personal answers. Then she shares the results of the inventory with the class by telling them about it. This is not a public speech, so the oral report should be done casually—in a circle, in small groups, or from seats.

10. Each child writes a paragraph on "I like friends who . . . ." This assignment should be preceded by a class discussion of how we choose friends, the values we hold for friendship, and the point that not everyone becomes a good friend. Then each child writes his feelings on liking friends. This is another excellent assignment to combine person-to-person interactions with giving meaning to writing.

ADVANCED LEVEL EXERCISES

1. Each child writes a poem that is about her as a person. The first three lines might begin from a Rod McKuen poem:

Listen
I don't apologize for being hard to know
I am what I am . . . .[4]

Children then write their own descriptions of their feelings and thoughts. Poems can be gathered, shuffled, and read aloud by a student. The class tries to guess who the author of each poem is. This assignment readily coordinates with English studies.

2. Each student writes a paragraph on "I am important because . . . ." This combines development of a sense of self-pride with making a purposeful writing assignment. We have chosen writing for this assignment with the realization that initially children may be reluctant to communicate such personal information orally.

3. Each student makes a positive personal inventory poster. This poster should fold into three sections. The center section is headed, "Things I do well." One side is headed, "Things I want to do," and the other is, "Things I have to do that I like." This lesson may be combined with art, and the concentration can be on lettering or on drawing responses in each section.

4. Each student makes a negative personal poster. This poster is three-sided as in the previous lesson, and it should be the same size. Then both positive and negative can be fit together to form a personal hexagon. In the negative personal poster the center heading is, "Things I do poorly." One side is, "Things I won't do," and the other is, "Things I have to do that I hate." It may be necessary for the teacher to discuss that the negative poster doesn't represent anything wrong with a person and that these behaviors may be an asset.

5. Each student names elements or things that are like him and tells why. This assignment is designed to combine with science and the elements may pertain to the current study. For example, "I am like ice because I appear cold, but I melt when the heat is on " or "I'm like a lily because I close up and stay to myself when night comes," or "I'm like selenite because I crumble easily."

6. Each student becomes a match or a contrast. This lesson is a companion to the previous lesson. As soon as students have the idea of comparing themselves to another element, then another more advanced assignment is tried. In this lesson a student announces a comparison, and another student must match or contrast. Suppose, for example, students are studying animals. The student says, "I'm like a horse. I want to be free to run over fields and feel the wind in

---

[4] R. McKuen, "Thirteen," in *Listen to the Warm* (New York: Random House, Inc., 1967).

my hair." Another says, "I'm like a horse, too. But I want to be a show horse that has his own room, is fed, curried, and cared for." In response to the same statement a student might say, "I'd rather be a cow standing and chewing my cud and just watch the horse run." These statements should involve recognition of the first person's statement and then add a match or a contrast.

7. Students participate in helping a person work out a problem. This assignment is most effective in small groups, and reading groups may offer such a pre-arranged group. Each person takes a turn as problems occur, reporting, "I'm angry . . . ." or "I'm hurt . . . ." or "I have a problem." Then the group finds out the details, suggests solutions, or whatever is appropriate. The primary goal is to be able to talk about it. The teacher may need to provide a number of examples before the group can begin to share. No doubt, the teacher can supply real examples, such as, "I have a problem. My car won't start. What can I do?" or "I just found out that Mr. Jones says our class is too noisy." Just as the teacher uses real examples, the students should use real examples. The teacher should encourage all students to take a turn but must guard against having a problem manufactured because it is time to take a turn.

8. Each student interviews family members to get their opinion on what is personal freedom. The teacher should give the students the question and then ask each of them to talk to at least two people in his family to see how they answer the question. The next day the class discusses the results of the question.

9. Each student interviews a person to find out about his or her career. In advance, the class should discuss careers and together make up a list of questions for an interview. The students may choose to ask a parent, a neighbor, or a stranger, but the important task is to seek and record answers to certain questions.

10. Each student participates in interviewing an historical figure. The class is divided into five or six groups. Each group selects an historical figure they want to interview. It may be Abraham Lincoln on freeing the slaves, or Jackie Kennedy Onassis on speaking a number of languages, or Alexander Graham Bell on the telephone. The group must read information on the person and the topic. Then one member of the group assumes the role of the person to be interviewed. The other members form a panel to interview that person. Students would enjoy interviewing that person in the format of a modern television program.

5

Group Communication

OBJECTIVES

At the end of this chapter you should be able to:

1. Explain the concept *group* and discuss the role of groups in contemporary society.
2. Describe how communication is central to the life of a group.
3. Explain feedback response, network, and social structure in group communication.
4. Describe the process of role emergence and the function of various roles in group communication.
5. Discuss how supportive interaction is critical to group functioning.
6. Distinguish between a task orientation and a process orientation in understanding group communication.
7. Discuss how the general and specific level competencies are designed to yield, by the time of exit, an elementary mastery of group communication as currently conceived.
8. Explain how the general exit competencies represent broad goals that accompany each specific level competency.
9. Match each exercise to the general exit competency or competencies and the specific level exit competency or competencies that the exercise addresses.
10. Explain why the successful completion of one exercise does not fulfill the objective of the competencies.
11. Design additional exercises for the fulfillment of the stated competencies.

Some business people in Honolulu were talking about their problems one day to a manager from the mainland home office. "We've got a real problem here," said one of the Hawaiians. "There's a *hui* in the accounting department that's making life miserable for everyone who has to work with them."

"What's a *hui*?" asked the mainlander.

"Oh, that's an Hawaiian word," the first replied. "It means a small group of people who stick together because they share the same concerns and don't care how much they disrupt the office just so long as they have their way."

"It's a clique," said another, "almost a gang."

"Well," replied the mainland officer, "perhaps we better appoint a committee to look into the matter."

Group communication suggests a wide variety of situations, some of them more desirable than others, some of them more easy to notice than others, and all of them presenting an opportunity to use communication skills. The business people talking with their outside manager constituted a group; so did the *hui* they were concerned with, and if they appointed the investigative committee to learn about the *hui*, that, too, would be a group requiring the use of skills in group communication. Families can be groups, but they are not always. School children often form groups of friends, and teachers form their classes into groups for many learning situations. The entire class of students may be a group, but, again, it is not necessarily always the case.

People form groups for play or recreation, they join groups of social functions, they act in groups to make decisions and get work done, and sometimes they try to solve personal adjustment problems by interacting in a group. And, of course, some people avoid groups, either because they prefer to do things by themselves or because they just do not feel comfortable or effective in groups. But even these loners find it difficult in modern society to make it through life without ever having to function in a group. The fact is that the nature of contemporary society is such that an enormous part of life's activities occur within the context of small groups. And the mechanism by which groups come into existence, function, and complete goals is communication. The conclusion is obvious: skill in group communication is fundamental to functioning in today's world.

THE CONCEPT

To understand the concept of group communication we must first look at the meaning of *group*. Sociologists, social psychologists, and communication scholars have all struggled with the meaning of that word. The first point that must be made is that group, or small group, is not defined by a certain number of people. Certainly it takes more than one person to make a group, but that is hardly a definition. We can look to literature to find some examples of the difference between a collection of people and a group. For example, there are dramas about passengers on an airplane who get on in ones and twos, pay little attention to each other, and would typically finish the trip without much acknowledgement of each other. But then trouble strikes the plane. The Captain has a heart attack and the First Officer is knocked unconscious as he tries to help the Captain. No one else knows how to fly the plane. Now the passengers share a common fate (actually, they did before, but were unaware of it). They begin to talk among themselves about how to get out of this situation alive. Some people emerge as ones who can help treat the pilots; others emerge as able to quiet the fears to hold off panic; still others address the problem of flying the plane until one or two are found with some flying experience; and still others figure out how to seek assistance from the ground. The collection of people is fast becoming a group.

As the drama unfolds, we might expect to take some time to look back on the lives of the people involved. Flashback after flashback will introduce us to these people and help us come to know them as individuals rather than as faces on the

93

plane. Some conflicts can also be expected. There is usually one loudmouth smart aleck who swings between rude behavior toward others and abject fear. The passengers quickly establish some ways of proceeding, which include restraining the loudmouth, taking turns at talking rather than screaming all at once, letting those with special expertise deal with their kind of problems, and concentrating on survival. When the plane finally lands safely, everyone cheers, they hug each other, vow undying love for one another, and maybe make plans for a reunion a year hence. Now we really have a group.

A classroom of children on the first day of school presents a similar situation. They come in twos and threes and tend to by shy with others they do not know. During the first recess they may play a game that requires teams and during the game team members must work together to play well. Some turn out to be talented players and may emerge as leaders while others may prove to be friendly and supportive and be embraced by the team. After school, the same people who formed a team may play together on the way home and gradually develop into a group. Within any classroom there may be several groups, some social, some oriented toward school work, some centered on games. Membership may change as the activity changes, but often well formed groups stick together across situations. However, different people may have influence depending on the activity. One person may be easily accepted as team captain on the playground while another may take the lead for a spelling bee. Sometimes, group hierarchies become so firmly established that it is Julie's group no matter what, and then membership depends on Julie's whims and Julie is the leader regardless of the activity, whether she is the most appropriate or not.

Conceptually, then, a group can be characterized as a number of people few enough to be aware of each other and have mutual reactions, who share a common purpose such that each one succeeds as the others succeed, who use oral communication as a significant factor in their behaviors, and who operate on the basis of norms and procedures accepted by all. This concept is developed in greater detail by B. A. Fisher.[1]

But our concept is not yet complete. We must focus on the concern of this book, which is communication. Scholars speak of "groupness" to call attention to their claim that groups are something more than the sum total of individuals in them. Groups can then be conceptualized in terms of the mutual structuring that occurs. Now we begin to see the application of the *system* concept discussed earlier. Just as the heating system in a home is interlocked so that detection of temperature is locked into the heating elements which are locked into the temperature of the home which is tied to the thermostat all of which is tied together infinitely, as long as the system continues to function, the mem-

---

[1] B. A. Fisher, *Small Group Decision Making*, 2nd ed. (New York: McGraw-Hill Book Company, 1980), Chap. 1.

bers of a group are interlocked. And the cement that holds them together is communication. Group communication, then, is characterized as the *interlocking acts* that occur when people speak, one person speaking after another in predictable patterns that have emerged in the functioning of the group. It is the pattern of interaction that allows the group to operate as a system, and it is the pattern of interaction that determines the presence of groupness. The ideas of process and transaction, discussed in relation to person-to-person communication, apply here as well.

Operationally, people communicate with each other in a face-to-face situation so that patterns of interlocking behavior are created. The specific behavior involved in the process cannot be specified absolutely, but we can call attention to some that are usually important.

People come together for a variety of reasons, some of them quite casual and some quite purposeful. Let us look at a couple of examples in order to begin the operational description of group communication.

It is the first day of school, and as Laura walks up to the still locked door she sees four other kids standing outside waiting to be let in. Two obviously know each other as they are talking. The other two are standing by themselves. Laura takes up a position by herself and waits. She is new to the school and does not know the routine. They could stand like this, as a collection of individuals waiting for the door to open. Laura walks over to one of the others standing alone and says, "Do you know what time they open the doors?" The other girl shakes her head and walks away. A communicative act has occurred; there was both an informative response to the question and a relational response that said nonverbally, "I don't want to talk to you."

Not to be discouraged, Laura approaches the two who are talking and says,

"Are you in room 10?"
"Yeah," says one, "are you?"
"Are you a sophomore?" says the other.

Another communicative act has occurred with both informative and relational elements. The girl identified herself as being in room 10 and said, in essence, "I would like to talk with you so I am asking a question that invites a response."

With this opening, the start of what can be group communication has occurred. Now Laura can identify herself as being assigned to room 10, she can introduce herself as new to the school, she can exchange names with the other girls, plan to sit with them in class, and even eat lunch with them. They may become a group. Communication took place, and an important behavioral element was the character of the *feedback response* which set up a potential pattern for continued communication and the development of groupness.

Consider another example. Five people from different grades have been assigned to serve on a planning committee for the school picnic. They were told to meet in the principal's office after school. They arrive, are seated, and look at each other. The silence is unnerving. Someone needs to say something. They thought the principal would attend to get things started, but she is not present. As long as they expect the principal to come, the five could sit there for a long time without saying a word. But if one person decides to speak, it can open up the floodgates, "Does anyone know if we are supposed to wait for Dr. Meese or should we go ahead and talk about the picnic?" The response to that inquiry can make a big difference. Look at two possibilities.

"I think we should wait."
"We may as well go ahead and start talking."

The first feedback response could well continue the silence whereas the second could at least generate a discussion of whether to wait or talk. Feedback that contributes to the development of group interaction is a behaviorial characteristic of group communication. The original plus a response is a basic unit of group behavior.

The *network* in which communication occurs within a group is also an important element. If you let any five or so people talk in a group and keep track of who speaks to whom, you will notice various patterns among different groups. Quite often, one or two people will do most of the talking, and most of the responses will reasonably be directed back to them. Some will do little talking and will accordingly have little talk addressed to them. In other groups, there will be a more balanced network of communication, with all members speaking to each other and being spoken to with about the same frequency. At still other times, a group may reveal a network in which two people on one side talk to each other while two on the other side speak between themselves, with little or no communication across subgroups.

Groups will form some kind of network of communication. Whether the network formed is the most useful to the group will vary from time to time, and no one network is best for all groups. It is possible to influence the nature of the network formed by the assignment of roles such as leader, but that may or not be helpful to group functioning.

Finally, a *social structure* is characteristic of communicating groups. Often, a social structure is imposed from outside the group. For example, many groups meet for the first time with a chairperson already assigned. By virtue of that assignment, the chairperson occupies a high-status position, will probably initiate and receive more interaction, and may exercise more influence on the formation of group norms, procedures, and outcomes. Consider the example of the classroom. Students enter the room for the first time and dutifully take their seats while the teacher steps to the front of the room, remains standing, and initiates the class. The teacher has been assigned this high-status position and the students accept it. What would happen if that procedure were violated?

It was the first day of the Spring Quarter and the students enrolled in Speech Communication 205 walked in and took seats. The bell rang; the students waited. Ten minutes later a nervous shuffling began and some students began to look at the man seated in the fourth row center wearing a suit and tie and looking older than the typical student. Finally, one student turned to him and said, "Are you the teacher in this class?"

"Yes," answered the man.
"Well," continued the student, "are you going to teach?"
"What did you want to learn?" the man replied.
"The course is group communication. Why don't you teach that?"
"What did you want to know about it?" the man countered.
"How about talking about this topic in the text on the meaning of group communication," said the student with some impatience. But before the man could reply, another student, sharing the impatience, said that he knew something about group communication and would be glad to tell the class about it. The man nodded approval and the student stepped to the front of the room and began to teach.

While it was a strange way to begin a class, and the students were eager to know why the teacher did it, they soon learned that the odd approach had helped establish a social structure in the class quickly and in quite a different way than that to which they were accustomed. The two students who had helped get the class started never lost their high status.

Social structure, then, is a characteristic of group communication. There is more than just high and low status involved. Groups have a variety of needs at different times. Sometimes they need a person who will try to get talking started; sometimes they need someone who has valuable information; sometimes they need people who can detect hurt feelings or shyness and talk to people in a way that encourages them; sometimes they need people who merely ask for information or suggest ways to divide up the work of the group, or encourage more effort, or build cohesiveness. Through communication, this social structure can emerge.

We use the term *emerge* consciously. Behaviorally, research tells us that groups tend to function in a way that people try to perform roles such as initiator, information seeker, conflict manager, and the rest of the group either accepts and reinforces the person in that role, or they do not. If they reject the effort of one person to perform the role, someone else will make an effort to assume the role. That person, too, may not be reinforced and will abandon the effort. Eventually, people making attempts to do work are reinforced by the others and they emerge in that role, at least for a time. Instead of consciously selecting people to assume various roles within the social structure, then, groups will more likely proceed by a method of residues: those who remain in roles by virtue of the supportive interaction of the others can be said to have emerged.

This same supportive interaction works to reinforce comments people make and thus determines the kinds of topics discussed and conclusions reached.

What do we mean by supportive interaction? Often it is merely a relevant response. If one person makes an attempt to be an initiator by suggesting that the group talk about a certain topic, a response which says that topic sounds good or even begins to discuss that topic will be supportive. At other times, a smile or nod from someone will be supportive. At still other times, direct responses such as, "That's a good idea. Why don't you take the lead?" will be used. On the other hand, nonsupportive responses can range from actually ignoring a comment by replying on a totally different subject, or directly rejecting it by saying, "I don't think that's what we should do."

THE TRADITION

Early in this century the focus of communication studies was on *public speaking and debate*. Groups intending to make a decision or accomplish a task were expected to use argumentation to yield a reasoned decision. This came out of the formalist tradition which we will discuss in Chapter 8, "Reasoning."

But some people were unhappy with this model. They thought the use of argumentation created tension and interpersonal conflict and also seemed to work every question into a two-sided debate defended by advocates. This, they said, defeated the objective of obtaining good decisions by people who were satisfied with the experience. Questions are not always two-sided, they argued, and the use of advocates creates a rigidity that works against compromise and the discovery of alternatives. Besides, argumentation can be an abrasive form of communication, which many people avoid and thus remove themselves from participation.

In place of argumentation and debate, these critics proposed a form of Socratic *dialectic*, which is characterized by a face-to-face question-and-answer form of communication in which the participants are not advocates but mutual seekers after wisdom and truth. This is described more fully in Chapter 9 when we talk about Plato's ideas on persuasion. The key points in this proposal were inquiry rather than advocacy, face-to-face interaction rather than a series of debate speeches, and an effort to look at all alternatives rather than debate one proposal at a time.

From this beginning, studies in *group discussion* emerged. For many years, the objective of teachers of this subject was to discover ways to apply the scientific method to consideration of human problems. Science was seen as a form of inquiry, in contrast to debate which was seen as advocacy. John Dewey's steps in reflective thinking were modified to constitute an agenda for scientific group discussion: (1) perceive a problem or felt need for inquiry; (2) define and delimit the problem; (3) analyze the problem (as we discuss in Chapter 8 on reasoning);

(4) suggest possible alternatives and set the criteria for selecting among them; and (5) select and implement a choice. As you can see, these first steps at group discussion put most emphasis upon a decision making task, such as we discuss in Chapter 7.

Common Ways of Thinking about group communication still reflect considerable emphasis on the task-oriented small group. Much attention has been given to discovering the ways one can become an effective leader in a group, and lists of traits associated with leadership are frequently discussed. At the same time, people have become increasingly aware of the human elements in group behavior. It is now common to recognize that total concentration upon the task elements of a discussion overlooks the fact that people are doing the communication and they must establish an acceptable network of interpersonal relations if they intend to maintain a functioning group. If there are some members who rarely talk, that creates problems for the entire group. If there are people who have what is called a "hidden agenda" or personal objectives that may not be shared by other members, that agenda must be brought out and addressed if the group is to work. If some people are angry at each other, or feel put down by other members, or feel unappreciated, or lack a sense of commitment to the group, they must be dealt with. If the group fails to develop a set of working norms and procedures acceptable to the members, that must be done before task issues can be effectively discussed.

The Current Perspectives are now more clearly coming from an interest in the *communication behavior* that occurs in small groups. The traditional tendency to divide issues into task problems and social-emotional problems is being set aside in favor of attention to what people say, the sequence and timing of what they say, and the ways in which the *process* of communication works to take the group from place to place in whatever it is doing, whether it is to make a decision, exchange ideas, engage in learning, deal with personal and social adjustments, or just be sociable. Prescriptions of how people should conduct discussions, or how they should be good leaders or good group members are now given less attention. Instead, descriptive studies about how people communicate in small groups are being reported. We are finding that many of the prescriptions are not useful because they do not relate to the ways in which people actually communicate.

The View of This Book, accordingly, is not that we should try to teach group communication skills by the recitation of a series of prescriptions. We look instead to the skills that come from continued experience in communicating in groups. The same skills that were begun in the study of person-to-person communication will carry into the group situation. The sensitivities developed in work with nonverbal communication and listening will also be valuable. Children, we believe, need multiple opportunities to talk together in groups and become sensitive to the ways in which people relate to each other and how they process ideas. Children particularly need experience in observing the processual character of group communication, as roles are allowed to emerge through interaction and ideas are processed not in a scientific or logical series of issues but in talk that moves from place to place and slowly grows to consensus by the method of residues discussed earlier. They will then learn to appreciate the ways in which group communication can be of value in personal, interpersonal, and task-related ways. They will also learn that for a group to be effective much attention must be given to the development of satisfactory patterns of communication. Finally, they will see that groups do not always constitute the most desirable forum for communication. There are plenty of times when communication can be done better in other forums. Then, they can choose wisely when and if to engage in group communication.

COMPETENCIES TO BE DEVELOPED

General Exit Competencies in group communication call for the ability to

1. Communicate actively in a group situation.
2. Responsibly assume a variety of roles relative to a group's needs.

The upshot of much modern research is that the best way to become skilled in group communication is to participate in it. A common problem of groups is the tendency of a few people to do all the talking while others remain virtually silent. Research also tells us that the silent member of a group is a problem both for the person and the group. For the person, there is a sense of dissatisfaction with the experience, of not being an active and involved member, of not contributing to the product, whatever it may be. For the group, the silent member constitutes at the very least a noncontributor, and at the worst, the silent member acts as an ambiguous stimulus, a distraction. Studies that have intentionally placed a silent member in the group have discovered that the other members become concerned with the silence, try to figure out what it means, seek to bring the other person into the discussion, and finally resign themselves to the presence of someone who, for reasons not quite clear, chooses not to participate. On the other hand, active participation does not mean talking all the time or everyone talking with about the same frequency. There are people who talk infrequently who are active participants and who are well satisfied with the experience. They communicate to the group that they are involved even though they say little, and they do contribute from time to time when they have something to say. As long as the individual and the rest of the group understand this, relative silence can be active participation.

Group communication operates on a series of conversational or discussional rules. There are rules that govern how one gets the floor to speak, rules that regulate the time one can occupy the floor, and rules relating to the ways in which others may interrupt without taking away the floor from the speaker. These are not necessarily universal rules; research is only now starting to look into them. Most likely, each group will develop its own adaptations of ordinary conversational rules, and the members will learn and contribute to them by participating.

Similarly, groups develop patterns of interaction which allow prediction of the sequence of communications. At the simple level, if someone asks a question, it is predictable that someone else will offer an answer. We can even begin to see patterns in three and four comment sequences.

Also, we are starting to discover ways in which groups communicate in terms of their interpersonal relationships. For example, some comments merely continue the interaction whereas others may also communicate status levels by showing deference or dominance to the previous speaker. For example, if one person says, "Marilyn, what do you think about my idea?" she may reply in several ways. Showing submission, she might say, "Whatever you think is okay with me." Or she may show dominance by stating, "I don't think it's very well thought out. Surely we can find a better solution."

The point of this discussion, in relation to the first general exit competency, is that students must gain the competence to participate actively in groups and by so doing they will learn the ways in which groups go about their communication process.

The second general exit competency carries this learning process into the assumption of the many different roles that must be performed. Two aspects of this competency deserve special comment: there are many roles played in groups rather than a single one of leader, and roles should be assumed and performed in relation to group needs.

As we have said, traditional literature has spoken of group leaders as if there were one person who directed the activities of any group. This is not so. Depending upon the purpose of the group interaction, there may be need for someone to initiate discussion, someone to seek information, someone to summarize and recall ideas, someone to help establish others in their roles, someone to help establish cohesiveness, someone to bring silent members into the discussion, someone to propose decisions, someone to provide information, and so on. It is not to be expected that one or two people will always have the skills necessary to perform any role needed. On the contrary, the wide variety of roles will almost certainly demand different kinds of people at different times. At some time almost everyone should be found to be performing an important role.

Second, these roles are not often known in advance of group communication. It is rarely advisable for roles to be assigned in advance of group interaction. The needs of the group change from time to time and from group to group. Roles, therefore, must be allowed to emerge in relation to the needs of the group at the time. The group will determine, through its response to those who seek to perform roles, whether the role fills a need at the moment. Part of skill in group communication, therefore, is not just to be able to perform roles. It is to be able to recognize group needs and meet them either by one's own action or by supporting the action of someone else.

Beginning Exit Competencies call for the ability to

1. Interact socially in a small group.
2. Complete a task that requires the cooperation of a small group.

A first step in learning skill in group communication is taken by moving out of the childish individualism that characterizes most young people and many adults, and become comfortable in relating to other people in a group situation. Notice we have spoken of "childish" individualism. To be a successful group participant does not require one to adopt a "group think" or herd mentality. It does not call for a rejection of some of the admirable aspects of individualism so powerfully supported in our nation's history. One can be an individualist and still be able to move into a group situation and relate to other people through active communication.

The childish individualism of which we speak is characterized by the view of one's self as the center of the universe. It can be manifest both by the feeling, "I don't care about those other people," and by the feeling, "I'm afraid I'll do something silly or wrong in front of those people." Either reaction is self-centered.

At this first level we hope children will see that interacting with other people is an easy, natural, and satisfying experience. They will discover that others have the same uncertainties and fears they feel as well as the same concern for their own needs and interests.

In the second beginning exit competency, children are asked to learn how to accomplish a task requiring others' cooperation. This will be their introduction to the fact that many of life's jobs cannot be done alone and that by working with others one can accomplish more, achieve more personal satisfaction, and discover the pleasure that comes from working with others. They will begin the process of discovering the various needs involved in group action. They will see that each member can have something to contribute. They can learn how to let people do what they can to achieve a group objective. In Shakespeare's *Midsummer Night's Dream*, Nick Bottom literally made an ass of himself by trying to play every role in the little drama prepared for the wedding. He had not learned the skill of sharing in order to fulfill a need.

102

Intermediate Exit Competencies ask students to demonstrate the ability to

1. Assume an externally assigned role in a group.
2. Share information in a group.
3. Participate in the division of labor to complete a group task.

Now we can begin to work systematically to build some specific skills connected with group communication. Although we have said it is rare that externally assigned roles will prove to be directly relevant to group needs, there is a reason to do so in early practice. Children without experience will need help at first identifying roles to be performed, and the teacher can provide that help. Moreover, in later life it will still happen that a boss, a parent, or a teacher will assign roles for group members, and they may as well learn to carry them out.

Notice in the exercises accompanying this competency that no one person is assigned the role of leader. This is done consciously to avoid communicating the idea that this is a necessary element of every group. It is not. Groups will do their own selection of high-status roles. It is also done to prevent the teacher from falling victim to the tendency to pick favorites from among a limited number of class members.

Notice also that in these exercises every group member has an assignment. It is useful to learn that in groups every member is important and that a person should be able to do the job assigned without infringing on another's task if the group is to carry out its mission. Research literature supports the notion that if a group cannot develop a division of labor it will fail to take advantage of the unique possibilities of using groups. Students will begin to learn skill in division of labor by performing these assignments.

The second intermediate exit competency begins work on an unusually important skill: making what one person knows a part of group knowledge. Think of it this way: if five people come together, they have a theoretical storehouse of information equal to the sum total of knowledge held by each individual. But the actual supply of information on which a group can base its operations is limited to that which becomes group knowledge through communication. A common comedy routine has a family frantically searching for a lost child while the four-year-old is pulling on Daddy's coat and waving her hand. She knows where the lost child is, but no one will pay any attention. Later, when the crisis is over and she is able to say she knew all along what happened, Daddy foolishly asks with exasperation, "Why didn't you tell us?"

The group cannot process information it does not share. Even saying something may not be enough. The group must listen and understand. It may be necessary to say it again and again in different ways. We know from studies of group communication that often a piece of information is offered and quickly is forgotten because the group did not appreciate its value or was not at a point

103

to use it. Later in the discussion the same information is offered and snapped up as a valuable contribution. Sharing information is more than just saying it; is more than saying it twice. It must be *communicated*.

At the last intermediate step, students can begin their learning of the ways in which they divide their own labor to do a group task. Remember two important aspects of this skill: labor must be divided if the time and effort of using a group to perform a task is to be worthwhile, and labor divided by the group itself in the course of doing something is more likely to reflect the particular needs of the group and the particular abilities of each member. The more a division of labor is responsive to the needs of the group and its members, the more productive the group is likely to be.

The teacher will need to show restraint at this point. The group will not always divide labor in the way the teacher would. They may not divide labor equally among all members, they may let a member perform a task which someone else could do better, and they may sometimes let one or two members do all the work. The important point to remember here is that the group did the division. They may want to talk about their division of labor later. They may see ways in which they could have done it better. They will use this knowledge to improve in future assignments. But what appears to be an improper division of labor to the teacher may be quite satisfactory to the group and its task. It should not be challenged.

Advanced Exit Competencies look for students to show the ability to

1. Participate in the selection of the individuals to perform leadership roles.
2. Assume the roles of group leadership.
3. Express supportiveness and difference of opinion in a task oriented group.
4. Express supportiveness and difference of opinion in a socially oriented group.

Only when students have a well-established repertoire of group communication skills should they turn to the business of selecting specific leaders and serving in such roles. We have tried to emphasize that traditional literature on leadership has proved to be misleading in suggesting that a certain number of innate traits are required for leadership. Books have suggested, for example, that only intelligent, good-looking, articulate, talkative, self-assertive, friendly, considerate, kind, obedient, cheerful, thrifty, brave, clean, and reverent people can be leaders. It just does not work out that way. Studies of United States Presidents, for example, have discovered that some of the best were not very intelligent in an academic sense. Lincoln was certainly not good-looking. Some were able to be downright nasty at times, and many were not always considerate of others.

Two skills are stressed in the first two advanced competencies: children should be able to select as leader that person or those persons able to do for the group what it needs to have done, and children should learn to accept gracefully a

leadership assignment and do the job. Because our society operates on the practice of selecting leaders, the skill in making that selection is an important one.
This requires communication. Often among students as well as adults, open communication about who might serve in a leadership capacity is an awkward one.
We fear hurting someone's feelings. If Marilyn wants to be leader, we often just
go ahead and select her without considering alternatives. Studies of juries, for
example, show that most commonly the first person to speak in the jury room is
selected foreman. Even though the group's assignment is to decide someone's
fate and there may be others on the jury better qualified to lead this particular
discussion, there is rarely much talk about what a foreman does and who might
do it. The result, of course, is frequent poor selection and the possible miscar-
riage of justice.

It is often common to play the role of reluctant leader. We act as if we must be
dragged kicking and screaming into a leadership role. It is considered unseemly
to seek out leadership in our society. If one plays false modesty or exercises the
self-centeredness mentioned earlier so as to decline leadership assignment, the
result again is frequent inappropriate choice. Students must learn the skill of
accepting such assignments, knowing that at another time with another task
someone else will be asked to serve. Practice in acting in a leadership role will
build skill in this communication task and build an ease and naturalness in
accepting responsibilities. Furthermore, having been a leader, however briefly,
increases one's tolerance and appreciation of those who lead.

Studies of communication within groups show that typically it is necessary for
group members to communicate support of another's point of view as well as
difference of opinion if the task is to be accomplished. The third advanced competency addresses this behavior. Thinking back to our discussion of the residues
processing of ideas in task-oriented small groups, mutual supportiveness is the
medium of reinforcement and ultimate decision. If each member continually
makes comments without response from others, there will be no growth of ideas.
An important role is response—supportive feedback—when it is appropriate. Just
as important is being able to express difference of opinion in a way that neither
diminishes the person who made the comment nor weakens the cohesiveness of
the group. Without difference, there would be no testing and developing of
ideas. Supporting, testing, and differing are the means by which a group reaches
a better outcome than could have been obtained by the best single individual
working alone. It is this that makes group tasks worthwhile.

Finally, students are asked to develop their skills in being supportive and expressing difference in a socially oriented group. Here they will call upon their
skills in interpersonal communication already developed. Research in group communication reveals the not so surprising fact that people can express differences
and support more easily on task issues than on social-emotional ones. One problem of many groups is their determination to focus only on substantive issues
and pretend the social, interpersonal ones do not exist. This, by the way, fre-

105

quently makes it impossible for groups to do tasks fully. The final advanced competency demands that students build their skills of support and difference in a socially oriented group so as to see that they are able to do the interpersonal processing that is so important.

This will predictably be more difficult. Students will need to be perceptive of the personal and social needs within the group. They will put their skills in listening to good use. Then, they will need to develop the ability to communicate openly not just their support of another person in relation to the group but to express differences so that such expressions are productive of personal and group needs. The time for self-centered perspectives is over. These skills will call for a sensitivity to human beings as they relate to one another.

Sample Exercises for Group Communication

The following exercises provide samples of group communication activities in accordance with the general exit competencies and those at each level of instruction. Group communication skills depend on the listening, nonverbal, and person-to-person communication skills, but the attention at this point becomes directed toward actively participating in a group. Young children are egocentric in their early years. Young children exposed to group activities tend to parallel play instead of communicating or cooperatively interacting with the other group members. So even those children exposed to preschools will not have experienced group interaction. Thus the initial experiences in group communication will be new for the children. As they become more experienced, group communication will become an important factor in their lives. Group communication is often seen as working together, completing a task, or accomplishing a goal. Although this is one of the purposes of group interaction, another important purpose is social—enjoying the company of others, finding a support group, and identifying with others. The following exercises are designed to develop group communication skills, both socially and task-oriented.

Decision making is one function of a group. We have intentionally separated decision making in groups from group interaction, because it seems apparent that children need to communicate in a group before they try to complicate the interaction by making decisions. Thus group decision making has been reserved for more experienced communicators and is discussed in Chapter 7.

The teacher may be concerned with what size a group should be. In the elementary classroom, a group may range from three people to the whole class. However, small groups (three to five people) usually provide more opportunity for all individuals to interact. Thus, as children are learning group communication, the majority of the activities are planned for small groups. It is further suggested that group members should be varied so children may experience communicating with others they scarcely know as well as with others to whom they feel close. The most important part of group communication is for the teacher to be certain that each child becomes a part of some group. In these activities no child is to be left to do the assignment alone.

BEGINNING LEVEL EXERCISES

1. Preestablished small groups have refreshments. This lesson involves a section of the room that is set aside for eating. If snacks are not provided every day, set aside a special day to have food. Juice, carrots, apples, or cookies may be set out on the counter. Then small groups can go together and help themselves. Of course, they must clean up their own mess. It is wise to select reading groups or math groups because this mixes children who may not be friends. Each group is told that as soon as their work is finished, they may go as a group to the snack table. Thus everyone has the opportunity during the day.

2. Spontaneously formed small groups play a game. This is an excellent activity for recess period on a rainy day. The teacher has preselected games that involve group activity, such as Candyland, Go Fish (cards), Sorry, or a place to play house. Each activity is set in a separate area, and children are told to select one game. The teacher should clearly mark each area with a number to indicate how many people may do this. The only control is that no more than the number specified may join the group.

3. The class separates into assigned small groups for a field trip. Teachers frequently use a buddy system to organize the class on a field trip. This assignment is an expansion of the buddy system. The teacher assigns groups of four who must stay together on the trip.

4. Small groups pretend they are members of another group and assume their roles. This lesson is planned to combine with social studies, and Thanksgiving time is an excellent opportunity. The class discusses how different groups might have celebrated Thanksgiving. Then the teacher assigns small groups to act as those they have discussed. One group can become pilgrims and Indians; another can be cowboys and farmers (the musical *Oklahoma* sets the stage for this); another can be a modern family, and so on. Each group can dress up as who they are, and then each group sits at their table while all have Thanksgiving dinner. The "dinner" may be pretend, or small treats, or a dinner, depending on the teacher's resources.

5. Newly formed small groups represent a method of transportation. As the class studies transportation, the teacher divides the class into groups. The teacher gives each group a type of transportation they must join together to show. For example, one group forms an airplane, another becomes a train, and so on. This is an excellent time for the teacher to assign groups of children to work together who would not usually join as a group, because the children will enjoy making themselves into a plane or a train or a car. Of course, the group becomes one plane, not five separate planes.

107

6. Small groups make a "Vegie Friend" or a "Fruit Friend." This lesson can combine with a health lesson on foods or a science lesson on growing plants. The activity is similar to building a snowman but this is a "Vegie" or "Fruit Friend." Originality and creativity of the group should be encouraged. After each group has finished, the friend is given a name. Then the groups explain to each other what the friends are made of.

7. Small groups paint a picture. This assignment provides a variation for art class. Each picture must be a group product. Newsprint or wrapping paper will provide a surface large enough for a group picture project.

8. Small groups build a miniature town. Each group builds one building in the town. Children would enjoy building a pioneer village or a mining town, and such a project would combine with social studies. Plain blocks, Lincoln logs, and similar products may be used for the building materials. This is another activity that is good for combining groups of children that would not usually work together.

9. Small groups prepare for a class party. The entire class can discuss plans for a party. Children volunteer to join a group to prepare at school one item for the party. Some foods for a party are easy to prepare at school, such as popcorn, Koolaid, or juice, and cereal snacks. However, the teacher may want to ask for parents who would be willing to supervise small groups as they prepare the food. Other groups of children can set the tables, decorate the tables or room, and write place cards.

10. Small groups invite a guest to join them for the party. This activity is designed to accompany the previous lesson. The small groups may remain the same or may be changed as the teacher sees fit. As soon as the refreshments are ready, each small group goes together to bring an important guest from the school to the party. Guests might be the principal, the vice-principal, the secretary, a janitor, a cook, or any of the special teachers such as the speech clinician, the counselor, the music teacher, and so on. When each group returns, children sit with their guest. In the previous exercise place cards should indicate such groups. The teacher is advised either to have the children write invitations or ask special guests in advance if they will be free to join them when the group arrives to escort them to the party.

INTERMEDIATE LEVEL EXERCISES

1. A small group assumes duties as a clean-up crew. Each day the teacher names a group of children who will be "The Neat Niks" for the day. He also gives each child a specific duty, such as, "Sally, you pick up the paper; Tom, you erase the board; Bob, you straighten up the books." The object is for each individual to assume assigned duties so "The Neat Niks" do a good job. This assignment should continue for weeks until every child has participated. The neatest

"Neat Niks" can be given a reward after all groups have taken a turn. This task is a good one to form new groups.

2. Small groups assume duties to complete a science project. Again, the teacher assigns each person in the group a job. For example, suppose the project of each group is to grow bean sprouts. In each group one child can put the sprouts in, another can add water, another put the screen on the top, another can add water later, and another can rotate the jar.

3. Small groups make a still life. This lesson is designed to accompany a history class. The teacher shows each group a picture of a famous historical event. Washington crossing the Delaware, the signing of the Declaration of Independence, the Boston Massacre, Washington at Valley Forge, and the driving of the golden spike are good examples. The teacher assigns each member of the group a person to be in the picture. Then the group looks at the picture and copies it by assuming the positions of those in the picture. As soon as all groups are ready, the teacher has each group come to the front and reproduce the picture. He tells the class the story of the picture while the class looks at the still life.

4. Small groups participate to put together a reading story. This assignment is planned to accompany reading, and reading groups form a preconstructed small group. The teacher duplicates a copy of the reading story and she cuts it into many sections as there are students in the group. Each child gets one section of the reading story. The students are instructed to read their own section, and each person tells the group his section. Then the group must fit the sections together so the story makes sense.

5. Small groups participate to put together a math problem in order to arrive at a certain answer. Each person in the group is given a number, and all except one number have a process. The entire group is given an answer. For example, the answer is 12. One child has "2," another "add 4," another "multiply by 6," and another "divide by 3." The group must fit the numbers and processes together in proper order to arrive at the given answer. This group communication lesson is for arithmetic and can be used with one group at a time or with a number of groups receiving the problem at the same time. Complication of the numbers and processes, of course, can be varied to fit the abilities of the group or groups.

6. Small groups fit together spelling words and definitions. The teacher gives each child in the group a few words and a few definitions. The group must read aloud words and definitions and the whole group works together to match the words with the definitions. This can be an innovative method to introduce a new spelling list or a review of previously learned material.

7. Small groups make a centerpeice. This project is designed to be used in combination with art class. As this is an advanced group communication task, it may occur later in the year. This project might be an Easter centerpiece or May

baskets. The purpose is for the group to work out on their own the contribution of each member of the group. However, as children first try to decide tasks in a group or on their own, the teacher should rotate among the groups to be certain that each child contributes. All members of the group need not contribute equally, but all members should do something. For example, the child who does not make the basket, make the flowers, or bring the flowers or anything else can be responsible for delivering a May basket.

8. Small groups design an invitation. This project is for art class, and the medium used to make the invitations should be something that can be copied. Each small group is to design an invitation to an actual event such as a school program or parent's night. The winning design is chosen and copied to be used for all invitations. Again, the groups are to interact on their own, except that the teacher may need to help see that every person in a group makes a contribution.

9. Small groups write a story. The class is divided into groups and each group writes a story. The teacher may name a topic for the story, if she wishes. But the story is to be the project of the group. In this lesson it may help in advance for the teacher to discuss ways a group can work together. Each child can write a line or two, or one person may do all the writing while others tell the story, or several people may write. It is important for the group to divide their own labor as well as ideas in any way they choose, even if suggestions are given in advance.

10. Small groups become clean-up crews and divide their own assignments. This is a return to an assignment used early at this level, except now that the children have experience working in a group, so they should share responsibility as they choose. The teacher should name those in the group and stay while the work is done. It is suggested that the teacher stay in the room in order to avoid any physical confrontation among group members as well as to check the work after it is completed. It may be noted that in some groups one child does all the work; in others, one child may order all the others and do nothing; or in another, one child may loaf or cause trouble. Such are the problems of groups working together, and the children should face them early. However, they are asked to assume this interrelationship only after considerable guided experience. The task means more if the children can discuss how the job was completed or not completed and how they felt after all groups have had the experience.

ADVANCED LEVEL EXERCISES

1. The class participates actively in the election of student officers for the school. Most schools have a student council, and students vote on council members and frequently on student body president. If this opportunity exists in the school, classes at the advanced level should have active discussions on what the responsibilities of the offices are. Students may volunteer or be selected by the class to run for available offices. Then groups should be appointed to help that person, and specific jobs should be given to each group, such as making

posters, distributing written information, talking to other people informally, and so on until all are involved.

2. A class selection committee selects students to fill class offices for the month. The teacher appoints the selection committee consisting of new members each month. The selection committee is given two mandates: no person may succeed herself in an office, and every person must fill at least one office during the year. The committee needs a list of all students and previous offices held. The teacher should also provide a list of class officer titles. In large classes, the list may need to be expanded. Suggested officers are president, vice-president-social, vice-president-academic, secretary, treasurer, room manager, and recess coordinator.

3. Each class officer selected in the previous assignment has to fulfill the duties of the office. The teacher should begin by giving minimal duties and allow the individual to expand those as appropriate. For example, the social vice-president would be in charge of social activities, including parent's night, PTA meetings and class parties; the academic vice-president might be in charge of collecting assignments, passing out tests or new books, and making suggestions for academic activities; the room manager might be in charge of the lights, the windows, the projector, and the neatness of the room; and the recess coordinator might be in charge of leaving for recess, monitoring the rest rooms, taking out play equipment such as balls, and deciding which groups use the ball diamond. As part of the duties, the class officers should have weekly meetings (remember, they hold an office for only a month). The president should chair those meetings and the secretary should take notes that are read to the class. The group would take care of its own business and provide a cross-check to see that individual officers are assuming their roles. The teacher should be an ex-officio member.

4. Each class officer becomes chairman of a small group appropriate to the responsibilities of the office. In some classes the small groups can be established as soon as the officers begin, but in other classes the children will need to assume their own duties before they can chair a small group. The purpose of the small group is to advise the officer and to help carry out the duties of the office. Experience with college students indicates that it is easier to learn to do all the work oneself than to chair a small group to help make decisions or assume duties. Part of being a leader is learning to let others help, and students need this experience.

5. Small groups complete a science project. The teacher should provide the class with a list of possible projects over a unit or several units. Then the class is divided into groups by having students count off one to five. Then all ones are a group, all twos a group, and so on. All groups may not be equal in number. Each group selects a project to complete from the prepared list. A project may be selected by several groups. The project should be one that requires some effort to put together, for instance, materials to be gathered as well as several steps to complete the project. Each group should work out the division of labor on its

own. A warning to the teacher is that if a grade is to be given, all students in a group do not have to receive the same grade. The teacher can circulate to observe who is doing the work in each group and talk about the project after it is completed to determine who contributed what.

6. Small groups report on a place for a great vacation. Once the place is selected by each group, the group divides the responsibilities in order to give a report on the place chosen. Reports can be given as a panel discussion with each person contributing his share. This lesson coordinates well with geography and may be limited to a specific country, to the United States, or expanded to allow a report on any place in the world. The teacher should alert the students in advance that they will need extra materials such as maps, picutres, travel brochures, or personal reports gained in interviews. In other words, this should not be an assignment to be derived just from an encyclopedia.

7. Small groups select and read a book. This assignment is naturally planned for reading groups. It is suggested that the teacher let the group select any book they want to read. Previous to the selection, the group visits the library or the bookmobile. Children are so used to being given reading lists that they will enjoy the freedom to select a book on their own. Of course, the requirement is that everyone in the group reads and discusses the book.

8. Small groups present a panel discussion on a current event problem. The teacher divides the class into groups, and each group selects a current event they want to read about and report on. In this assignment each group is told that the problem must be specified and possible solutions should be presented with advantages and disadvantages. The advantages and disadvantages may be obtained from newspapers, from interviews with people, and from personal opinion. Each group should choose a team leader to coordinate the responsibility of each person and to see that the reports are complete. Students should be allowed plenty of time for this project. Each panel presents a report to the class. The class discusses whether the problem was delineated and whether possible solutions were provided with advantages and disadvantages to each solution.

9. Small groups plan and participate in a scavenger hunt. The class is divided into groups. Each group is told to make a list of things to be found on a scavenger hunt. The teacher may want to restrict the students to items that can be found in a limited area. She may also need to restrict the number of items that the list may contain. Each group has a number. Its number is put on the top of the list. The teacher checks the list for spelling and clarity in writing. As soon as all lists are complete and corrected, the lists are then given to another group to go on the actual hunt. This activity can be planned in advance and then used during recess or a class party. As the teacher decides, the hunt can be conducted in the building, around the block, or in the town. The restricted area must be specified and be the same for all groups. In addition, depending on local circumstances, the teacher may need to set rules that prohibit stealing. The main pur-

pose of this lesson is social interaction, but the lists could contain items for an art project, a class party, or a science experiment, as well as a just-for-fun list.

10. Small groups delineate and discuss a social problem. Prior to this, the class might discuss social problems as a group. They may mention some school rule, people who are noisy in a movie, smoking, drugs, activities at parties, bossy people—the list has no limit except those things that really concern children. Then the class divides into small groups. This is an excellent time to allow students to self-select the group they would like to interact with. All groups do not have to be the same size, but no student should complete the assignment alone. Each group discusses a problem of its choice. Then the groups informally discuss the problem with the class. Again, the teacher returns to asking was the problem specified and were the pros and cons of solutions discussed. Although the talk should be informal, the criteria of specifying a problem and presenting both sides to possible solutions must be required. The purpose is to provide a support group, and any judgment of right and wrong should be avoided. There is a difference in saying, "I understand what you feel and I feel differently" and in saying "You're wrong."

6

Public Speaking

At the end of this chapter you should be able to:

1. Describe the distinctive characteristics of public speaking.
2. Explain the behaviors involved in preparing and presenting a planned speech.
3. Distinguish between the traditional idea of oratory and modern concepts of planned speaking.
4. Explain the importance of audience analysis in achieving shared understanding through public speaking.
5. Discuss how the general and specific level competencies are designed to yield, by the time of exit, an elementary mastery of public speaking as currently conceived.
6. Explain how the general exit competencies represent broad goals that accompany each specific level competency.
7. Match each exercise to the general exit competency or competencies and the specific level exit competency or competencies that the exercise addresses.
8. Explain why the successful completion of one exercise does not fulfill the objectives of the competencies.
9. Design additional exercises for the fulfillment of the stated competencies.

Leaving home and going to school involve entry into a public situation in contrast to the private environment of home, family, and neighborhood. We sacrifice some of the privacy and supportiveness of primary groups in order to gain many benefits found only through interaction with others in a larger community. Many benefits come from the acceptance of opportunities and responsibilities that include speaking in a public situation. In spite of folklore that associates public speaking with a few highly talented national leaders, almost all of us need the ability to speak in public if we are to be fully functioning members of society.

THE CONCEPT

Our discussions of person-to-person and group communication have stressed the transactional nature of the concepts. People have been characterized as participating in on-going, relatively spontaneous communication in which they are simultaneously speakers and listeners. Let us now consider another situation.

Yesterday, the class divided into groups to discuss various aspects of the spring carnival to be held in two months. Chris, Ruth, Milt, Parry, and Neff were assigned to pick the location of the carnival. After some discussion, they came up with two possible places but they were not sure the lots would be suitable and they did not know if they could get permission to use either one. Milt said he would go look at them after school and talk to the people who owned them and report back to the group tomorrow. Today, when the group gathered again, Milt said he had a report to make. He said he had looked at the two sites, had talked to the owners, and concluded that the lot on the corner of Scott Street and Underhill Avenue would be big enough, was closest to the school and that the owner said the school could use it for the carnival. While he was talking the others listened carefully and remained silent. Milt had made notes for his report and he presented his ideas clearly and in order. Although discussion within the group resumed after his report, Milt had made a public speech.

Conceptually, then, public speaking suggests a form of communication that involves some advance preparation, some attention to the ways in which ideas can be communicated consecutively to achieve maximum understanding by those to whom they are presented, and a single person acting as speaker while others remain silent and serve as listeners. The term *public* suggests an audience consisting of people outside our closest, primary groups. It may, however, be as small an audience as the other four members of our school group and they may be people we know very well. The speech may be a talk with only a little preparation and lasting only a few minutes. The defining characteristics are advance preparation, concern for communicating to others in a public situation, and a single person acting as speaker for others who are, at least for the time, members of an audience. Speeches may be oral reports, the sharing of experiences, providing descriptions or explanations, they may be instructional or persuasive. Speeches may be presented to a few people or a few hundred people. Some speeches last for only a few minutes and some may require more than an hour.

Whereas small groups of people can work out their common problems or interests through discussion in which all may freely interact spontaneously, if a large number of people need or want to share the same ideas, spontaneous interaction may need to give way to a more formal and organized method of communicating in which all remain quiet while one speaks so that everyone can hear what is being said. Because the one person speaking may have a limited chance to talk before the next person gets a turn, because a quiet audience denies the speaker a chance to hear them talk back and show what they understand and where they agree, and because communicating to many people at once demands careful adjustment to a more complex variety of backgrounds, public speaking calls for careful preparation. The preparation requires understanding about how one communicates to a public.

Operationally, then, public speaking involves behaviors in which the individual:

1. Makes note either in written or mental form of an idea or ideas that he or she wants to communicate to a group.
2. Makes note of the people in the group—who they are, how they relate to

her, how they relate to the ideas she wishes to communicate, what their beliefs on related ideas are, what their general values are, how old, how well educated, how interested they are in the ideas to be presented.

3. Revises the notes on what is to be said in the light of this knowledge about the audience.
4. Considers the language most appropriate to the audience and phrases the ideas accordingly.
5. Plans what is to be said, either in written form, orally, or both.
6. Integrates the gestures, movements, visual aids, and other physical objects that will contribute to the language used to communicate the ideas.
7. Rehearses the entire speech with all elements combined with oral performance now used as it will be in the actual speech.
8. Delivers the speech.
9. Seeks the reaction of the audience by talking to the members and/or observing their behavior.
10. Notes how future speeches can be made more effective on the basis of this speaking experience.

The most fundamental—at once the most elementary and the most sophisticated—behaviors in public speaking are those involved with relating ideas to the audience through advanced preparation. This is the operation that best characterizes public speaking and distinguishes it from other communication skills. Look at the difference. In most communication experiences, people talk face-to-face spontaneously speaking and listening, acting and reacting, telling each other what they think and what they think the others think on the basis of their understanding of what was previously said. It is best described as a transaction: people jointly communicating and building simultaneously a shared meaning. Public speaking typically does not allow this. The very term *audience* suggests a group of people whose role it is to be listeners. They do not verbally interact and mutually build shared meaning with the speaker. They sit and listen and build whatever meaning each person chooses or tends to build, and they do so with little or no return communication to tell the speaker what that meaning is. A speech to a group of 100 people may generate 100 different meanings, and there will usually be no chance for the speaker to learn that and try for common understanding. So it is of prime importance that the speaker know as much about the audience as possible in advance of preparing the speech and that he prepare the speech so as to achieve the maximum liklihood of common meaning.

THE TRADITION

Of all communication skills, public speaking has been the most intensively studied skill for the longest period of time. Texts on how to give a speech can be found in documents from ancient Egypt and Greece more than 2,500 years ago. There is too vast an array of theories and methods available to summarize here. Probably the most *common way of thinking* about public speaking is to view it as a form of literature in the sense that focus is placed upon the structure and phrasing of ideas. Use of the term *orator* conjures in the mind images of Demosthenes, Cicero, Webster, Bryan, Churchill, and their equals. Oratorical eloquence is associated with achieving an almost poetic quality in speech, because the emphasis is put on the use of rhetorical devices such as metaphor, personification, alliteration, repetition, and a sublime use of language. When ideas and their development are examined, it has tended to be in terms of their inherent depth and quality rather than the extent to which they communicated something to an audience.

This common focus has been so widely accepted that today it is often turned into a caricature of the original: to criticize someone's speech by suggesting it contained no substance or quality and was instead nothing but exaggeration and bombast, one may call it "mere rhetoric." The focus on speech as a literary specimen has created genuine problems for speakers and audiences today. The speakers today dare not appear too "eloquent" and audiences are quick to ridicule those with whom they disagree by calling them "nothing but orators."

Current Perspectives among communication specialists would put public speaking down a peg or two and recognize it as nothing more or less than one of a variety of forms of communication. Without denying that at times great orators have truly spoken poetry to the people, specialists are now more interested in the day-to-day instances of ordinary people trying to say something to a group of listeners. Particular interest is given to the character of society, its communication needs, and the ways in which public speaking serves those needs.

If people lived alone or among a small group of others as in a family or small tribe, there would be little or no call for public speaking. They would be able to talk interpersonally to reach common understanding needed for survival. As societies grew more complex, as social functioning and survival required more and more people to share ideas, it became more and more appropriate that a kind of public speaking be developed for those instances in which communicative efficiency would be best achieved by having the many listen to each other individually speak. Then, a person needed to develop the ability to express ideas before the group so that the group could benefit from those ideas. The value of the public communication, then, is measured by the extent to which the speech resulted in shared understanding—that true communication occurred. Public communication, in this view, is then seen as a right and responsibility not only of the few who act as leaders but of all the people. The highly developed democratic society in which we now live makes public speaking a requirement of citizenship. Those who remain the "silent" majority or minority are not really a part of the society and have no business criticizing the policies of those who do participate. Perhaps it is for this reason that in recent years in the United States the so-called silent majority has ended its silence with a bang.

There is a significant divergence of perspective today between communication specialists on the one hand and many elementary and secondary teachers on the other. Communication specialists have long ago rejected the traditional conception of public speaking as great oratory. They have concentrated on the more common situations in which a person has something to say to a group. In this sense, the frequent oral reports students make in class are public speeches. Making an announcement in the assembly, telling the class what happened during the summer, explaining to the student council that more time is needed for recess, asking the class to vote for class officers, explaining what a story was about, trying to get the class to vote in favor of a field trip, convincing the faculty to participate in a faculty-student variety show, teaching the class how to put on SCUBA gear are all potentially public speeches.

Many elementary and secondary educators, on the other hand, see these situations just mentioned as ordinary parts of the education process, fail to perceive them as forms of public speaking, and thus fail to give them the attention needed to help children learn to speak in public. Children are just asked or allowed to do them. At the same time, teachers who work with forensics or debate programs actively encourage students to participate in oratory contests for which the students are carefully coached to speak in formal and stilted ways. Gestures are rehearsed and performed in the old elocutionistic manner. Speeches are written according to Ciceronian prescriptions suitable for few modern speaking situations, and children memorize and deliver them in an ancient way that has not been practiced in the United States, with the exception of occasional presidential inaugural addresses, for fifty years or more. The forensic contest situation and the lack of communication education among teachers has allowed the perpetuation of the most outmoded practices in public speaking.

The View of This Book derives directly from the current perspectives among communication specialists. Public communication is seen as a basic skill to be developed in all children as a part of their preparation for adulthood and citizenship. It is a part of fundamental literacy. The stress given to reading and writing is premised upon the assumption that to be educated we must be able to gather ideas from others and give our ideas back to them. No matter how private it may seem when you read this book or write a paper of your own, this is part of public communication. Writers cannot engage in a communicative transaction with readers—they cannot see you and will probably never meet you. Yet, we write with you in mind and hope to share our ideas with you just as you will do with the future readers of your papers.

The parallel of the individual writer and the audience and the individual speaker and the audience is apparent. Somewhat less apparent is that the ability to address a group of listeners in a public speech is a fundamental and necessary skill if one is to be a fully participating member of society. Public speaking is the oldest method of public communication and it remains a readily available and vital form for the expression of literacy. To read and to write are a more private form of communication for the majority of people. Most of the children you teach will communicate their thoughts to the public through speech rather than through writing with more frequency in the course of their lifetime.

COMPETENCIES TO BE DEVELOPED

The exit competencies listed and discussed here are first, general competencies, and second, those organized according to levels of accomplishment. The general competencies express the overall purpose or goal of every level. As in previous chapters, levels do not necessarily relate to ages or school grade. As a child is able to perform at one level, he should be moved to the next.

General Exit Competencies include the child's ability to do the following:

1. To deliver a planned speech alone to a group of listeners familiar to the speaker.
2. To speak with the purpose of communicating specific ideas in a manner that is easily understood by the audience.

We have concentrated upon teaching children to be competent participants in communication by listening effectively, and we have dealt with various aspects of interpersonal communication which involve largely unplanned discourse within relatively familiar situations. For most of us—children or adults—moving from interpersonal to public communication involves a step into a less familiar and thus a potentially more threatening situation. Even standing before a group of classmates who are perceived as friendly and supportive is quite a challenge.

Fearless public speaking begins at the basic level and no better opportunity exists to establish positive public speaking experience than in the elementary classroom. The first general exit competency calls attention to the need for advanced planning for public speaking and the ability to present the speech while standing alone in front of a group. Although group communication, discussed in the preceding chapter, moved the children from unplanned talk to that which required some advanced planning, it is in public speaking that fully planned discourse is demanded.

Children will need help in thinking of topics to talk about. It is possible that some of the subjects that have been discussed within a group may be organized into a public presentation. In any case, children should choose to talk about things that are familiar to them. Before they get up to speak, the teacher may find it helpful to talk quietly with each one to find out what will be said. "What

121

are you going to talk about?" "What will you say first?" "What comes next?" Then, some supportive statements such as, "That sounds fine. I think you will do a good job," will be helpful. You should not anticipate that any child begins school with a fear of talking to a group because the child has never had this experience. The teacher's job is to provide repeated experiences in a positive atmosphere to speak to a group. The teacher should talk about how much "fun" it will be to share ideas. During the beginning and intermediate levels, the teacher should be the first speaker, demonstrating by her model (appropriate to the level of the children) what the children are to do. The children should know in advance when each person's turn will be. Each series should be started with volunteers. You may have to help the more shy children think and plan in advance what they have to say.

In terms of each child's performance, several factors can contribute to the enjoyment of public speaking. At the lowest level, the first speeches, you should sit in a small chair in front of the classroom and have each child stand by you as she talks. After several speeches you need to move your chair to the side and then subsequently to the back of the room. By the end of the beginning level, the teacher should be a listener in the back of the room. During a child's speech the teacher should say nothing except to initially insert questions to help the child continue the content, or occasionally the teacher may need to courteously thank someone for talking and cut off a child who is occupying excessive time and attention. A teacher should *never* interrupt a speech to correct English or speech skills. Improvement of skills is accomplished by continued practice. At the advanced levels the teacher may write notes during the performance or talk to each child privately to offer suggestions for improvement. But the class should hear the teacher make *positive comments* after every speech. Positive comments are the effective method to point out what is desired and at the same time to help each child develop confidence.

We need to make a comment about the danger of establishing fear through negative pressure to talk. We remember a classroom in which we were demonstrating the teaching of the most basic task—stand and tell your name and address. The regular classroom teacher decided the method to make each child talk was to rap him on the head with a ruler if he didn't stand up immediately. When we suggested this was unacceptable, she yelled for a few minutes at each child. Of course, such techniques are unacceptable and fear-producing. Children will talk in a supportive atmosphere, not a negative one.

The second general competency puts emphasis upon communication of specific ideas that the audience can understand. The objective is that the young speaker should think about the audience in relation to what she wants to say. Comments and reactions to a presentation should focus on whether the audience *understood* the speaker. That is the test of success. It is neither helpful nor relevant for the teacher or the class to impose their sense of correctness upon the speaker by commenting on whether he stood up straight, twisted and turned while speaking, stuttered or said "ah" a lot, tapped a foot on the floor, repeated himself, used incorrect language or grammar, used slang expressions, talked too softly or loudly, too fast or too slow, or whatever. Talk instead about what the child said and about how delighted we are to have her share those thoughts with us. Have the speaker, the audience, and the teacher focus on the information communicated. This competency is, of course, interwoven with the first competency, and the specific techniques stated are applicable here as well.

Beginning Exit Competencies include these three steps:

1. Plan in advance the ideas to be communicated.
2. Make three or four consecutive and related statements without prompting or interruption.
3. Talk about something concrete.

Recall that one of the distinguishing characteristics of public speaking in contrast to most interpersonal communication is the need to plan what is to be said. Why plan? Because here there will be less (perhaps no) opportunity to build mutually the shared meaning with the audience. The lack of the transaction of joint communication increases the need to think in advance. With the potential apprehension of standing before a group rather than interacting as a part of it, the chances of losing track of ideas increases as the mental powers decrease. The more confident the person is in what is to be said, the more clearly thought out the subject is, the less likely it is that when he finally gets his chance to talk he will have nothing to say.

To move the child into the frame of mind that allows participation in public communication, the transition from interpersonal communication must be started. Specifically, in interpersonal communication people take frequent turns in speaking; if one person starts a statement another person may jump in and finish it. If one pauses in search of a word, someone will probably supply it, "I saw a firetruck go by and I heard its . . . . ah . . . ." "Did you hear its siren?" "Yeah, that's it, a siren." In public speaking, even though every member of the audience is thinking "siren," they do not say it. They wait for the speaker to come up with it. So, the speaker must learn to handle the communication without prompting or interruption for three or four consecutive and related statements to meet the beginning competency. Planning the delivery of a few statements is accomplished at this level by thinking about it before you say it.

Talking about something concrete—something we can see, touch, taste, smell, hear—is a good place to begin public communication. Abstract ideas—symbols, values, feelings, attitudes, beliefs—are much more difficult to cope with when starting out in formal communication, and they can well be left for the more advanced students. The most basic form of public speaking is to talk to others

123

about something that the speaker knows or has experienced. The younger speaker's cognitive abilities are developed in concrete concepts and experiences. So, when children first begin public communication, they can do the job with fewer demands on their own communicative competence by working with concrete objects.

Intermediate Exit Competencies introduce the following tasks:

1. Plan a communication with some sequence to the ideas.
2. Speak for about one minute on the same subject.
3. Talk about the occurrence, function, or operation of something concrete.

A step toward putting ideas into a sequence begins development of one of the most critical elements in public communication. As we shall see in the discussion of advanced competencies, the pattern of organization is a matter of choice and is a function of the relation between the speaker, the subject, the audience, and the circumstances or environment in which the speech will take place. When the students go on to more sophisticated study of communication in high school and college, they will learn the theories directing the choice of speech organization or sequencing of ideas. They will learn that different sequences are better suited to different topics, audiences, and purposes.

For now, it is enough to alert children to the importance of planning some sequence to what they have to say. As they think about the speech or presentation, they should be urged to think about what they will say first, next, and so on. The audience may be able to talk about what was said when it is over, and report the sequence of ideas. This will help students see that audiences are sensitive to their comments and that some parts of the speech are more easy to recall than others.

With more experience in planning, and with more confidence in the experience, it is reasonable to ask students to plan to talk for about a minute on the same subject. This is no small challenge. Although many youngsters can talk almost incessantly in spontaneous interchange, even adults can find a full minute of planned talk before an audience to be difficult. Two problems are likely to occur here, and for some people they continue into adulthood. Many will find that what they thought would surely last for a minute is over in less than half the time, or some will ramble and add additional clauses to the same sentence and find themselves unable to reach a conclusion and stop. Both problems are a function of need for work in planning and organization. At this stage, it is important for them to learn to speak for about a minute, plus or minus ten or fifteen seconds.

At the intermediate level, students should begin to develop their concepts more fully. Now they can show the occurrence, function, or operation of a concrete object. No longer restricted to communicating about what is present and

124

visible, speakers can now tell about other places the object can be found, where it comes from, what happens to it later, what it can do for us, and how it does it. This helps students learn to take advantage of the important functions of communication that allow people to deal with more than immediate experience.

Advanced Exit Competencies take the students to the highest level reasonably expected at the elementary level. These are the abilities to

1. Organize a speech with an introduction, a body, and a conclusion.
2. Organize the body of the speech according to a prescribed plan of organization, including chronology, authority, and problem solution.
3. Present about a three-minute speech using notes.
4. Give an informative report with supporting objects, occurrences, or ideas, using research, oral, or printed sources as the basis.

Fundamental to all speeches is the overall structure that includes an *introduction, body,* and *conclusion.* To provide emphasis and increase the chances of audience comprehension and recall, virtually all public communication—written or oral—operates on the old principle that first you tell them what you are going to say, then you say it, and finally you tell them what you have said. Within this principle, each main part has a function.

The *introduction* serves three functions:

1. Establishes contact with the audience and invites their attention.
2. Announces the topic to be discussed.
3. Gives a brief overview of what is to be said, generally by indicating the main points to be covered.

The *body* of the speech serves two functions:

1. Restates more fully the main ideas of the speech.
2. Provides development, explanation, or support of the main points.

In the *conclusion*, for the level of speeches dealt with at the elementary level, three functions are served:

1. Restates and summarizes the main points of the speech.
2. Emphasizes the importance of the ideas of the speech.
3. Gracefully disengages from the speaking situation.

Consciousness of sequencing remarks, which was introduced at the intermediate level, can now be taken into the development of specific plans of organization. As children learn a sense of time—yesterday, today, tomorrow, a year ago, many years ago—they can structure a speech according to *chronology*. In talking about a flower, for example, a speech can be built according to time: first there was a seed, then it became a shoot, then a bud, and finally a flower. The order for the speech is determined by the time order in which things occur. If a talk is to have three points, which is common, then the first point is what happened first in time, and so on.

Use of *authority* (reference) as the controlling plan of organization is another form of sequencing. Here the speaker will have prepared by seeking material from several familiar authorities—people who because of their education, profession, experience, or status have the qualification to be considered worthy of belief. If three references have been consulted, the teacher, the principal, and a parent, for example, then the speech will be organized according to what each one said. The first point would be, for instance, what the teacher said. Then, the principal's comments would be summarized, and finally, the parent's point of view would be given. The use of authority may also be written authority such as an encyclopedia, a book, or an article written by someone else. The use of authority is the introduction to the use of research in the preparation of public speeches.

Problem solution structures are most common in public speeches. This two-point organization is obvious: first, the speaker takes time to point out a problem and to explain the importance of doing something about it. Having thus interested the audience in the problem and having moved them to be interested in a solution, the speaker presents the solution he or she prefers as the second major segment of the speech.

At the more advanced level children can be expected to prepare *longer talks*, from three to five minutes, and they can be taught to prepare *notes* which will usually be necessary for that length. At this stage the notes may consist of cards on which the substance of what is to be said is written. The important element here is that speakers gain experience in speaking from notes without totally losing eye-contact with the audience. Although children may initially write a speech in full, they should never deliver a public speech by reading a manuscript.

Finally, students can be expected to prepare and deliver an *informative report* with supporting objects, occurrences, or ideas that have been gathered from *oral* or *printed sources*. Two elements, basic to public communication, are introduced in this competency: supplying support for ideas presented to increase the credibility of the speech, and discovery of that support by doing research.

It is well established in public communication that a speaker will typically need to offer some grounds that are external to the speaker and relatively free from his bias to help satisfy doubt in the audience. The form of this in a speech comes as a statement: "Greece is a country with much history (idea) as we learn from an article in *National Geographic* last month (support)." The experience of finding sources of support, either by reading or talking to others, is an excellent start toward more complex forms of public speaking to be learned later.

126

As the teacher plans assignments to develop the competencies, he should remember that these are *exit* competencies and that the learning of each competency at each level will be accomplished by progressively difficult tasks and expectations of the performance.

Sample Exercises for Public Speaking

The following exercises provide suggestions at three levels of ability in elementary school for experiences in public speaking. Each exercise should be conducted with the previously specified competencies as the guideline for skills. Most of the exercises are designed to be conducted over a series of days.

Public speaking requires that one person stands and speaks to a group of listeners. The effective method of achieving a productive experience at the elementary level is to have a limited number of children (usually about five) speak in one day. They must, of course, be told in advance that on a certain day they will be asked to do the assignment. The specific assignment is then continued for a week or more until every child has been a speaker. In such a manner the speaker can attend to the task and listeners will not become restless. To do otherwise tends to produce the chaos of the nonproductive, traditional "show and tell" or other types of class participation. Furthermore, our method incorporates speaking with various subject matters, augments other class work, and does not occupy an extensive amount of time. At the advanced levels more than five students can give speeches in one day. In fact, if the speeches contain the essence of another subject matter, the teacher may want the students to talk in immediate succession. However, the listeners must be able to listen and learn from the speaker. Experience suggests that speeches are therefore best presented in limited time periods throughout elementary school.

BEGINNING LEVEL EXERCISES

1. Each child stands in the classroom and tells everyone his full name, his address, and his parents' or guardians' names. When the child's memory will allow, he should add his phone number. This is a basic communication task that teaches an essential element of safety and survival, and should be taught at the first of the year in the first year of school. This task may be developed by adding one fact each day, until finally each child is able to confidently give the information in its entirety. As soon as the child can accomplish the whole exercise in the classroom, others such as teachers, the principal, and the janitor can randomly ask the children to do this in the halls, the lunchroom, or on the playground as they meet.

2. Each child brings an object, usually a toy, from home, and tells about it. The teacher may need to insert prompting questions. Ultimately, the child should be able to plan all that she has to say in advance so that no prompting is

127

required. The teacher should avoid allowing any child to occupy center stage too long. A simple "Thank you, Sally for talking to us. Now it's time to have someone else talk" is sufficient to keep the speech limited.

3. Each child tells about his pet, the neighbor's pet, or a pet he wants. To give this experience meaning, the child may bring a photograph of a pet or a picture from a magazine of the desired animal. If it is possible in adherence with school rules, a parent or a friend might bring the animal to school briefly for each of two or three children a day.

4. Each child brings a favorite book, story, or poem, and talks to the class about it. This is an effective expansion of beginning reading classes. Of course, the children do not read the written material they bring; they talk about it. But this assignment incorporates oral communication and an interest in reading.

5. Each child brings something that grows (a plant, a flower, a vegetable) and tells everyone its name and something about it. This assignment is, of course, designed to be incorporated into a science class. The child should be ready to tell you where it grows (in the ground, in a pot, in my neighbor's yard) and what we do with this thing that grows.

6. Each child is appointed on a different day to give the weather report. This is another assignment that is designed to be incorporated with science, if the teacher desires. Expansions would include what it looks like, how it feels, what one wears, and possibly some effects such as "rain makes the grass grow."

7. Each child tells about a member of his family. This may be incorporated into social studies. He can name the person, tell their relationship, and what they do, or some other interesting fact. The child may bring a picture of the person, or as the best of all choices he may bring his mother, father, grandparent, brother, sister, or cousin to school to "show" them to their class while he talks about them.

8. Each child tells about a community helper that she knows. This assignment is naturally an adjunct to social studies. The nature of this speech makes it more advanced because the chances are that the child will not have a picture or be able to bring in person her doctor, a policeman, a nurse, janitor, or the checker at the grocery store. Expansions of this will include describing the person and what he does for her.

9. Each child talks to the class about a song he likes to sing—what its name is, where he sings the song, and eventually who sings this song with him. In this task he may be able to bring the sheet music or a record of the song for everyone to enjoy. The assignment is designed to coordinate with music and can be effectively used to increase music appreciation, especially if it is assigned in advance so each child has time to plan the speech and what he might bring.

10. Each child has an assignment to plan to talk to the class about a picture she likes. The child should bring a poster, a print, a painting, a drawing that she has in her room or her home or, if this isn't possible, one she's drawn. This speech is designed for planned oral communication in the art class and can be

expanded to add what is in the picture, where it hangs, what colors were used. Such a lesson can increase the art experience of all the students.

INTERMEDIATE LEVEL EXERCISES

1. Each child tells about his last or his favorite vacation. This is a basic task that should provide experience in accurate reporting and in sequencing events. The speech should be used early at this level in order to provide experience in expanded speaking and organization using a familiar event. Some children will have traveled to interesting places; others will have stayed home and played. Anything they did provides ample subject matter for this speech.

2. Each child explains what she did when she learned to do something. By the time a child is ready for this speech, she will have learned to ride a bike, to swim, to skate, to ski, or to read.

3. Each child tells the class how to play a game. The game may be Scrabble, Sorry, card games (such as Concentration), or dodge ball, baseball, and so on. The speech should provide enough explanation that the listener at least understands the kind of game and the basic skills involved.

4. Each child describes an event when someone was hurt or sick. She may want to talk about herself or a family member or a friend. This speech will change the experience because the focus will be on the functioning of the human body and sequencing those occurrences. This should provide an adjunct to health and/or science classes. Actually, the initial attempts may be recording of experiences, and after planned health classes the talk can involve consideration of parts of the body, the effects of germs or fever, the characteristics of diseases such as measles, mumps, as well as elementary first-aid procedures from a concrete experience.

5. Each child explains how to make something. This speech may run the gamut from cookies to popcorn to clay or paste and even to mud pies. Such a speech could be incorporated in a craft period where the listeners have the opportunity to try to produce some of the things described.

6. Each child explains his mother's or father's work. He tells what the person does, what the job involves, the hours of time spent, and so on. The word *work* has been used intentionally in place of occupation, so that children from nonprofessional families, part-time employed parents, or unemployed parents can describe the tasks their parents do as well as can the child from a professional family. Of course, this lesson is an excellent adjunct to social studies.

7. Each child selects a fundamental substance and tells how it exists, is used or combined, and the results of this. These substances can be natural such as water, dirt, or sand, or a product such as metal, flour, or paint. For example, a child may explain the making of compost or that water on iron results in rust. This speech can readily be incorporated in science classes and should be used after class discussions have prepared the children for the necessary concepts.

129

8. Each child talks about the feelings and actions of a character in a story that she has read. She can talk about the feeling, why the character may feel that way, and what the character did. For example, the three little pigs were scared, little Bo Peep was sad, Winnie the Pooh was hungry, Charlotte was loving, or Charlie was happy. At this age level nursery rhymes are too juvenile, but because they are familiar to all the children, they are good examples for the teacher to use. Each child should use a character in a story she is interested in now. This speech is naturally compatible with reading class. This subject matter is recommended as the initial attempt in teaching children to talk about feelings, because the description in the books should provide assistance, and it may be easier to discuss feelings and actions of someone else.

9. Each child selects a piece of music and describes how it makes him feel and how he acts when he listens. He may describe feeling quiet and relaxed, or he may say, "It makes me happy and I want to dance." Expansion of these experiences into a speech of about a minute can help to make the children aware of feelings as well as augment a music class.

10. Each child gives a talk about a situation in which she was happy, sad, angry, emotionally hurt, or worried. This speech should be expanded to include not only the situation and the feeling but subsequent actions. The older a person becomes, the more the person learns to hide emotions, and at any age it is difficult to see that actions are often the result of feelings. Children are not so inhibited, and a speech can increase understanding. After these speeches have been given, such experience can be utilized for successful solving of individual problems in the classroom, on the playground, or in the halls.

ADVANCED LEVEL EXERCISES

1. Each child gives a speech on his autobiography, organized in chronological order. This speech coordinates well with a writing assignment. As with all the following assignments, a public speech should not consist of reading aloud a fully written manuscript. However, an English assignment could require that the material be written. At the completion of the writing project, each student could make notes and then deliver the speech orally from the notes. This is a good initial assignment at this level because it teaches preparation, organization, and delivery without requiring outside sources for the material.

2. Each child talks about the activity, the purpose, and the importance of something in which she participates. The source of the information for such a speech should be a conversation with an authority on the matter—either the child's parents or the adult in charge of such an activity. Examples of the subject matter might include Little League ball, ballet, the library, scouts, a class in school, and so on. This speech is a good assignment for the initial use of information from an authority. Such an assignment could also coordinate with a writing task.

3. Each child gives an oral book report. This speech is traditionally associated with reading. The students should plan the organization; a chronological report of the story is perhaps the easiest method.

4. Each child tells the class about a problem in a story and the solution to the problem. Such a speech coordinates readily with reading class.

5. Each child talks about a math problem and presents the solution. Arithmetic classes are frequently overlooked as a possibility for a public speech, but the oral presentation of a problem and the solution to the problem is an excellent teaching device for math as well as for oral communication.

6. Each child gives a speech about a famous person. This speech requires the use of written sources, frequently an encyclopedia. A speech on this topic is amenable to almost any subject matter. For example, in English the persons could be famous authors; in science, famous scientists; in music, composers; in art, artists, and so on.

7. Each child gives a speech about a certain animal, bird, horse, or dog. The speech would require special research on the animal, usually from books or magazines dedicated to such a purpose. This speech could coordinate with an art class in which the student also drew or painted the animal or, of course, as a writing assignment for English.

8. Each child selects an historical event and presents a speech about that event. Such a topic is a natural subject to discuss in chronological order. However, this topic may also be presented in a problem–solution type of organization. Outside research is necessary. This speech is designed to coordinate with history class.

9. Each child presents a travel report on a different state. Such an assignment coordinates easily with geography. The project could include writing a letter to the particular state's travel bureau and requesting the information. Then after allowing sufficient time for the information to arrive and be read, the speech could be prepared and delivered.

10. Each child gives a speech on a current event. The assignment should include reading authorities and it is hoped that contrasting views could be presented. The reporting of varied opinions makes this assignment the most difficult at this level. Combination of different sources may be difficult for many students, but frequently *Time, Newsweek,* and *U.S. News & World Report* offer differing perspectives. Such a speech coordinates well with social studies.

7

Decision Making

OBJECTIVES

At the end of this chapter you should be able to

1. Define decision making.
2. Describe the behaviors involved in decision making.
3. Distinguish between an idealist notion of problem solving and a modern idea of decision making.
4. Explain the importance of human interaction to decision making.
5. Discuss how the general and specific level competencies are designed to yield, by the time of exit, an elementary mastery of decision making as currently conceived.
6. Explain how the general exit competencies represent broad goals that accompany each specific level competency.
7. Match each exercise to the general exit competency or competencies and the specific level exit competency or competencies that the exercise addresses.
8. Explain why the successful completion of one exercise does not fulfill the objectives of the competencies.
9. Design additional exercises for the fulfillment of the stated competencies.

"No problem is so big or so complicated that it can't be run away from," says Charlie Brown. "I just let lots of things sit on my desk for a few weeks," says the administrator, "and you'd be surprised how often decisions are made for me by people losing interest or deadlines passing." "I hate to be on committees," says the student, "because I never seem to have anything to contribute until I get home, and then it's too late."

The class was given a choice among several different kinds of cookies with the limitation that they could choose only one kind. The first student selected an oatmeal cookie and loved it. Every other child picked an oatmeal cookie, apparently because the first student had made that choice. Most of them did not like their choice after one bite and wanted to take one of the others. But they had made their decision, and they had to live with it. On the playground, the teacher allowed children to choose the activity to do for that period. They selected quickly, and after a few minutes many became bored and wanted to do something else. The teacher said they had made a decision and they had to stick with it until the end of the period. The next day the teacher gave the same decision opportunity. The students took a good deal more time making their decisions, and they were happier with their choices. They had learned something about decision making.

Making decisions is one of the most difficult and still the most necessary of human actions. Not making decisions is virtually impossible because inaction is a decision in itself. The problem is to make decisions in a way that is satisfying and rewarding.

THE CONCEPT

Decision making can be distinguished from behavior which we do unconsciously or automatically on the one hand and problem solving on the other. There are many actions we take daily that may look like decisions but, in truth, reflect merely behaviors done without thinking or planning. After getting out of bed each morning, there are few, if any, people who ponder whether or not to wear clothes that day. On the other hand, we often have to make a careful decision as to what clothes to wear. But, looking to the other extreme, it is rarely a case of discovering the single correct solution to the problem of dress. Typically, it will involve a choice among various alternatives, all of which would do, but with some better than others, depending upon the criteria employed. Similarly, people living in the threat of an oncoming hurricane rarely think much about the relative merits of living or dying—the desire to live is strong in most of us. However, there probably is never a single correct response to such a threat; it is not a matter of discovering the true solution that is "out there" and waiting to be found. The whimsical behavior of storms is such that we may not know for sure even after the storm has passed whether it would have been better to evacuate or stick it out. So it was a decision making problem.

Conceptually, decision making is recognizing the alternatives and choosing among them on the basis of selected values or other criteria and then carrying out the decision. Because of the nature of human problems, because of the inadequacies of our investigative abilities, and because decisions usually must be made within some time constraint, finding the single correct solution is either a fruitless hope or an impossibility because one does not exist. On the other hand, if we had to make a conscious decision about everything we do, little would get done. Imagine having to deliberate on whether to get up in the morning, whether to dress, whether to go to the bathroom, whether to eat, whether to walk rather than run to school, and so.

Decision making, then, addresses situations of choice important enough to warrant the cost (time, effort, money, loss of other things) of reaching a decision. Most often, these are the kinds of choices that involve others, either as resources for our understanding of our problem or because others must share in the decision. To the extent it involves interaction with others in any way from processing to announcing the decision, decision making is a communication skill.

An *operational* definition of decision making is most difficult because various experts prescribe various patterns, and people tend to do their decision making in ways that dissatisfy the experts. Probably the best compilation of behaviors recommended by experts is presented by I. L. Janis and L. Mann[1] who broke the process into seven steps which we summarize as eight behaviors.

1. Survey a wide range of alternative possible decisions.
2. Survey all the potential objectives to be gained and the values implied in each potential choice.
3. Weigh as carefully as possible the costs and risks of a negative or a positive outcome to the decision.
4. Look for all the information that can be found to help evaluate the alternatives.
5. Look objectively at all the information that comes out even though it does not support what seems to be the favorite alternative.
6. Go back and look again at all the positive and negative consequences of all the alternatives, even those labeled as unacceptable at first.
7. Make a decision and announce it.
8. Make detailed plans to implement or carry out the decision, including what to do if the worst fears of failure come to pass.

THE TRADITION

Idealists at least as far back as Socrates have been inclined to see every problem that the human mind can conceive as susceptible to one and only one correct solution. Whether they were calculating the path of the planets, determining the boiling point of water, finding the cause of disease, establishing a form of government, learning history, or distinguishing between good and evil, they proceeded as if each question could be answered clearly, correctly, and finally. From ancient idealism to modern positivistic science, answers, solutions, or decisions (whichever they choose to call them) are perceived as being external to human choice. It is not a matter of what you want or how you see the problem, they would say, it is finding what is "right."

Even Aristotle, whose work indicated some problems with absolutism, divided the world of issues into two groups, one containing questions capable of certain answers such as mathematics and science, and one including questions capable of contingent or uncertain answers such as those emerging from human problems: right and wrong, war and peace, values, and public policy. For questions in the first group, Aristotle believed the means of solution could be found in some form of calculation as in math and logic. For human problems, he believed that rhetoric or communication was the appropriate methodology.

Over the years, perhaps the most *common way of thinking* about decision making has been to give priority to the *idealistic approach*. Even Aristotle's

---

[1] I. L. Janis and L. Mann, *Decision Making* (New York: The Free Press, 1977).

division has been blurred with the emergence of naive social science, leading to such schools of thought as those advocating problem solving. Here the suggestion is that even human problems can be addressed through scientific methods to yield correct solutions.

Current Perspectives are in a state of transition. Many observers still advocate calculation over communication on the theory that bringing people into discussion merely confuses issues and opens the possibility of irrational decisions. In the middle are those who follow an essentially Aristotelian position by dividing questions into those that can be calculated to correctness and those that can be discussed to decision. At the other end of the continuum are an increasing number of physical scientists, social scientists, and humanists who reject the belief that calculation can ever do the entire job of decision making. They argue that calculations play an important role in many decisions, but they invariably reflect the values of the calculator: computers do not make any decision or do any function that is not a result of the values and choices of the programmer. Similarly, no logic, no scientific study, no mathematical formula operates apart from the perspectives, concepts, values, or choices of the experts using them. Therefore, in this point of view, human interaction underlies and controls all decision making.

Furthermore, as experts come to believe that decisions are in people and not external to them, greater attention is being given to purely human choices. In economics, buying and selling are seen as a function of what the market will bear and not merely a computation of the costs of land, labor, capital, and government. Labor-managment relations have been based upon the bargaining strength of the parties and not just a product of relative economic conditions. International relations are seen as predicated upon the effectiveness of diplomacy. Law resolves more problems through bargaining in both civil and criminal cases than it does through trials. Even the decisions of juries and appellate courts are now recognized as trade-offs among competing human perspectives and values rather than the finding of "facts" and knowing the "law."

The *perspective of this book* advances the position that human interaction underlies all decision making. We use the term *decision making* consciously to indicate our belief that all problems (personal, social, scientific) are resolved at any given time through human choice. We would relegate problem solving to subordinate specific tasks which, although they may make an enormous contribution to the final choice, do not make the choice. They only provide data on which human beings may base their choice. Human beings choose the mathematical, logical, or scientific systems to apply to problems, human beings analyze and evaluate the results, and human beings interact to decide when and if to accept and act on the results of calculation.

For this reason the communication skills involved in decision making are fundamental to human functioning. When in the past we have pretended that human interaction could be ignored, we have allowed ourselves to be controlled by more subtle uses of communication.

COMPETENCIES TO BE DEVELOPED

Three *General Exit Competencies* can be identified for communication skills in decision making. These are the ability to

1. Make a conscious decision and communicate it to others.
2. Interact with others to make a mutual decision.
3. Assume the responsibility for living with and carrying out a decision.

In a manner of speaking, we make decisions all the time. Some of them come from habit, social norms, general learning, or response to the lead of others. For many, if not most, of these, we do not even recognize the fact of having made a choice. Sometimes, people do not perceive themselves as having a choice when in fact they do. The goal of the first general competency, then, is to acquire the ability to perceive choice by recognizing that alternatives exist, to be able to evaluate the alternatives according to consciously selected criteria, and to be able to make the decision public. Even when the decision is personal, communication is involved. It is through interaction with others that we learn what alternatives are open to us. From childhood on, many people believe that their problems are unique, their feelings and values are unique, their sense of being obliged to take certain courses of action is unique. It is only when they share these feelings with others that they discover these problems are common and that through sharing, alternatives which may prove more satisfying are available.

Research tells us that the public announcement of a decision is an important step. The oral statement of a decision tends to make it more fixed and clear. When others know of a decision, we tend to become more committed to it. When someone has decided to make an important change in lifestyle, for example, experience says that it should be announced to significant others. If you want to break a bad habit, change the way you relate to others, or try for an important goal such as getting a part in a play, making the team, improve school work, telling friends about the decision will strengthen your ability to see it through.

Part of the problem of making a conscious choice is the ability to do the reasoning (see Chapter 8) needed to evaluate alternatives. This research process calls for skills that may come only in advanced students even though the decision itself is not so complicated once they are informed.

The second competency addresses the special problems and skills required to work with others to reach a mutual decision. Here the focus rests on the quality of the interaction in relation to the quality of decision desired. Obviously,

138

authoritarian structures such as usually characterize elementary classrooms can yield a mutual decision easily as long as the students, for example, are willing to let the teacher tell them what to do. As long as the teacher or other authoritarian truly knows best, this can be an efficient decision making approach.

The trouble with authoritarian group decision making should be obvious. Most important is the fact that valuable input from others in the group is lost. Even very young children can provide insight into some problems that could improve decisions: they know what they understand and what they do not; they know what they like to do; they even know what teaching techniques help them learn best and what ones are not very productive. Another problem with authroitarian groups is the loss of group satisfaction with interaction and the ultimate decision. Evidence shows that democratic group decision making generates significantly more satisfaction among members of the group and more commitment to carry out the decision.

But to achieve a group decision, as opposed to one dictated by the one or two high-status members, a fully functioning communication network must emerge. There must be time for members to establish themselves in appropriate roles, such as those discussed in Chapter 5, "Group Communication." There must be some division of labor in working on the decision so that maximum productivity can be achieved. All members of the group must have the chance to contribute to the decision-making process, if they choose to do so.

Finally, our general competencies call for students to be able to assume the responsibility for living with and carrying out a decision. Making and even announcing a decision is not enough. It must be done in such a way that those involved are satisfied with the choice and can devote some energy to its fulfillment. Furthermore, a decision made but never effected is empty. An individual must assume the responsibility of carrying out his own decision. In groups, interaction must occur, leading to assignment of roles and responsibilities in doing the labor connected with seeing a decision through to completion. Again, unless this is done through mutual communication, the decision will either fail completely, or its accomplishment will fall on the shoulders of the one or two willing members. This leaves the rest of the group relatively uninvolved and leaves the willing workers feeling used. It also puts total reliance for the success of the decision on those who accept the full responsibility, and they may not be the ones best able to see it through. Ultimately, successful social decision making requires that all involved accept the decision and work for its completion.

Beginning Exit Competencies include the ability to

1. Think about a decision before announcing it.
2. Announce a choice.
3. Take the responsibility of carrying out the decision.

139

A first step toward the awareness of the world of choice is to think about a decision before making a commitment. So often, both children and adults commit first and think later, when it is too late. The waiter in the restaurant comes by and asks, "Is everything all right?" and a common response is, "Sure. Fine." (It is as if it were a ritual greeting: "How are you?" "Fine.") Then you discover it would really be nice if you had some more butter, but by then the waiter is gone. Too late you realize that the waiter was presenting a decision opportunity, and you should have thought before responding. The issue here may seem to be assertiveness, but one cannot be assertive until a decision is made.

To recognize the difference between rituals (as in the greeting) and genuine decision opportunities is an important first step. This calls for development of a habit of thought and interaction. The old comedy routine is not far from the mark; the beautiful flight attendant says, "Can I do anything for you?" and the lecherous old man says, "What did you have in mind?" If the question is what do you want to drink with dinner, instead of calling for what you always have, you might ask instead, "What's available?" A child might get something more exciting than milk once in a while. Some of the initial exercises are designed for children to learn this first basic step, making a choice. In making a choice, they must learn to realize there are alternatives, study the alternatives, and then make the decision. This simple first step is basic to more sophisticated action required later.

We have already said that the announcement of a decision is critical to the decision process. Sometimes this is a surprisingly difficult task. How often have you seen people avoid commitment with such phrases as, "Oh, I don't know. What are you having?" "Whatever you think is okay with me." "I guess we could go to the movies, but we don't have to if you don't want to." In this second competency, children will learn that it is neither socially unacceptable nor unduly pushy to state clearly what their decision is.

Finally, at the beginning level, children can begin to assume responsibility for their decisions. This will move them toward more realistic selection of decisions. For example, in some research, we gave children a chance to select a gift for their teacher. They finally decided to buy her a tape recorder even though the only way they could afford to do so was for one student to exhaust his life savings. Had they been required to take responsibility for the decision, they would have quickly adopted a more realistic choice.

Intermediate Exit Competencies include the ability to

1. State the basis on which a decision was made with several related utterances.
2. Announce in advance and realistically the actions required by a decision.
3. Participate in making a group decision.

140

Having developed the habit of thinking before deciding, children can now learn to communicate the bases for their decisions. This step accomplishes at least three things. First, it makes the individual aware of the elements of her decision; second it opens the way to developing common criteria for decision within a group. This is a necessary step to social action. It is one thing to have criteria that satisfy you. It is quite another to contribute your criteria to a common pool of those mentioned by others. Third, announcing criteria establishes the possibility of interacting critically. That is to say, you learn to hear others point out problems with your criteria without your being crushed. You also learn to express problems with the criteria of others without hurting them. Only in this way can the benefits of group decision be realized.

Making a realistic assessment of the actions required by a decision in advance of its selection establishes the ability to evaluate decisions wisely, and it establishes the sense of responsibility that goes with mature decision making. Even for personal decisions, as we have said before, communicating with others on the consequences of decisions increases the quality of the assessment process. For group decisions, it is absolutely essential to be able to communicate with the others on the impact of any particular decision.

Finally, at the intermediate level, students establish the ability to participate in an actual group decision. This will draw heavily upon the skills developed in the study of group communication in general. In addition, students at this level will learn to engage in decision-oriented group interaction and to come to responsible consensus in the sense of seeing what is needed to carry out a decision.

Advanced Exit Competencies that students should display are the ability to

1. Evaluate alternatives to a decision individually and in a group.
2. Interact in a group to evaluate alternatives for mutual decisions.
3. Interact in mutual division of labor and acceptance of roles in making and carrying out a decision.
4. Participate in a small group that makes a decision for others.

Most of the research in decision making has dealt with the task of evaluating alternatives. This is difficult enough for a person acting alone for a personal decision. It is still more difficult when the evaluation must be done in a group where several persons must agree on the relative values and costs connected with alternatives. At the advanced elementary level, students should be able to do both tasks at a preliminary degree of sophistication. That is, they should be able to recognize the goals sought through the decision and talk about the extent to which various alternatives promise to meet those goals. They should also be able to notice the relative disadvantages of the alternatives. For example, if the purpose of the decision is to decide on a class project and the alternatives are for each person to do their own project or for the class to do one together, the evaluation might come out as follows. If each does an individual project, everyone would be involved equally, but the quality of the projects would be variable according to the talents of the students. If they do a group project, the quality of the product would be high but not everyone would be able to contribute equally. The students would need to state and evaluate these pros and cons.

This, obviously, leads to the second competency in which the group makes this evaluation mutually. They would need to respect the wishes of all members and take them into account, but the would also need to engage in compromise and creativity to generate a final outcome that satisifies the greatest number of members. The students will need to learn to agree and disagree positively, without damaging the cohesiveness of the group through hurtful exchanges.

An advanced competency at this stage is the ability to allow appropriate roles to emerge and to build a division of labor that will yield a decision reflecting the inherent strengths of group decision making. We have already spoken of role emergence. In decision making, the focus is upon those roles that will facilitate a good decision. Most appropriate are the suggesting of decision alternatives, providing information, seeking information, encouraging critical interaction, supporting others, and identifying the emergence of a consensus. It is also important that the students display the responsibility to generate roles which lead to carrying out the decision. Once a consensus has been identified, they will move immediately to discussion of the ways in which various members can do the work necessary to seeing the decision through to completion.

The final competency is the most difficult and requires that students use their understanding of the decision process in a mature and responsible way to act in a group that makes a decision for others. The expansion suggested here is the focus on the suggestion and evaluation of alternatives with the needs, values, and desires of a larger group in mind. It is quite common in our society that committees are appointed to make a decision for a larger group. This is done for efficiency as well as quality. A small group can consist of those best able to deal with a particular subject matter, and a small group can interact more efficiently than a large one. But committee operation only works when the members of the committee can represent the others to be affected by the decision. Thus, the evaluation process is a bit more complicated, as is the business of reporting the decision to the larger body in a way that enables them to understand and appreciate the work of the committee.

These competencies are all exit competencies both overall and by level. They may be accomplished by providing practice in making decisions of graduated difficulty.

Sample Exercises for Decision Making

The following exercises provide samples of types of decision-making lessons for the elementary classroom. The three levels of exercises should be conducted with the previously stated competencies as the goals for each level. Decisions are made by individuals, by small groups, and by large groups. These decisions have varying effects, ranging from little or no effect to controlling others. The practice in making decisions includes informed choice, announcing the decision, and taking the responsibility to act in accordance with the decision. Human interaction and communication are different in the decisions of an individual, of small groups, and of large groups. In addition, different decisions involve different experience and knowledge. So the following exercises are organized into individual and group activities and the order takes into consideration the knowledge necessary to reach and to carry out an informed decision.

The teacher must remember that any decision skill assignment has to be a real experience. That is, decisions should not involve "pretend" situations. Some of these tasks may be completed at one time, and some involve a series of days or weeks. The nature of the lessons should make the time period obvious. All the tasks are designed to coordinate with regular activity in different subject matters and should not appreciably increase the teaching time.

BEGINNING LEVEL EXERCISES

1. Each child looks at a row of pictures and draws a circle around the one that is different. This is a basic task that is familiar to every teacher who has taught reading readiness. However, rarely does the teacher or the child consider this as decision making, which, of course, it is. The teacher should tell the child that he is to make the decision. Decisions such as this are a part of the entire educational system and clearly point to making a decision and living with the consequences. However, sharing of the decision is usually only between the child and the teacher until children are mature enough to grade each other's work.

2. Each child selects something to eat from a variety of items. This is another task that involves a private decision that others may not see; consequently, it is a low-level assignment. Such an activity is a teaching adjunct to a birthday or a holiday party. Each child is presented a variety of cookies or sandwiches and must select one without handling the others. If possible, it augments the lesson to have enough to give each child a second selection after the first is consumed.

3. Each child chooses an activity to do during a free time. Such decisions are the essence of the open classroom and have an appropriate place in the structured classroom. This choice is a private one, but it involves not interfering or disrupting another person's choice. This task involves completing more difficult subsequent actions in that the child should be responsible for getting the material, working with it, and putting it away, whether such a choice is the tape recorder, a puzzle, the paints, or number rods.

4. Each child selects a person to give a speech about and announces to the class who that person will be. This assignment is designed to be the initial step in the public speaking assignment proposed for social studies in Chapter 6.

5. Each child selects a chore to do in the classroom. The teacher keeps a list

of the chores selected. This decision should be made for a week in advance, with different children responsible each day, to allow experience in making decisions for the future.

6. Each child decides in advance what picture they will draw and they announce the decision before they begin. Of course, this assignment is designed for art class.

7. Each child describes whether she will read a paragraph or two of the reading lesson aloud or silently and then tell about it. This decision task provides a variation to participation in the reading group.

8. Each child selects a study partner and then studies with that person for the day or the week. The turn must be rotated so that one half of the class selects, and then the next day or week the other half of the class selects. Such a decision is probably best designed for spelling, because students of differing academic abilities can work together as one child reads the words to the other and checks the spelling. The teacher may also consider using this decision as a modified sociogram.

9. Each child decides upon a song from the repertoire the class knows for the class to sing. One or two children a day may make such a decision until each child has had a turn. This assignment will involve more thinking in the decision-making process if the person who is to make the decision knows in advance when he must announce the decision. Of course, this is designed for music class.

10. Each child selects something that grows to talk about, and that selection must be different from the items chosen by any other child. This may be an initial step in the public speaking assignment suggested for science classes, but the task becomes more difficult if each one must select a different item. Children will learn the advantages and disadvantages of quick and delayed decision.

INTERMEDIATE LEVEL EXERCISES

1. Each child decides what he will do during a recess period that allows individual choice. As with all exercises at this level, the child must be able to announce the decision and resulting actions required in advance of having to carry out his decision.

2. Each child announces something she wants to learn to do. She may want to learn to play marbles, to play baseball, to play a piano, to be a ballet dancer, or even to drive a car. This exercise should involve a more complicated discussion of the results of such a decision, including considerations such as other people who would have to participate, possible cost, and the ability or age required for such a project.

3. Each child selects someone to do something for that day or tomorrow. He should announce the person and the act in advance and explain the decision. Then he needs to explain what he will have to do to carry out the decision.

4. Each child decides what public servant is most important to him. This involves a discussion of the other person's job and actions and the effect these actions have on the child. This discussion would augment a social studies class.

5. Each child decides whether to complete a work assignment during a study period at school or whether to complete this assignment at home. Such an option may be an occasional variation in arithmetic classes. It is excellent practice in making a decision, anticipating in advance the consequences, and carrying out the action of a similar decision that each child makes throughout his education.

6. A preestablished small group decides what school work to do next. This assignment is designed for reading groups. The teacher selects several stories that could be read next, and the group decides which story they would like to read. Decisions of the children are frequently more motivating than decisions of the teacher, and this decision provides a variation for reading groups.

7. A newly established small group selects a project to complete from among a list of teacher-proposed options. The teacher should be certain that a decision of the group involves a complete discussion of the choices available. This decision could coordinate well with a science class in which group projects are to be completed.

8. The class decides what book, story, or poem the teacher will read aloud. Teachers often read aloud to the class to expand literature experience, but usually the class has no vote on what is read. The teacher should provide several options with a brief summary so the class can make a somewhat informed decision.

9. The class decides what field trip to take. This task is a candidate for any subject matter in which a field trip may be taken. The teacher should preselect viable possibilities for class discussion and decision making.

10. The class decides what gift to get for a person such as the teacher, the janitor, or a special visitor. This task is advanced at this level, because the possibilities are open and the discussion will have to involve such practicalities as the method of obtaining money, if necessary, the acquisition of the gift, and its presentation.

ADVANCED LEVEL EXERCISES

1. Each child selects a school activity he wants to participate in during the year. This is a good task for early in the school year. The class should be able to see a prepared list of school activities that may include safety patrol, teacher's helper, water the plants, acolyte for chapel in parochial school, and so on until many jobs are listed. The child's name should be put on the list beside the job as soon as he decides what job he'd like to do. Such a decision does not mean he'll get the job, but it does mean he has chosen at least one extracurricular activity he'd like to do and that he'll submit a request to do it.

2. Each child participates in bargaining for a trade of actual objects. This task may be completed by arranging a flea market in which every student brings several items they own and are willing to trade. Time is allowed for all items to be displayed and viewed. Then students are given time to circulate and arrange to trade any item they have. The decision of each individual is her own and may range from no trade to acquisition and repeated trading. The teacher would be well advised to notify parents of this assignment so that someone does not bring an unpermissible item to trade, such as a tape recorder or an older sibling's new poster.

3. The class selects books to comprise one of the various reading lists for independent reading during the year. This assignment coordinates with reading and with public speaking. Every child can nominate a book to include in the list by first giving a speech summarizing that book. Then the class votes on which books they want to have included in the list.

4. A committee is appointed to decide the songs the class or the chorus will sing for a school program. The songs should be selected from the repertoire the class has sung. Naturally, such a small group decision is planned for music class.

5. The class decides procedures for evaluation on one section of completed class work. In this decision the teacher should give the class a list of possible options. The options may include what day to be evaluated, whether to take a short answer, true/false, or multiple choice test, whether to have a test or a written assignment, and so on. Although the teacher presents options, this assignment requires experience in methods of evaluation and thus becomes an advanced assignment.

6. A group of class officers makes decisions on rules, duties, and some assignment of work. These officers should change monthly so that every student has the opportunity to be a part of the decision-making group. Depending on the nature of the group of students, the teacher should decide whether the officers are to be elected, thus combining the task with a persuasive campaign speech, or whether the officers should be appointed. But every student needs the experience of serving. The decisions this group makes may include class rules, duties such as who is hall monitor or who ushers at a program, and may include handling certain discipline problems. The range is as broad as the teacher's imagination. These groups must begin early in the year if everyone is to have a turn, and this task is suggested for the most advanced elementary students.

7. Each child selects a project to complete on the basis of a series of personal or telephone interviews with older students who completed similar projects a year or so before. The teacher must announce the task far enough in advance so that interviews may be completed before a decision is made. The task can be a part of any class, for example, selecting books for English, a project for science, or a project for art.

8. Each child decides a person he most admires from a group of persons he has researched. This decision coordinates well with history and may also include

public speeches on the person. Each student conducts research and writes a resumé on three famous people before the decision is made.

9. The class plans a project and appoints committees for each responsibility that must be carried out to complete the project. Then the committees meet and make decisions concerning their section of the project. This is a double assignment with some decisions by a large group and some by a small group. The project may include a booth at a school fair, an overnight trip, or a field trip and is applicable to any subject that has the possibility of such a responsibility.

10. A committee plans a class party and then appoints committees for each responsibility necessary for such a party. This is a double assignment that involves a series of small groups making decisions.

8

Reasoning

OBJECTIVES

At the end of this chapter you should be able to

1. Distinguish between having an argument and giving reasons.
2. Describe reasoning as a communication process.
3. Define the elements in reasoning.
4. Contrast prescriptive concepts of logic with a descriptive analysis of reasoning.
5. Explain why reasons are not necessarily valid or invalid, right or wrong, but derive their quality from the way people use them.
6. Discuss how reasons vary in content and form.
7. Discuss how the general and specific level competencies are designed to yield, by the time of exit, an elementary mastery of reasoning as currently conceived.
8. Explain how the general exit competencies represent broad goals that accompany each specific level competency.
9. Match each exercise to the general exit competency or competencies and the specific level exit competency or competencies that the exercise addresses.
10. Explain why the successful completion of one exercise does not fulfill the objectives of the competencies.
11. Design additional exercises for the fulfillment of the stated competencies.

"Mommy, Sue won't let me play with her doll!"
"Well, Laura, it's her doll and she doesn't have to let you play with it."
"Yeah, but if she's not playing with it she should share, right Mommy?"
"Yes, it's nice to share. But she doesn't have to if she doesn't want to."

A great deal of our communication does not call for reasoning, but there are situations such as the foregoing exchange where reasoning is important to transactions with others. Laura wanted to play with Sue's doll, but Sue was unwilling. In the face of this disagreement, Laura had a number of choices. She could have gone to play with something else and there would have been no further conflict. Many potential differences are avoided in this way. In fact, it can be burdensome and even offensive if we choose to make arguments time and time again.

But Laura really wanted to play with the doll and she wanted to talk about it. Walking away would have left her feeling unsatisfied. Besides, she did not see any *reason* why she should not be allowed to play with it. We do not know what went on between the two girls before Mommy was brought into the picture, but we can imagine. Sue may have merely rejected the request or she may have added a reason, "It's mine." Laura may have found that insufficient as a reason by replying that Sue should share her possessions if she was not playing with them herself. It was a stand-off again.

They could have then resorted to having an argument: shouting, crying, pushing, taking, instead of giving reasons. This alternative is not limited to children. Unfortunately, adults do it frequently, and even nations resort to war when they can't get what they want.

But Laura chose to seek a reasoned resolution of the problem. She presented her reasons to a respected and unbiased arbitrator (Mommy), who heard the points to be made and gave a reasoned decision. Now Laura might still feel disappointed in not getting her way, but she has the satisfaction of knowing that her reasons were heard and fairly considered. The decision went against her but she knows why—that is, she had a rule to understand: sharing is voluntary, though nice, and does not transcend the force of possession. Beyond that, Laura has behaved in a way our society recommends. We discourage shouting, crying, pushing, and taking in the presence of disagreement, and we recommend reasoning in its place.

THE CONCEPT

Reasoning is a basic communication skill. Two words in that sentence may be surprising: *basic* and *communication*. As we will explain in the discussion of the tradition of reasoning, people have often perceived reasoning as an advanced skill available only to those who are specially trained and expert. Now we know that even three-year-olds are typically making their first tentative efforts at reasoning, and the skill becomes more and more a part of their communication behavior with each additional year. By the time children reach school age, they use reasoning strategies similar to those used by adults.

Reasoning is also a *communication process*. Everyone has private thoughts in which ideas are developed and potential solutions are worked out for problems, but reasoning is most effective as a *social process* in which people exchange points of view, with the objective of preventing or resolving mutual differences. No matter how sensible our thoughts may seem privately, it is only through reasoned communicative transactions that shared knowledge or agreements are developed. They result from mutual understanding and commitment to mutual rules. Thus, reasoning is inherently a communication process.

Conceptually, reasoning consists of speech acts that expand communication in a way to explain a person's position, whether disagreement is present or absent. At its most basic level, a reason may consist of a single utterance: "The doll is mine." Commonly, reasoning involves an utterance plus some additional communication designed to provide support for it. By support, we mean verbal or nonverbal communication that increases the likelihood the person or persons to

151

whom the utterance is addressed will agree with it: "The doll is mine. See, it has my name on it. It has red hair, and you know my doll has red hair."

In our studies of children's reasoning, we have found them using a variety of utterances. Consider some examples:

THREAT: "If you don't do it, a policeman will come and get you."

"His mother'll kill you."

"You're too little, not big like me."

DESIRE: "'Cause I said so. I want you to."

DEMAND: "You better give it right now."

BRIBE: "I'll give you an apple if you do."

"He can play with you, and he'll be much nicer."

MORAL OBLIGATION: "He wants to be out. That what. He just wants to be out."

"He needs his mother around him."

"He can't breathe."

"He hasn't did nothing to you."

SOCIAL PRESSURE: "You should let him go. 'Cause it's nice."

"You know you are just being bad."

"Everybody will see you in your shorts."[1]

Although this is by no means a complete listing of reasons used by children, it illustrates the concept. It shows that single utterances are quite common.

The concept of reasoning implies a communicative transaction, not a series of statements by one person. We all know that children develop an inquisitiveness early on. They want to know *why:* why do we have that; why did you do that; why did you say that; why is it called that; why, why why? They learn that *why* is a legitimate question, and that it usually gets a response. That response is usually a reason: *because.* . . . Through such transactions, reasoning works to develop shared agreements and knowledge by establishing mutually acceptable grounds for claims. In our studies of children's reasoning, we found them constantly wanting to know why the other person did something, or why the other person did not accept their reasons. They readily gave reasons and sought reasons. Children seem prepared to learn how people evaluate reasons within certain contexts so as to identify those that would satisfy the people involved and yield agreement. This is the essence of reasoning: making claims, supporting them

---

[1]M. L. Willbrand, "Child Reason in Supplicatory Discourse: Rules to be Refined," in G. Ziegelmueller and J. Rhodes, Eds., *Dimensions of Argument* (Annandale, VA: Speech Communication Association, 1981), pp. 595–608.

with reasons, listening to others' claims and their reasons, responding with modified claims or additional reasons when agreement does not emerge, and continuing this reasoned transaction in the search for agreement.

Operationally, the elements of reasoning are explained by S. Toulmin, R. Rieke, and A. Janik,[2] who present in detail the following information. *Claims* are identified as statements that communicate what the person is asking others to agree to as a result of his or her argument. *Grounds* present the information (observations, common knowledge, statistical data, personal testimony, previously established claims, or anything perceived as "factual" data) that tells others the foundation or basic support for the claim. *Warrants* are assertions of the legitimacy of the grounds in support of the claims. That is, they tell why, given the grounds stated, the claim should be agreed to. They consist of values, rules of thumb, legal principles, and cultural truisms. *Backing* serves to support the warrant, to provide material such as that in grounds—factual or verifiable statements—which serve to establish the acceptability of the warrants. *Modal qualifiers* are statements that suggest the force with which a claim is advanced: *usually, possibly, probably, unless something happens, the good Lord willing,* and *the river don't rise,* and so on. In other words, not all claims have the same force. Sometimes we want to say something with certainty: "You can hold me to this no matter what." At other times, we may be willing to advance a claim, but we do not want others to take it without reservation: "I really think that's what the teacher said to do, but I'm not certain." The qualifier tells others how much stock to put in the claim and how much you are willing to be held to it. Finally, *possible rebuttals* are the statements that explain the qualifier. They identify tnat virtually any claim is susceptible to rebuttal with the exception of those few that are certain and necessary, such as the answer to an arithmetic problem, given the mathematical system being used.

Look at the example on page 154. Everyday we hear the weather report and try to make claims based upon it. Operationally, these arguments can be charted.

As we have already said, in practice, neither children nor adults speak in such fully developed arguments as that charted here. Often, they.exchange a series of single statements, which are sometimes grounds, sometimes warrants, sometimes qualifiers, sometimes backing. Often the claim is presumed and never actually stated. This operational definition is an analysis of a fully developed argument which reveals the potential elements and their relationship. This analytic process is an operational concept of the elements involved and does not presume to prescribe how children must accomplish reasoning in either everyday conversation or in planned speeches.

[2] S. Toulmin, R. Rieke, and A. Janik, *An Introduction to Reasoning* (New York: Macmillan Publishing Co., Inc., 1979), Chaps. 2 through 7.

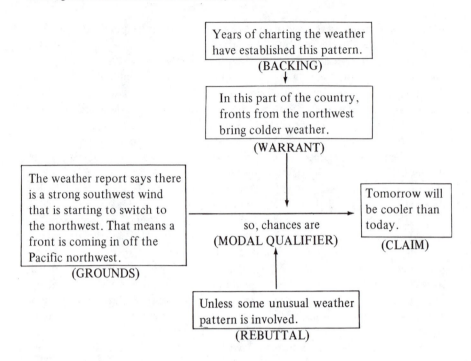

THE TRADITION

The tradition of reasoning in communication goes all the way back to Aristotle's work on rhetoric in ancient Greece. He modeled his comments on rhetorical reasoning after his extensive work on logic and thereby set a pattern based on the syllogism that persisted for almost 2,000 years. Modern work in symbolic logic has been added so that it has been common to try to test claims people make in communication according to the rules of consistency and noncontradiction, which work in more formal systems.

Common Ways of Thinking about reasoning and argumentation during this century in the United States have been highly influenced by the work of George P. Baker at Harvard. Writing at the turn of the century, Baker adapted ancient rhetoric to modern needs by bringing together the work of philosophers and rhetoricians to present a pattern of reasoning designed to serve all situations. It was a prescriptive system in the sense that its purpose was to teach students how to make correct arguments by following the modified rules of logic combined with established tests of evidence. It recognized the importance of being able to communicate arguments effectively, but the test of a correct argument remained intrinsic to the reasoning process rather than the communicative transactions.

Current Perspectives show a growing tendency to look for the quality of reasoning within the various communication situations in which it occurs. More and more, writers are talking about *fields of argument*. That is, they look to the kinds of reasoning inherent to law, science, politics, art, religion, and the general argumentation that takes place within interpersonal communication. The prescriptive pattern of the past is giving way to *descriptions* of how people reason. Still, many writers hold to the belief that there are certain correct, or more effective, ways to reason. The descriptive work on fields is only just starting. Particularly in writing intended for students doing competitive debate in schools, there are clearly set patterns of argument prescribed.

The View of This Book is based upon the descriptive, field-oriented theories of reasoning. We believe reasoning to be more a *communicative act* than one of logical analysis. There are situations in communication in which people need and want to present claims so that others will find them valuable too. In this process, different persons develop their own patterns of making, supporting, and responding to claims. Our objectives in building this communicative skill are to sensitize students to the reasoning process, give them some experience in supporting and responding to claims, and provide them with the ability to learn the more specialized forms of reasoning as they move into other groups, whether they be advanced levels of school, professional activities, or as citizens functioning in a democratic society.

Considering that the perspective of this book is *descriptive reasoning* rather than prescriptive, it is our intention that children experience reasoning. The intention is not for the teacher to pass judgment on good or bad reasons, allowed or disallowed reasons, or right and wrong reasons. Through experience a person may learn which of his reasons are viable to his audience. In the everyday world, the validity of reasons may change with the situation and the audience. Experience, rather than prescriptions, seems better preparation for reason giving.

COMPETENCIES TO BE DEVELOPED

Two *General Exit Competencies* can be identified for reasoning skills in communication. The child should possess the ability to

1. State a claim (proposition) and present consciously developed reasons in support of it.
2. Present a reasoned response to another person's statements on the basis of analytical listening.

These two competencies embrace the essence of reasoning. Regardless of the situation or the field, reasoning calls for stating a claim or claims, offering reasons designed to make the claim valuable (sensible, sound, reasonable, and logical) to the others involved in the communicative transaction, and the ability to listen analytically to the claims and support given by others and communicate a reasoned response. We have described reasoning as relevant to disagreement, but that does not mean it always occurs in the presence of disagreement. On the contrary, much reasoning is done to prevent disagreement from ever emerging. For example, "I'm not going to Bob's party even though I know it is expected, because I just don't like him and I'm uncomfortable in his presence." This statement includes a claim: "I'm not going to Bob's party." It offers two statements in support: "I don't like him and I'm uncomfortable in his presence." It recognizes and rejects a possible rebuttal: "Even though I know it is expected." And it is stated with maximum force: "I'm not going. . . ." instead of any one of a number of qualifiers such as "I may not go," or "I really don't want to go," or "I probably won't go." Thus, it is a rather fully developed line of reasoning. But it could well have been said in advance of any disagreement, and because it is so clearly stated, the expected response might well be, "I see your reasons and I think your decision makes sense. No one expects you to go to a party if you will be uncomfortable." The response represents analytical listening and is also reasoned, but it reinforces rather than disagrees with the claim.

The disagreement relevance of this reasoning lies in its ability to anticipate and dispatch disagreement before it occurs. Of course, the listener would be fully within bounds to say, "You ought to go anyway. Others expect you to be there, and they will be disappointed if you don't show up. Besides, you can just avoid Bob with the exception of a brief 'hello' and then you wouldn't be uncomfortable." In this case, disagreement has emerged, and the two people can continue the transaction until a reasoned decision is reached. The first person might change her mind and decide to go to the party, she may stick to the original claim and not go, or she may reach still another decision that comes from the reasoning exchanged. The reasoning is still disagreement relevant. This pattern is quite common in interpersonal reasoning.

The same kind of reasoned communications take place in group decision making. As we learned in Chapters 5 and 7, groups go through a period of cooperative reinforcement of others' claims, both early and late in the decision-making process, and typically have a period of overt disagreement somewhere in the middle. Group decision making allows and encourages reasoning aimed at preventing or reducing disagreement, and some decisions are made with virtually no sustained disagreement. In fact, often the better prepared people are to make and support well-researched claims, the less likely it is that disagreement will be a significant factor.

Debates are quite a different communication situation. *Debate* is a form of communication designed to deal with disagreement that already exists and cannot be readily resolved through interpersonal communication or a conference. Debaters are advocates: they have a proposition to advance or oppose and part of their function is to see that the best case possible is communicated to the person or persons who will decide the issue. In law, for example, your attorney will argue your case throughout the trial so that the judge or jury will have available all that can legitimately be said in your behalf. The opposing attorney will undertake to argue the other side of the case, and when the decision is made, it will reflect a thorough exposure to the elements of the case. Political debate is not quite the same. Here the advocates may change their minds during the debate and ultimately support another side of the proposition or some compromise proposal. In this instance, the advocates are also the judges. Student councils use political debate.

But this is not to say that debate is necessarily an antagonistic or unpleasant forum of communication. Although it becomes that too often, the basic premise of debate is a cooperative one. It is an agreement to disagree so that the decision will be stronger for having all points of view developed and tested. All lawyers in a trial are officers of the court; they function to serve the cause of justice, not just to win. Legislators represent the various perspectives of their constituents, which often puts them in conflict with each other, but ultimately they are "officers" of the government, dedicated to making policies and law that will serve the best interests of the country. The important point to be made here is this: in our language the word *argument* may refer to an angry exchange, often involving shouting, name calling, and other efforts to hurt the other person; or argument may refer to the systematic exchange of reasoning around a central issue with the purpose of generating a sound decision. The debate we are talking about involves the latter meaning, where there is no room for anger, shouting, name calling, or words designed to hurt the other person.

Beginning Exit Competencies include these three steps:

1. Give reasons in response to a request for them in support of an utterance for which reasons are appropriate to the context.
2. State something believed or desired with at least three reasons in support, with prompting for more reasons if necessary.
3. Agree or disagree with another person's statement and say why.

Clearly, not all utterances are suitable for reasoned support. If you greet a friend in the morning with "Hello," and she asks, "Why?" you will be properly confused. You have not made a claim and it seems unnecessary to be asked for reasons. On the other hand, if you greet your friend by saying, "You'll be sorry you came to school today," she will most likely ask why you said that. The goal of the first competency is to sensitize students to the kinds of utterances that call for reasoned support and to alert them to the kind of reasons they give spon-

157

taneously. As we have already reported, our research shows that by the time children reach school age, they already have a well-developed repertoire of reasons. They need first to become aware of how and when they use them.

In the second competency, this reasoning process is made more deliberate by asking students to give a series of reasons in support of the same utterance. It will probably be necessary at this stage to continue prompting by asking for more reasons, but if children are able to state three reasons without prompting, so much the better. By calling for three reasons, the students will become aware of the fact that there are various ways to support the same claim.

The final beginning competency calls for providing reasons when agreeing or disagreeing with someone else. Although it may be sufficient for the individual's needs to do nothing more than say, "I agree," or "I disagree," these unsupported utterances are insufficient as a basis for *shared understanding*. When you listen to people talk, they will often supply their own reasons when accepting another's claim. For example, "I think we better go home because it's getting dark." "Yeah, our folks will be wondering where we are." This developed or supported agreement adds to the original claim and renders the shared understanding more robust. It reinforces the first person and develops a stronger basis of agreement.

Merely to disagree leaves the others involved without any basis for further communication. Imagine a discussion in which one person regularly says, "I don't agree," but never offers any support. How can any dialog around the claim develop? How can the others understand and respond to the one who disagrees if they cannot discuss the reasons? If, instead, support for the disagreement is provided, a more full and meaningful interaction can occur. For example, if in response to the claim that we should go home because it's getting dark, the other person had said, "We don't have to go yet because it's only 3:30 and we don't have to be home until 4 o'clock. That's just a cloud that makes it seem dark," then the original claim maker can talk about the disagreement. They can come to a mutually satisfying agreement.

Intermediate Exit Competencies include the following:

1. State something believed or desired with at least three different reasons without prompting.
2. Prepare and present a one- to two-minute speech that presents a claim and supporting reasons.
3. Prepare and present a one-minute, reasoned evaluation of some other communication.

At the intermediate level students can begin to be more conscious in their reasoning. Rather than acting spontaneously, they are now asked to do some thinking about their reasons before they give them. At this point, they can build upon their already established understanding of the communication process. They can ask themselves whether the reasons they have will be meaningful to the others. They can ask whether their reasons are ones other people not only understand but share. We are not asking the teacher or other students to comment on whether the reasons are good or bad, but we are suggesting that intermediate students can consider the extent to which the reasons they think of are ones other people can relate to.

This becomes particularly important in the preparation of the speech with reasons and in the evaluation of some other communication. Here the students are to establish the basis for a dialog on a claim. It is not so important at this stage that other people accept the claim on the basis of the support given, but it is important that students be able to communicate in such a way that others can see their point, understand their perspective, and understand how a reasonable person could make the statements.

Students at this stage of development can begin to think about the structure of reasoning. Although unplanned reasoning frequently is fragmented, involving a series of single statements that may or may not include the clear statement of the claim, in these planned exercises students should be encouraged to state their claim specifically, state their reasons in support, and then restate the claim. For example, the presentations can be structured this way:

CLAIM: At first, the Indians helped the colonists, because
REASON: 1. They taught them how to plant corn,
REASON: 2. They showed them where to hunt for game, and
REASON: 3. They shared their food with them, so
CLAIM: The Indians did help the colonists, at least at first.

Advanced Exit Competencies are as follows:

1. Prepare reasons supporting one point of view on one issue.
2. Prepare and present a two-sided perspective on some proposition and include outside sources of support.
3. Participate in a mini-debate, including presentation of one point of view on one issue and an extemporaneous response to what a classmate has said on another side of the same issue.

The first competency builds upon work done at the intermediate level by asking the students to become aware of the various issues that go together to make a full discussion of a proposition or major topic. This is an introduction to *analysis* in reasoning: the breaking of a major topic into its various component issues. For example, in a discussion of a career goal, the major topic might be whether working as a paramedic might be attractive. But to answer that question, a number of subordinate questions or issues must be addressed, such as:

1. Does paramedic work provide excitement and satisfaction?
2. Must a person have a college education to be a paramedic?
3. Is paramedic work dangerous?
4. Does paramedic work offer good pay?
5. Are there openings for paramedics?

In the first competency, students are asked to select one subordinate issue within a larger topic and prepare a claim that answers the issue and provides reasons in support of the claim.

In the second competency, the process of reasoned analysis is carried further by asking students to discuss reasons on two sides of an issue. For one to be competent in reasoning, it is important to understand the points that can be made for and against a particular claim. Here they will learn that few claims are open to one and only one answer. They will become sensitive to the legitimate reasons supporting another answer, even if it is not the answer they would originally select. We are not asking students to argue against their beliefs or to be unethical. In the second competency, they are still free to say which answer they prefer, but before doing so, they will have reviewed the arguments that could be made for the other side.

This analysis will be assisted at this stage by doing some outside research. That is, students will gather information from outside sources—interviews, reading of textbooks, newspapers, newsmagazines, encyclopedia, or other books and magazines found in the library. With this information, they will discover support for the two sides of the issue. The presentation, then, might take on this format:

ISSUE: Does paramedic work provide excitement and satisfaction?
CLAIM: 1. Yes, paramedic work provides excitement and satisfaction, because
REASON: a. They are on the scene of dramatic, life-and-death situations, as reported in the newspaper article on paramedics . . .
REASON: b. They have the satisfaction of saving lives, as we learn from incidents reported in the newspaper . . .

CLAIM: 2. No, paramedic work is not so exciting and satisfying, because
REASON: a. They spend many hours with little to do but wait, which I learned from talking to a paramedic in our town.
REASON: b. They are often frustrated by seeing people die, which I also learned from my interview.

In the final competency, students put together their understanding of reasoning and analysis by participating in a mini-debate, in which they can present their arguments for one side of an issue, hear another student give arguments for the other side, and extemporaneously respond to the other person's arguments. To do this, the teacher can select a major problem area such as the prospects for a career in the paramedics. Then, with the class participating, a series of subordinate issues, such as those suggested here, will be selected. Then, the class is divided into small groups of varying size to debate each issue. At least one person is assigned to prepare a presentation on one side of each issue, with another person assigned to prepare a presentation on the other side of the same issue. Then, each student will present the prepared arguments, and each student will be given a rebuttal time immediately following the first presentations to respond to what the other person has said and try to show the strength of their chosen answer.

When the class is ready to discuss more challenging issues, groups of two, three, or four can be set up to defend each side. The students in a group will speak in alternation, one from the "yes" side of the issue, followed by one from the "no" side, until all have spoken. Students may choose to combine with the preplanned speech some rebuttal of what the other side argued. Regardless of the material, they are to restrict their comments to the specific issue in question and avoid straying over into other issues that other groups will discuss.

Sample Exercises for Reasoning

The following exercises provide suggestions at three levels of elementary instruction. Each exercise is designed with the previously stated competencies as goals for the skills to be developed at each level.

Because reasons are a basis for some feeling, action, thought, or decision, it is apparent that reasons may be developed silently and never expressed orally. But it is not possible for a listener to know, to understand, or, if necessary, to respond to the speaker's reasons unless those reasons can be communicated. Thus, each exercise is designed for the *oral expression* of reasons. Reasons may be highly personal such as "I like. . ." or "I want. . ." or may include outside sources of facts. A reason statement is indicated by the context and is not necessarily marked by "because."

The assignments are designed to help children to give reasons. They are not designed for judging whether a reason is a "good" reason, an "unimportant" reason, or a "bad" reason. Even when the listener disagrees, each person has provided his own reasons that are viable at least to him. While the highest level lessons provide experience with debate, it is not our intention to imply that debate is the ultimate goal of all reasoning. Giving reasons occurs in a variety of circumstances and includes many contexts that involve no debate. Assignments are designed to be incorporated with a variety of classroom subjects and in each subject matter the teacher needs to consider the context, keeping alert that a student's self-concept is being built up, not torn down.

The following suggested exercises may be augmented by expanding any of the

161

decision-making assignments in Chapter 7 to include reason giving. Once a student is experienced in decision making that is unencumbered by requests for her reasons, she can then learn to give reasons for a decision.

BEGINNING LEVEL EXERCISES

1. Each child has looked at rows of pictures and selected the picture in each row that is different. The teacher then asks each child what picture he selected in a given row and why he chose that picture. This is an example of an expansion of a decision-making assignment. In the request for a reason, the teacher may use requests such as "Why did you choose that one?" or "Give me your reason." In early stages of reason giving, the children should be expected to respond to a request for a reason rather than freely generate a decision followed by a reason.

2. Each child is given a picture in which something is missing, such as a person without a hand, a skirt with one button missing, or a house without a door. This is a familiar task to elementary teachers, and perception tasks such as this can be readily expanded to have each child orally explain what is missing and give a reason for her decision. Again, the teacher may need to request a reason each time.

3. Each student participates with classmates in giving reasons for an everyday occurrence. This task is an excellent opportunity for role playing, and children usually enjoy such experiences. The teacher may assume the role of a child who won't eat his dinner. The class members are to be the parents. Each child (playing a parent) in turn tells the teacher (playing a child) why he should eat dinner. This task is planned so that each student must think of one reason, but that reason must be different from any other given. When different reasons are exhausted, the teacher (playing a child) says "O.K. I'll eat dinner, but I won't go to bed" and the lesson continues with as many changes of topics as necessary until each child has given a reason.

4. Each child gives more than one reason for something desired. This activity is also amenable to role playing. The teacher may become a witch who has a little baby bear in a cage (put a toy bear in a cage) and won't let it go. The children are told they should give the witch (the teacher) reasons that she should let the bear go. As each child gives a reason, the witch does not respond by letting the bear go. Instead she says "no," or "why should I?" or "give me another reason," or "I'm still not going to let him go." In this task each child should give two or three reasons, and the teacher may expect the need to prompt with a question or statement for each reason. Of course, the witch lets the bear go after every child has given a number of reasons. The reasons in this task will probably contain repetitions. The task is designed to get a series of reasons from each person but not necessarily different reasons.

162

5. Each child names something appropriate to wear in a certain situation and gives reasons for selecting such an item. For example, the teacher might use situations such as in the rain, in the snow, at the beach, at school, or picking berries. Of course, the situations need to be appropriate to the experiences of the children in the class. The children would probably enjoy having the teacher add taking a bath because one usually does not wear clothes there. As each child gives her reasons for her selection, she should be asked to give another reason and another. This lesson could coordinate well with either a science lesson on weather or a health class.

6. Each child states something you "should" do when you leave school and gives a number of reasons he believes this. Examples of responses in this lesson might be, "Don't talk to strangers. They might hurt you. My mother said so," or "Look both ways before you cross the street. Because you have to. A car could hit you," and so on. Safety lessons are necessary in elementary school and are often given as rules from the teacher. The chances are good that a safety lesson will have more meaning if the children state the rules and give reasons. Then the teacher can expand, if necessary.

7. Each child tells why he thinks a character in a story did a particular thing. Once again, the child should be encouraged to give more than one reason. Of course, this assignment is designed to incorporate with a reading lesson.

8. Each child responds to a series of statements made by agreeing or disagreeing and then giving reasons. The statements may be prepared in advance by a teacher. Some suggestions include school is fun, hamburgers taste awful, peas fall off a fork, Daddys can't cook, pigs are pretty, and so on. These can be general or adapted to a specific subject, but it is not intended that they be a true/false test. The items should be statements to which there is no right or wrong answer. This task could also coordinate well with a writing lesson in that the student could write yes or no and then several reasons. If written first, the answers should be given orally afterwards.

9. Each student names a place she would like to go on a vacation and gives reasons. Such an assignment incorporates well in social studies and is more effective if the student prepares her answer in advance and includes information from parents or a friend. The assignment can be expanded by asking various other students if they would or would not like to go to that place and why.

10. The class participates in a "why time." The teacher names a limited time period (10 minutes, 30 minutes, an hour, half a day, or whatever is appropriate to the students in a particular class) and says that during this time the students may ask "why" about anything. Another day, the teacher asks the students "why" about whatever comes up. Another day, the students ask each other. Of course, the person asked "why" must respond with reasons. Careful attention to limited time periods and equal turns per student should avoid chaos.

163

INTERMEDIATE LEVEL EXERCISES

1. Each student names something she likes or doesn't like and gives reasons for her feelings. The students should be encouraged to think of reasons in advance so that two or three reasons can be offered with no prompting from the teacher. This assignment may be a general one and used as a form of getting acquainted, or it might be incorporated with a health lesson on foods or in a physical education class in games.

2. Each student discusses whether he would have responded (in action or words) to a situation as the character in a story did. Then he gives reasons that he would or would not have responded in such a manner. The student should think of reasons without prompting between reasons. This reason task may be incorporated with students reading aloud or silently or with the teacher reading a story aloud.

3. Each student looks at a picture and tells why she likes it or doesn't like it. This is a good assignment for beginning art appreciation, and the pictures used might be a variety of well-known paintings from the old masters to Picasso.

4. Each student reads a story problem in arithmetic and then explains the answer to the group by giving numbers as reasons. Every class has story problems in math, but students might not realize that numbers are excellent reasons.

5. Each student talks about an historical event and tells why it happened. This should be a speech prepared in advance and it is hoped the history book will provide the reasons. This assignment might well extend for a number of weeks until enough historical events are covered and every student responds.

6. Each student selects a book that he has read and tells in a short speech why it is an interesting or fun book to read. This assignment should be prepared in advance. Students have been previously trained in public speaking and decision making. The substance of the speech is reasons to read the book. This task incorporates well with giving students a list of books to read outside of class.

7. Each student takes a turn on succeeding days and predicts the weather for tomorrow and gives reasons for the prediction. This weather forecast should be prepared in advance and may be based on a radio, a TV, or a newspaper report, or augmented by the student's own opinion. The following day the accuracy of the prediction can be checked. The lesson naturally fits with a science class.

8. Children read a story or the teacher reads a story aloud and the class as a group discusses whether the story or parts of the story are believable or not. The teacher may consider books such as *Charlie and The Great Glass Elevator* by R. Dahl (New York: Alfred A. Knopf, Inc., 1972). Fantasy is fun and the purpose is not to reject fantasy. The purpose of this lesson is experience with a type of evaluation that is different from "I like" or "It's interesting because. . . ."

9. Each student reads a newspaper or magazine article and gives a prepared

report on it. She tells whether she could understand it or not. The student gives reasons for her opinion. This lesson fits with social studies or reading.

10. The teacher gives the students a list of possible rules and each member of the class has time to review the list and prepare reasons that the rules seem reasonable or not. The teacher might choose to have fun with such a list by including some statements such as, "all fourth graders should wear coats backwards" or "students may not use the sinks to wash their hands," along with axioms such as, "no shirt, no shoes, no service." This assignment could add an interesting variety to a writing lesson, but should also be given, at least in part, orally.

ADVANCED LEVEL EXERCISES

1. Each student plans a city of the future and gives a speech on his city with his view of reasons for each thing in the city. This assignment could be associated with art or science or social studies, depending upon the function of the project on which the teacher wants to focus.

2. Each student reviews information about a place that could be a vacation choice and then gives a speech on whether this is or is not a good place for a vacation. Facts should be used to support the viewpoint taken. This assignment could fit well with a geography lesson and in such a case the teacher may want to assign certain locations, or countries, or cities. However, it may also be an adjunct to a creative writing task in English. Outside sources such as *National Geographic*, the encyclopedia, travel magazines, or a travel bureau should be used. Students should already be versed in giving a speech using outside sources. The critical element in this assignment is that each student presents one viewpoint and organizes the presentation to support that position.

3. Each student selects a controversial topic and presents a speech on one side of the issue. Newspaper editorials are excellent sources for such issues. However, newspaper articles or magazines such as *Time* that present both sides of the problem also provide such information, depending on current political or social issues. The teacher should be certain that enough information is available and have a list of suggested sources for the students. This assignment fits well with social studies or English.

4. Each student selects a season and gives a speech about the season and the things she likes and does not like or about how the season is both pleasant and unpleasant to experience. This lesson coordinates well with a science lesson on seasons. The purpose of each speech is to present two views of the same topic.

5. Each student selects a method of transportation and gives an oral report on the advantages and disadvantages of this method. The transportation means might inlcude walking, running, cars, buses, trains, planes, boats, and so on. Outside sources should be used in addition to personal opinions. The teacher should expect to guide students with at least one reference on each topic.

6. Each student selects a career to talk about and presents advantages and disadvantages of this career. It is suggested that this assignment be preceded by inviting members of the community including parents to talk about their careers. After the talk, assign a limited number of students (dividing the class in proportion to number of careers presented) to use the techniques learned in interviewing (Chapter 4) and interview the person to learn advantages and disadvantages. The outside basis of the student speech is established by this method. If this approach is not possible or limited in scope, it can be augmented by having each student interview his parent or a friend outside of class.

7. Each student gives a speech about a first-aid procedure and presents a list of "dos" and "don'ts" for such a procedure. For example, some topics may be helping a person in an accident, applying a tourniquet, or treating a burn. Of course, this lesson is designed to accompany class lessons in first-aid or health.

8. Each student participates as a member of a team in a mini-debate on an historical issue. Possible general topics for this debate are the American Revolution, the Civil War, the Boston Tea Party, the Panama Canal, or the Stamp Act debate. For guidelines on facilitating a mini-debate, look at the discussion of the advanced competency in this chapter. This lesson is designed for history class, and the history book is a rich source of material.

9. Each student participates as a team member in a mini-debate on a scientific issue. Possible broad topics might include environmental protection, protection of an endangered species, alternate energy sources, or fluoridation of water. The lesson is planned for science classes, and outside sources should be used to provide data. The advanced competencies explain techniques of the mini-debate.

10. Each student as part of a team participates in a debate on a political issue. The political issues chosen should be those that are interesting to children. Public issues such as dog leash laws, child labor laws, or gun laws should provide interesting topics. School topics such as year-round schools, bilingual education, or desegregation of schools might be important to the students. Outside sources of information are vital for these topics. Prior to utilizing the mini-debate technique suggested in the advanced competencies, the English teacher might require written reports on the topic.

166

9

Persuasion

OBJECTIVES

At the end of this chapter you should be able to:

1. Discuss the responsible use of persuasion and its potential effects on individuals.
2. Explain the variety of conceptions of persuasion.
3. Discuss persuasion as a coordinated behavior associated with communication.
4. State the steps leading to the persuasive goal.
5. Compare and contrast the views of persuasion held by Plato and Aristotle.
6. Discuss the value of being a critical receiver of persuasion.
7. Discuss how the general and specific level competencies are designed to yield, by the time of exit, an elementary mastery of persuasion as currently conceived.
8. Explain how the general exit competencies represent broad goals that accompany each specific level competency.
9. Match each exercise to the general exit competency or competencies and the specific level exit competency or competencies that the exercise addresses.
10. Explain why the successful completion of one exercise does not fulfill the objectives of the competencies.
11. Design additional exercises for the fulfillment of the stated competencies.

"This record is not available in any store. Order now!"
"All the kids are wearing GLORIOSO DESIGNER jeans. Get yours now."
"Your school is like your home. Keep it clean and enjoy it more."
"If you want to grow big and strong, drink more milk."
"Vote for Sally for Class President. She will organize a class party."

It is almost impossible to count the number of times each day someone tries to persuade us. Radio, television, billboards, newspapers, and even the sides of barns are obvious places people use to communicate a persuasive message. But there are many other ways used to persuade: parents constantly caution children to look both ways before crossing the street and to not talk to strangers; the clerk in the store wants us to buy; teachers exhort students to do their lessons; police want us to pay for things we take from stores; government leaders encourage us to be loyal citizens; charities want us to give them money and help them get others to donate; and so on. Person-to-person talk, public speeches, loudspeakers, walk-a-thons, marathons, telethons, talk-a-thons, rallies, grand openings, special appearances by celebrities, marches, sit-ins, demonstrations, pickets, sermons, retreats, posters, matchbooks, signs, songs, dramas, and even

168

balloons in the sky are means used to persuade. Whether we like it or not, persuasion is an extraordinarily important part of modern communication. Consequently, persuasion is a communication skill that must be studied carefully if children are to become effective users and respondents to persuasion.

This is a sensitive subject to discuss, and a word of caution is needed before we proceed. Of all the communication skills available to us, persuasion is particularly directed toward influencing the behavior of others: getting other people to do what you want them to do. Look at the examples at the opening of this chapter. The record may or may not be one you will be pleased to buy, but the seller wants you to feel as if you must order immediately or miss out. He is concerned with profits more than with your music interests. It may not be important that all kids dress alike, but the second statement is trying to use social pressure to sell jeans, again for profit. School may not really be like your home; the school merely wants to urge students to be neat. Milk does not guarantee big and stong adults, but the ad suggests—not promises—that it will. Is the most important task for a class president the organization of a party? It might not be, but the promise might get votes anyway.

The problem is that through persuasion, claim some critics, people can be made to do things that are not good for them. For that reason, continue the critics, we should not teach students how to be persuasive and we should discourage people from using the skill. Persuasion thus becomes a dirty word in some perceptions: what I do is inform; what those who disagree with me do is persuade.

We do not share this view. Instead, we would compare persuasion with a knife, as Aristotle did: in the hands of a surgeon, it may be used for good; in the hands of a murderer, it may be used for evil. It makes no sense to pretend knives do not exist or to try to outlaw them. Rather, with knives and persuasion, it makes sense to learn their responsible use and to understand their potential effect on us. That is the goal of this chapter.

THE CONCEPT

Over the years there has been a variety of approaches to characterizing the concept of persuasion. Some take the position that the critical point is the *attempt* to persuade. Regardless of what was communicated or what people did in response, the state of mind or motive of the communicator makes the difference: was she trying to be persuasive? In this view, you could say something moved people to act according to your wishes, but if you did not mean to persuade, persuasion did not occur.

Another point of view has been to define persuasion in terms of the kinds of communication used: the *stimuli*. Here the important feature is the content and structure of the message. Messages are seen in this perspective as either informa-

169

tive, descriptive, entertaining, inspirational, or persuasive. One can tell if a message is persuasive by looking at its structure to see if typical techniques of persuasion have been used.

A third approach to understanding persuasion has been by focusing upon *ability*. People talk about the power or art of persuasion as if it were a talent possessed by the few in the same way they might speak of an artist or musician. Some people, they would say, have the ability to persuade and some do not: you have to be born with it.

For many years a major conceptualization of persuasion looked to the psychological *effects* in receivers. That is to say, the concentration was upon the beliefs, attitudes, and values in people to be persuaded, and persuasion was defined as a change in attitudes, for example, as measured by psychological tests. A test would be given to an audience, then a persuasive message would be presented, and then a second attitude test would be administered. If a statistically significant change in attitudes was measured, then persuasion was judged to have occurred.

Finally, persuasion has been seen as a process of *alignment* or *identification* in which two or more people jointly create a state of commonality through the use of communication. Emphasis here is upon a process of people communicating to build a joint meaning and coordinated—not necessarily identical— behavior. Persuasion is not seen in this conception as one person or agency acting upon others in order to be influential. Rather, people or agencies are seen as interacting or transacting with the outcome being mutual influence.

Significantly, in the past 25 years or so, writers on persuasion have done the same thing we have done: they have given a series of possible definitions of persuasion, each reflecting a slightly different point of view. Although they ultimately select one they favor, as we will do, the discussions reflect the dynamic nature of persuasion theory. There is no clear majority that agrees on one concept of persuasion. We are dealing with something that is difficult to pin down. Theorists tend to agree that something happens among people communicating that should be called persuasion, but they are not sure precisely what it is or how it happens. Not many would still believe that persuasion can only be said to occur when someone makes an attempt, but many are uncomfortable with the idea that virtually anything can be persuasive. Almost no one still believes persuasion is an inherited ability that is limited to the talented few. We are confident that students generally can develop this skill. The form and content of communication is still seen as important, but theorists do not tend to put total concentration upon this element. Similarly, the psychological effects that occur in people being persuaded are still respected, but we just do not have as much confidence in our understanding of them as we once had. The concept of alignment seems most responsive to contemporary communication theory, but there is not as yet a substantial body of research data in support of it.

Nevertheless, we are inclined to work with the approach that is most consistent with our overall understanding of the communication process, and so we will join with C. Larson in saying that *conceptually* persuasion is the "... cocreation of a state of identification or alignment between a source and a receiver that results from the use of symbols."[1]

The complexity of the process of persuasion combined with the current theoretical uncertainty makes an operational definition virtually impossible. We could list the multitude of techniques that have been associated with persuasion over the years but that would be unacceptable for two reasons: it would put the emphasis back on the persuader alone, which we have rejected; and no one or group of techniques has ever been claimed as universally appropriate to all persuasion situations.

Therefore, we opt for a most restricted approach in which persuasion is characterized *operationally* as *coordinated behavior* associated with communication. Most important to notice in this statement is the idea that persuasion is manifest through behavior. Although communication may generate a variety of feelings, motives, beliefs, attitudes, values, or intentions to behave, persuasion becomes known by the way in which people act. For example, in a political campaign, voters may decide that they prefer one candidate over another, but that does not satisfy the objective of the persuasion. The voters must cast a ballot for their choice, or join in the effort to campaign for other votes if the effort toward political persuasion is to be fulfilled. Candidates who win praise but lose elections are not deemed to have been persuasive under this definition, unless the campaign did not seek election in the first place. Similarly, a charity drive that wins sympathy from people but fails to generate money through donations will usually be judged to have failed in its persuasion. Or a business that builds product recognition and high praise for quality but does not turn a profit will soon cease to be a business.

Not only is behavior the end of persuasion, it is the beginning as well. The operational definition would be a process one in which behavior is continuous: people act (and that includes communication behavior), and they and others observe their actions. As we observe our own actions, we form and modify beliefs, attitudes, and values of our own in an effort to maintain a consistency between our actions and our thinking and a consistency within our total belief system. So, in this way, we persuade ourselves. Similarly, others who would persuade us must first observe our actions and listen to us report on our thinking so that they may adjust their persuasive communication to fit our beliefs, attitudes, values, and intentions. For example, businesses study consumers to discover what they need and want before they try to devise products that they will try to persuade us to buy. Or politicians study the constituency in order to learn what the people want from government before seeking election on the

[1] C. Larson, *Persuasion Reception and Responsibility* (Belmont, CA: Wadsworth Publishing Co., Inc., 1979), p. 7.

171

basis of persuasion centered around appeals to those voters. So, in this way, those who are to be persuaded first persuade the persuaders.

Then, of course, once a potential persuader has observed the actions and communications of those to be persuaded, once he has adjusted his persuasive goals in accordance with the analysis of the audience, then he must devise the messages that will communicate ways in which his goals serve the needs and interests of those he would persuade. If the people respond with behavior consistent with the persuader's goals, they will observe their behavior and that will further influence their beliefs, attitudes, values, and intentions. It is a circular and continuous process. M. Fishbein and I. Ajzen discuss these ideas at an advanced level.[2]

Our concept of persuasion, therefore, views the process as one in which people are engaged in mutual persuasion through regular communication. It does not include a common perception of persuasion in which Machiavellian individuals and groups work their devious tricks and techniques to make people do whatever they want them to do. A great body of persuasion research does not support that perception. Lincoln had the idea when he said, "You can fool some of the people all of the time, and all of the people some of the time, but you can't fool all the people all the time."

THE TRADITION

No aspect of communication has a more lengthy and distinguished tradition than does persuasion. By the time Plato began writing, almost 400 years before the Christian Era, the teaching of rhetoric or persuasive speaking was well established. In fact, it was so well established that Plato felt moved to write a scathing criticism of the sophists or itinerant teachers of rhetoric and other subjects. The issues he drew between himself and the sophists remain of concern to the present day and deserve a brief summary here.

The sophists, claimed Plato, treated persuasive speaking as a knack or a set of tricks with which to fool people into believing almost anything. They dealt with appearances rather than reality or truth, said Plato.

Instead, Plato would demand that only after a speaker has learned the truth of the matter to be discussed could an effort to persuade others to that way of thinking be tolerated. In Plato's theory of persuasion, therefore, the important communication would take place among the experts—in his time, the philosophers—as they engaged in dialectic to discover the truth. The business of communicating these truths to people in general would then become a secondary process as most citizens would merely learn the truth from those better able to

[2] M. Fishbein and I. Ajzen, *Belief, Attitude, Intention and Behavior* (Reading, MA: Addison-Wesley Publishing Co., Inc., 1975).

discover it. To modernize a Platonic example, if an airliner runs into bad weather, the decision to change course or altitude does not become a matter for general debate among the passengers and the pilot. Rather, the pilot, in consulation with other experts on the ground, will make the decisions and the passengers will merely hear the report of that decision over the intercom.

The alternative, according to Plato, could be disastrous. What if one of the passengers turned out to be more eloquent than the pilot? Even though the passenger knew little or nothing about flying, her eloquence might be so great that the majority of the others would vote to follow her lead. She could be persuasive but wrong.

This is the issue that has become traditional in discussions of persuasion. Many philosophers have for centuries argued what is essentially Plato's position: the only legitimate and proper way for people to come to beliefs and take action is through logical discussion or dialectic. To them, persuasion is the tool of the propagandist or sophist.

Aristotle disagreed. He did not share Plato's contempt for the average person. On the contrary, he believed that Plato, by restricting the search for decisions to a small group of intellectual elites, ran the risk of failing to find the truth. His argument was that in advance of the decision we are not able to know what points are relevant and proper and what ones are merely propaganda. We must hear what everyone thinks; we must allow anyone who wishes to try to persuade us. Then, because truth and justice are stronger than their opposites, in the end they will win out. Thus, he defined rhetoric as the ability to find all the available means of persuasion on any topic. Then, if they are allowed to compete in a free marketplace of ideas (to use a modern term), people will choose wisely. The only time the sophist or trickster wins in persuasion, according to Aristotle, is when the people have not been exposed to all the available means of persuasion. This can come about when one or more points of view are suppressed or when the advocates for some points of view are inept in persuasive communication. For this reason, Aristotle believed that everyone should be skilled in persuasion.

Further, Aristotle rejected another point that derives from the Platonic position and continues to be repeated today: people should use logic alone as the tool of persuasion. We still find today some people who believe any appeal to emotions or any belief based upon acceptance of a speaker's authority or credibility should be avoided as dangerous. Again, Aristotle believed that any form of persuasion should be heard and considered. He said that there are three categories of legitimate persuasive appeal: (1) *logos*, or the use of reasoning; (2) *ethos*, or the character, wisdom, and goodwill of the speaker; and (3) *pathos*, or the feelings or emotions of the listeners.

At the time of the adoption of the Constitution of the United States, these issues were still paramount. Some of our Founding Fathers shared Plato's lack of confidence in the ability of the masses of people to make wise decisions. They would have set up our nation so that an aristocratic elite did the truth

173

finding and then communicated their decisions to the people. Others, however, had more democratic inclinations. In fact, they had strong suspicions about the desirability of allowing an aristocracy to hold such power.

Of course, the latter group won out and among other results was the First Amendment to the Constitution, which protects freedom of expression. The Supreme Court of the United States has typically interpreted that amendment as protecting the right of any citizen to seek to persuade the people even when that person seems to be dead wrong. They have given strength to the statement of Thomas Jefferson that ". . . error of opinion may be tolerated where reason is left free to combat it." Unless someone speaks with malice or reckless disregard for the truth, even erroneous statements used in an effort to be persuasive are protected and respected by the law. How can missstatements be respected? Only in the sense that we may not know in advance what will ultimately be deemed to be incorrect, or if we silence some people through fear of being punished later, we may fail to find Aristotle's available means of persuasion, do we respect error.

Thus, the central tendency of persuasion tradition in the United States has been Aristotelian: all people should be skilled in persuasion and free to employ their skills in virtually any way they choose in order to win others to their way of thinking and acting. To be sure, we become frightened at times and lose sight of our basic commitment: in time of war we have tried to silence those who opposed our policies, unorthodox religions have been suppressed, discussions judged to be obscene, blasphemous, or libelous have been punished. But, for the most part, freedom of persuasive expression has been protected and encouraged.

Common Ways of Thinking about persuasion reflect the variety of definitions discussed earlier. Many think of persuasion as a body of techniques to be used by communicators such as formulating persuasive goals, establishing a common ground with the audience, getting the attention of the listeners and orienting them to feel a need for a solution or answer, building a reasoned case for the persuader's position, mobilizing the beliefs, attitudes, and values of the audience members behind the persuader's position, and then moving the audience to take the desired action.

Others are still strongly committed to a more psychological approach to persuasion, which is predicated upon a thorough understanding of the state of mind of the audience members. They believe that if the persuader can learn the attitude of the audience toward the persuader and the subject, then persuasion proceeds by confronting listeners with ways in which the persuader's goal can serve their objectives and satisfy their psychological needs. In this way of thinking, the emphasis in persuasion is on analysis of the audience rather than analysis of the persuasive message itself.

It is now commonly believed that persuasive skill is not limited to the few

174

talented people who are the great orators of the day. Years of teaching in persuasion have established the fact that almost anyone can develop some skill as a persuader. True, they will not all become great orators, but they will have the proficiency necessary to function in society.

The Current Perspectives do not give preeminence to any one point of view; neither do specialists have the confidence they once had that we truly understand how persuasion occurs. At present, research in persuasion is almost at a standstill while researchers take stock of what we know and where we should go from here.

A good deal of attention is being directed toward understanding persuasion effects within an overall communication theory. Specifically, the idea that persuasion is a distinct process that can easily be differentiated from other forms of communication is now being challenged. The great body of research that has sought to explain persuasion as a function of attitude and attitude change has been shown to be lacking in evidence that attitudes can be directly tied to behavior. Other explanations have been offered in place of attitudes which are based on the interaction that takes place among people within a particular situation. That is, people will make alignments—find agreements—with different people and ideas, depending upon who is involved and in what situation the communication occurs. For example, ministers have observed that members of the congregation are more receptive to moral persuasion when they are in church. than when they are sitting in a bar.

Further, the tendency to distinguish persuasion from coercion is not as great today. Some writers now suggest that some coercive elements may be found in most persuasion. Negotiation, for example, involves persuasion that uses both traditional appeals as well as threats and promises. Salespersons coerce gently by suggesting that the consumer should buy immediately lest the price go up or the supply of products run out. Candidates for public office threaten the voters with possible diasters economically, socially, or militarily if the opponent is elected.

The View of This Book rests upon the generally accepted premise that persuasion is a significant communication skill that is exercised regularly in society and should be studied by students. In response to the current perspectives, we believe that persuasion should take its place alongside all other communication skills and not be separated as something distinct, more important, or more difficult than other aspects of communication.

We further take the position that skill in persuasion should reflect a thorough understanding of the psychological factors that influence those who are the objects of persuasive attempts, the impact of the situation in which persuasion occurs, the interaction among the people involved, and the message characteristics of the persuader's communication. We also assume that persuasion is

175

typically found within some form of campaign or ongoing series of communications rather than the product of a single speech to a single audience.

COMPETENCIES TO BE DEVELOPED

Three *General Exit Competencies* for persuasion suggest that students acquire the ability to

1. Understand yourself and others in relation to a persuasive goal.
2. Understand the persuasive situations in relation to the purpose.
3. Present a persuasive communication.

Those who would participate in persuasion, regardless of role, must be able to understand the psychological factors involved. If one is to try to persuade others, it is neccessary to understand what the action goal is and how that relates to one's own beliefs, attitudes, values, intentions, sense of self, and social situation. Who are you that you should ask others to do as you wish? Children may grow up thinking of themselves as the center of the universe with the right and power to direct the behavior of others on a whim: "Mom! Come here," usually obtains Mom's presence without further justification. But in society, things are different. Every request for action may not be met. People will be selective in their response, so the prospective persuader needs to evaluate herself to determine if this particular persuasive goal is one worth seeking, is important and relevant enough to expend the effort, is a goal worth being associated with, and is one for which she has the personal and persuasive abilities to obtain.

This necessarily leads to a consideration of the psychological state of those who are to be asked to behave in a certain way. Is the goal consistent with their beliefs, attitudes, values, sense of self, and social situation? Are there bases on which they can reasonably be expected to comply? How can the persuasion be communicated so that they will find the goal appealing? Where are the points of agreement and difference between persuader and persuadee?

Just as important is the ability to assess the situation in which the persuasion will take place. Is this a situation in which persuasion holds some promise of success? Not all situations are rhetorical; if you car won't start it does no good whatsoever to kick it, swear at it, or threaten to junk it. The Salvation Army knows that derelicts will respond better to exhortations to make something of themselves if they have a full stomach and a good night's rest. Parents are more likely to agree to a request just after the child has come home with a good grade card, and children learn this analysis of situations early on.

Finally, the general exit competencies call for the ability to present a persuasive communication. All the study and discussion in the world does not prepare students for the actual presentation.

In this competency we have used the expression persuasive communication in order to include a variety of experiences in persuasion that ranges from person-to-person to commercials to speeches. Although the advanced competencies include planned speech making, we are not implying that formal persuasive speeches are the ultimate in persuasion or the culmination of persuasion theory. It is a matter of practicality that the complicated knowledge required to deliver a persuasive speech can not be expected of students at lower levels. The ability to organize communication on the basis of a thorough analysis of self, others, and the situation is important, but ultimately children must acquire the ability to do the persuasive communication in a way that fulfills the goals. Because there is no set of universal persuasive techniques and each persuasive situation offers some unique challenges, presentation of persuasive communication must be learned through practice.

Beginning Exit Competencies involve the ability to

1. Recognize attempts by others to be persuasive.
2. State a persuasive goal.
3. Give a reason for acting or not acting on the persuasion.

A first step at the beginning level is to help students become aware of the multitude of persuasive attempts to which they are subjected daily. Even adults are sometimes naive about this. They may not be aware that in the grocery store a huge stack of potato chip bags is located near the checkout stand and not with the other chips for the precise purpose of getting them to buy that brand. They may not realize that their decision to purchase one brand of laundry detergent was made on the basis of the shape of the bottle or the color of the box rather than a knowledge of the quality of the product. They may not realize that their decision to purchase apples today was made not on a need for apples but on the fact that they were beautifully polished and neatly stacked.

A concern of critics of television is that children's shows are sponsored by manufacturers who wish to sell products for children. They fear that children may be moved to demand purchases of products by their parents on the basis of unduly urgent persuasion. The response of communication scholars, as we shall discuss in Chapter 11, "Mass Communication," is not to call for regulation of television broadcasting but instead to teach children to be more critical receivers of persuasive advertising. A first step in this education is for children to realize that people are trying to persuade them.

A second step in this educational process—becoming critical receivers as well as effective persuaders—is the ability to state persuasive goals. Children need to learn what it is they may be asked to do as a result of persuasion. For their future efforts as persuaders, they need to learn what they can reasonably expect to ask others to do. Here, the emphasis will be upon identification of action goals. That is to say, persuaders do not merely seek to generate a desire for a bicycle. They seek to persuade children to demand that their parents buy a particular brand of bike. The action will come in the communication behavior of the children as they say over and over to their parents, "I want a Schwinn bike. I don't want any of those others."

When the teacher talks at length about how nice it is when the room is neat, the children should realize that the persuasive goal is not simply an appreciation of neatness but is an action goal involving putting things away in their place. When parents compliment children for being nice to brothers and sisters, the children need to recognize that the goal is not just to make them feel good about themselves but to have them continue the desired behavior.

Finally, at the beginning level, children can start to recognize the bases on which they might be persuaded or persuade others. It is important that at this level children be allowed to state their own perceived reasons for acting on persuasion. Each persuasive appeal may involve a number of potential reasons for effectiveness, and different children may respond to different reasons. It will be interesting to see the various reasons children mention and allow them to discuss these different perceptions.

Intermediate Exit Competencies call for students to

1. Recognize the reasons used by others in relation to a persuasive goal.
2. Survey the opinions of others and report the results.
3. Present a one- to two-minute persuasive speech on points of agreement with the audience.

The first intermediate exit competency carries over directly from skills learned at the elementary level. Now reasons or bases for perusasion can be identified in relation to specific persuasive goals. Children may be asked to think about why they want a particular brand of bike and come to realize that it is a function of wanting to be like other children. They may discover that their desire to be neat in the classroom is a function of desiring the approval of the teacher. They may be able to see that the attractiveness of a certain toy was the realistic appearance it had in the magazine ad. Here the objective is to begin to tie persuasive goals to persuasive appeals.

In the second competency, the students move into the difficult but important process of doing audience analysis. They must, at this level, begin practicing the kinds of communication necessary to learn what other people think and believe. As they perform elementary opinion surveys and report the results, they will both learn the process of analysis and discover the ways in which their peers are similar and different from themselves.

By this point, children will be ready to make an attempt at presenting a persuasive speech on the basis of what they have learned through their audience analysis. Knowing, as they will, the ways in which the others agree with them, they can structure a brief speech that uses points of agreement to accomplish some persuasion. For example, a student may try to persuade the class to vote for a trip to the zoo, having learned that all the children love animals. Development of the speech may involve telling the audience about all the wonderful animals they can see, and that they might be able to pet some of them.

Advanced Exit Competencies deal with the ability to

1. Recognize the differences among persuasive situations.
2. Give an evaluation of the strengths and weaknesses of a persuasive message.
3. Deliver about a three-minute persuasive speech that uses outside authority and states the action goal.

The students have already been sensitized to the fact that persuasion varies from situation to situation. Now they can become more sophisticated in this understanding by concentrating upon specific situations. As they go through the process of recognizing some situations as allowing for relatively easy persuasion whereas others present a greater challenge, they will grow in their understanding of the need to analyze the situation before seeking to persuade, they will increase their understanding of their own susceptibility to persuasion in certain situations, and they will develop some ideas on ways a persuasive message can be adjusted to a particular situation.

Having become aware of the many attempts to persuade that occur each day, and having become sensitized to the bases on which persuasion rests, the class can now become critics of persuasion. They can examine samples of persuasion to notice the techniques used and make some comments on the ways in which they might find some persuasion acceptable or objectionable. In this, they will start the process of becoming critical receivers. This criticism serves the dual purpose of developing some protection to the widespread persuasive attempts that use undesirable techniques and of building awareness of the many ways one can be persuasive without violating ethical standards.

Now the students are ready to work with persuasive presentations in more detail. They can use their abilities in research to obtain some forms of support or evidence that give strength to their messages. That is, they can find authorities whose testimony will lend persuasiveness to their message. They can combine their understanding of points of agreement and disagreement in the audience with the statements by outside authorities that may resolve disagreement.

Further, the placement of persuasive messages within a campaign can now be tried. Because virtually all persuasion occurs as a part of a larger effort that uses a variety of messages in a variety of media over a period of time to achieve a goal, children need to learn how to function within this context. By working with an actual campaign, they will see that a full campaign is needed to accomplish most goals.

179

Sample Exercises for Persuasion

As in the other chapters, the following exercises provide suggestions for teaching persuasion at three levels of elementary instruction. The stated competencies provide guidelines for the skills to be developed.

Although an important part of persuasion is doing it yourself, persuasion is not just another kind of speech. In learning persuasion one must learn to recognize persuasion attempts by individuals, by groups, and by the media and learn to respond to those attempts as a thinking individual. Because an important part of persuasion is acceptance by another individual or group, in order for a person to be persuasive, he must understand his listeners.

The following exercises are designed to help young children begin to learn these concepts. The exercises build on the communication skills learned in all the preceeding chapters with particular relationship to skills in listening, decision making, reasoning, and public speaking. It might be predictable that these lessons will not be successful until prerequisite skills have been learned.

BEGINNING LEVEL EXERCISES

1. The children select one of three of the same articles displayed differentially. For example, in three bowls, the teacher arranges apples differently. In the first, cut slices of apples and allow them to turn brown; in the second, arrange apples that are unwashed; and in the third, arrange apples that have been washed and polished. This lesson might well coordinate with art class. The teacher can explain that the type of visual display is one method of persuasion. He should explain that all the bowls contain the same thing, but that visually the shiny apples are more likely to persuade a person to buy or to eat.

2. Each child selects a place she would like to go from a picture in a magazine. The children may use magazines at home or the teacher may collect and bring magazines to school. The purpose is to demonstrate that a picture can be persuasive. This lesson can coordinate with either art or social studies, depending on the desired other area of learning.

3. Each child names and describes a television commercial that he likes. This assignment should be made the day before so children can watch commercials for this purpose. Then, the next day, each child describes a commercial he likes. The purpose is to teach that both visual display and words can be persuasive.

4. Each student participates in giving reasons for an everyday occurrence with the understanding that he is trying to persuade someone. Return to exercise 3, beginning level in Chapter 8 (Reasoning). The exercise of the children (playing parent) trying to get the teacher (playing child) to eat dinner can now be seen as a type of persuasion.

180

5. Each child has the opportunity to state the goal of a persuasive effort of the teacher. This lesson can be done over an extended time period. It can be an effective method of reinforcing a desired goal. For example, suppose the teacher gives a persuasive talk on the need to keep the classroom neat. She can then follow by saying, "I'm trying to persuade you to do something. What is my goal?" Then several children restate the goal. The next day the topic of persuasion will change, but the lesson fits easily into a normal classroom routine.

6. Each child states how someone could be persuasive. Excellent stimuli to use for safety lessons are the Berenstain Bears books. (i.e. S. and J. Berenstain, *The Bike Lesson* (New York: Random House, Inc., 1964); or S. and J. Berenstain, *The Bears' Vacation*, (New York: Random House, Inc., 1968). In these books, persuasion on safety is approached by a stated safety rule and a demonstration that aborts the rule. This is an excellent opportunity for the children to think for themselves and to tell how the persuasion could be better demonstrated. The books are written on a beginning reading level and thus can be coordinated with reading groups.

7. Each child tells one thing that a parent, another adult, or a child tried to persuade her to do. This assignment should be made several days in advance. It can be combined with writing. Writing lessons are best taught with a practical purpose. So have every child write a sentence that explains the goal of an act of persuasion. For instance, she might write, "My mother wanted me to go to bed," or "My brother wanted to play with my ball," or "Sally wants me to sleep at her house."

8. The students state the persuasive goal and describe the persuasion used in poetry. Three poems, "Rice Pudding," "At Home," and "The King's Breakfast," by A. A. Milne in *When We Were Very Young* (New York: E. P. Dutton & Co., Inc., 1961) will provide good opportunities for discussion. This is a lesson to be combined with literature. After the teacher reads the poems he should have the children state the persuasive goal and discuss what actions were involved. The students can then discuss whether the persuasion was effective or not.

9. Each child discusses a persuasive goal of a television commercial and then tells whether he would act on it or not act on it. This lesson is an expansion of the first acknowledgement of television persuasion in Exercise 3. Now children should name the goal and make an individual decision as to whether they would purchase it or not. This lesson might combine with health class by asking students to look at commercials on food or health aids. For example, a student might say, "I like the commercial for X cereal. The little kids are cute. They say _____. But I won't ask Mommy for it. I don't like cereal."

10. Each child reads a persuasive argument, tells the goal, and discusses whether she would respond to that persuasion or not. The teacher may want to select a story from the reading book or advertisements from children's magazines. Of course, this lesson is designed to combine with reading groups.

INTERMEDIATE LEVEL EXERCISES

1. The students discuss how the display on a poster or advertisement is giving reasons to go see a performance. This assignment should coordinate well with an art class. The teacher may want to collect posters or ads from the newspaper about theater, music, or movie performances to show the students. For example, the children might note that the picture of a little girl and her dog is persuasion to see *Annie* or note cartoon drawings look interesting in an ad for a Walt Disney movie. They may note whether a G, PG, or R rating is persuasive, and so on. Of course, this can be followed by having the students draw an advertisement in a persuasive manner.

2. Each child selects a television commercial and identifies its goal and the reasons given to persuade you. They might note that the purpose of a commercial is to sell a certain soft drink. Among the reasons they can note are that it tastes good, that it is cooling, that people who have fun drink this, or teenagers or popular people choose this soft drink.

3. The teacher or principal makes an announcement asking the students to do something. This is an expansion of a beginning assignment. At this level the teacher may say "I was trying to persuade you to leave quickly and quietly during a fire drill. What were the reasons I gave?" then ask children to restate the reasons. This can be a clever way to help children review reasons for important action instead of simply following a power command. Research suggests that we might anticipate this lesson will be more difficult for children from lower socioeconomic levels, but all children need practice in understanding reasons for an action.

4. Small groups present reasons to classmates for their choice of the most important public servant, and the class votes to indicate their persuasion. The children have had a previous opportunity to decide individually an important public servant to them (Exercise 4, Chapter 7). Now the teacher divides the class into small groups and asks for a group decision with reasons for the choice prepared. After each group has finished planning, one group at a time presents its public servant to the class. The leader nominates the type of job, then each person gives a reason in support of the selection. After all groups have made presentations, the class is surveyed by vote (written vote is probably better) to indicate the opinion of the class. This lesson combines with social studies.

5. Students survey the class to obtain opinions about a class activity. In reading, the teacher may give a description of several stories that could be read, or in math, different types of problems can be described, or in music, different songs. After the descriptions have been given, assign four or five students to survey the class and report on the findings. The teacher then responds to the findings. The purpose of this lesson is to teach students to be aware of audience opinion. The tasks should be varied until every student has the opportunity to

survey. A clever teacher can vary the descriptions so she can see for herself what is the most persuasive to the student.

6. The class is surveyed before they study a topic for opinions. For example, in history, the teacher asks the class who they are most in sympathy with or who they think had the hardest time in the early years on the North American continent, the Indians or the Pilgrims. The teacher should keep the results of this survey. Then the class studies these people and events of the early years. When the unit is completed, the class is surveyed again. The two results are compared to see if information persuaded people to change their opinion. This class is designed for history, but any topic in any subject can be effective. We would suspect that closer attention and more involvement in the topic will occur if students express opinions early.

7. Each student gives a persuasive speech on a safety rule. The class selects safety rules they consider most important. The teacher should prepare a list of options before or with the class helping. Then as a group the class votes on the most important. Ask the class for reasons for their decision. Then take the top five or ten and assign those as topics for a persuasive speech. Of course, more than one student will give a speech on the same topic. The teacher should discuss with the students that persuasion is most effective when the speaker and audience have a common ground.

8. Each child gives a commercial on a health aid. In preparation, ask the class which health aids they think are important (toothpaste, soap, shampoo, adhesive bandages) and why. Then ask each student to give a commerical for a product that is real or imagined for the most chosen categories. They can look at television for ideas, but these commercials should be planned around what the class has given as reasons. For example, "Mothers want children to use X soap" may be a better reasons for young children than "You will smell good all day." Children like to do commercials, and this assignment can be an interesting method in health class.

9. Each child gives a commercial on a brand of food. In preparation, have the class discuss important foods and give reasons. Then each student selects a real or imagined brand of that food and gives a commercial on it. As in the previous assignment, the reasons of the class should be the basis of the commercial. After this assignment, discuss whether television ads use children's reasons or grown-ups' reasons in their ads. Discussion of foods naturally fits in a health class.

10. Each student gives a persuasive speech about a party and tries to convince the class to have a certain party. Prior to this, have the class discuss what they would like to do at a party. Note the previous lessons have required naming, but this preparation asks for a description only. Then students are to listen to the class, make their own decisions about naming a party, and give a persuasive speech about the party they think would be fun. Students have learned in decision making to carry out the decision so the teacher is advised to warn them

in advance to make realistic plans. The teacher may need to check this privately with each child before the speech. Suppose that the class decides they want to go outdoors to play games and to eat. Doubtlessly, several children will give a speech on a picnic party. But a more innovative child might say, "I think we should go to the zoo. The class wants to be outside. The zoo is outside. The class wants to eat. The zoo has good hot dogs and popcorn. Or we can take sack lunches to the zoo. The class wants to play. We can play games after we eat at the zoo picnic area. And I think it would be lots of fun to see the animals too. We can do what everyone wants and still have more fun at the zoo if we watch the monkeys." And so on with the persuasion. After the speeches, the class should vote on which idea they accept. Of course, this vote should be carried out with further planning and action. This is a good activity for the end of the year, because it involves so much more than just a persuasive speech. It can provide a realistic view of persuasion and the results.

ADVANCED LEVEL EXERCISES

1. The class divides into two teams for a persuasion relay race. One team has to name people who are easy to persuade, and the other, people who are hard to persuade. Each person on the team thinks of a person and then writes the name or title of that person on a paper. The name is passed to the next person on the team who reads it and passes it on. Teams do this in sequence so everyone can listen. But each team is timed, so the one with the best time wins. Of course, this lesson is preceded by a discussion of being aware of the differences in the people one is trying to persuade. Students may note that grandparents are easier to persuade than parents, that a friend is easier than a stranger, that a teacher is easier than the principal, that Tom is easier than Bill. They should discuss the reasons for such conclusions.

2. The class participates in making a list of situations that contribute to easy or difficult persuasion. The teacher puts two columns on the board, one for easy situations and one for difficult situations. He should have the students think of the opposite situation to put in the other. For example, the teacher writes, "You haven't done your chores at home and you want to go to the movie" in the difficult column. Then the students would perhaps decide, "You have been good all day and you want to go to a movie." The teacher may write, "Students may enter the building early with special permission and you need to complete an art project" in easy column; the opposite would be, "There is a rule no student may be in the building before school starts and you need to come in early to finish an art project." The teacher should vary his contribution from the easy to the difficult situations so students can experience changing both situations.

3. Students divide into groups of four and in pairs role play persuasion in the contrasting situations listed in the preceding exercise. The team of four plans

the role playing and helps each other prepare to role play in front of the class. This may combine with writing by having the scenes written before they are performed.

4. Students analyze the persuasion in the fence-painting scene in *Tom Sawyer*. The teacher reads aloud the scene to the class or each student may read it silently. It is such a good persuasion effort and may be enjoyed more if it is read aloud. Then the class discusses this indirect persuasion by demonstrating in such a manner that the audience persuades itself. Discuss whether this can be an effective persuasion. This lesson combines easily with literature.

5. Each child looks at advertisements in a mail order catalog and gives a critical review, comparing the picture with the actual size of the object. This lesson is designed to combine with math class. Each student cuts out an ad and shows it to the class. Then she reads the description aloud. Then she demonstrates actual size and compares that to the picture. Students will enjoy showing the size of a two-ounce jar of jam compared to the picture, or of a toy that is six inches high compared to the picture, and so on. The teacher may need to bring in mail order catalogs that certain stores distribute or that are usually mailed at Christmas time by bulk mail.

6. Each student prepares and delivers a campaign speech to vote for so-and-so for a certain office. This may effectively coordinate with social studies in an election year. Or it may be used in conjunction with a school election.

7. Each child selects a president of the United States whom he thinks was the most important president in our history and gives a speech to persuade the class that this was the most important president. This lesson is an excellent opportunity to get students involved in history class. Each student should prepare his speech on the basis of available reasearch (including facts and opinions) about this president. After all the speeches have been given, the class should vote on who they now believe was the most important president.

8. Each student prepares a critical review of a current campaign receiving wide recognition at the time. The newspapers and television as well as prepared brochures are excellent sources. In order for every student to participate, the teacher may select different topics and relate topics to various subjects. For example, a campaign to stop smoking relates to health; a campaign to reduce taxes relates to math; a campaign for enlistment in the armed services relates to social studies; or a campaign to send aid to other countries relates to social studies.

9. Each child prepares and presents a speech on a community action that she thinks is necessary. The speech contains facts and is designed to persuade the audience what action is necessary. Topics for such speeches may be a bike lane for a busy street, a traffic light at a corner of frequent accidents, a park in place of a refuse dump, a city recreation program, or making an unsightly area attractive. After the speeches, the class votes on the one project they think is most necessary.

10. The class members conduct a campaign to get the city to carry out the

desired action selected in the previous exercise. After the action is selected, each student interviews someone about their ideas on such a project. Parents, teachers, city councilmen, policemen, the mayor, and so on are all valuable sources. Then the class reports on the interviews. Each student prepares a persuasive speech considering the desires of others, the ideas of the class, and his own plan. The speeches are delivered to the class. Then the class and the teacher decide which of the speeches should be delivered to other classes, which should be given to civic groups, and which might be written as letters to the editor of the newspaper. All decisions should be carried out. The students will enjoy such a project, and it might result in action by the city (such as making a bike lane), or the city might allow the students to complete the project (painting an unsightly wall).

Literatures in Performance

OBJECTIVES

At the end of this chapter you should be able to:

1. Discuss the social impact of assuming roles.
2. Explain the meaning of literatures in this chapter and discuss how they involve both original and previously prepared material, both oral and written.
3. Explain the various specific procedures used in putting literatures into performance.
4. Discuss how oral performances of literatures make them come alive.
5. Distinguish between the personal development of students and the professional pleasing of audiences in performances.
6. Discuss how the general and specific level competencies are designed to yield, by the time of exit, an elementary mastery of literatures in performance as currently conceived.
7. Explain how the general exit competencies represent broad goals that accompany each specific level competency.
8. Match each exercise to the general exit competency or competencies and the specific level exit competency or competencies that the exercise addresses.
9. Explain why the successful completion of one exercise does not fulfill the objectives of the competencies.
10. Design additional exercises for the fulfillment of the stated competencies.

A kitchen counter was covered with crumbs surrounding a knife smeared with peanut butter. Next to the knife was a glass with two or three swallows of milk slowly growing warm in the afternoon sun. These signs gave unmistakable evidence that Laura and Amy were home from school. But they were no longer in the kitchen, having now retired to their playroom which was set up with portable blackboard and chairs to resemble a classroom. Their voices could be heard.

"I'll be Miss Van Trump and today we're going to do arithmetic," said Amy.

"I don't want to do arithmetic," replied Laura. "besides, you got to be Miss Van Trump yesterday. I'll be teacher and we'll draw pictures."

"Okay, but I want to draw pictures of animals."

"Now settle down, children. Take out your papers and crayons and think of an animal you want to draw . . ."

The children were playing. To the insensitive observer they might be said to be doing childish things, frivolous things, not serious or productive things. People acculturated with the Puritan work ethic look down their noses at play for any but the youngest children; they call easy and unimportant jobs "child's play," and in past years actors and actresses have been deemed rather disreputable because they were playing.

Today we know better. Play in all its forms to be described in this chapter is an important element in our communicative behavior that benefits both children and adults. Many of us have been influenced by the philosophy expressed in 1 Cor. 13:11, "When I was a child, I spake as a child, I understood as a child, I thought as a child: but when I became a man, I put away childish things." We will argue quite to the contrary. One goal of training in oral communication skills is the ability to retain, cherish, and take advantage of the marvelous ability we all display as children in expressing ourselves and interacting with others by assuming roles, telling stories, acting out experiences, sharing our lives, our culture, and our history through literatures.

Amy and Laura had just experienced a day of learning, some new experiences, and challenges. They had worked with a teacher and other children in tasks that were important to them and needed thought and reflection to be understood. Their medium of communication for this thought and reflection was play: they tried out different roles, they created scenes from their day, they rehearsed actions and interactions, they worked together in mutually deciding what to communicate and how to do it—the roles to be played and the stories to be relived. Now it was school that needed attention. At other times they play other adult roles such as mother and child, parents, cowboys and Indians, cops and robbers, Darth Vader and Luke Skywalker. Sure, their topics and methods are childish, but they are children. The communication skills they are employing—putting literatures into performance—are by no means childish. Curiously, this more than any other communication skill comes easily to children, but is gradually extinguished as adults teach them to put away childish things. Without nurturing at home or in school, these skills of communication diminish with age, and the product is a civilization of adults who are grievously inhibited in their ability to play, and accordingly in their ability to communicate some extremely important ideas and feelings.

THE CONCEPT

Shakespeare in *As You Like It* expressed the first essential element of the concept with which we are dealing: "All the world's a stage, and all the men and women merely players." During our lives we play many roles, more than just the seven ages Shakespeare described. We are variously students, teachers, professionals, lovers, comedians, friends, adventurers, victims, mourners, winners, losers, survivors, and so on. Each of these roles is a part of ourselves and a response to our circumstances, surroundings, and the people with whom we are relating. Who we are at any time, how we play the role, is a function of our history, culture, our symbols, rituals, philosophy, religion, our understanding of other people, past and present, real or imagined, and how they played their roles in various situations. It is a function of how we understand our impressions and interpretations, feelings and thoughts as shaped by what we have learned from others.

Art is the expression of the inner self. It is a medium through which we communicate thoughts, feelings, impressions, and interpretations that cannot be expressed as well with other forms of communication. Art is not the sole province of the gifted few, although some artists in each generation are unusually able to communicate artistically. But just as one need not be a great orator to be a participant in public speaking, children need not be great artists to participate in artistic expression. We have used the plural "literatures" in the title of this chapter intentionally to signal our belief that we are all participants in and creators of literature.

If you examine the dictionary, you will find *literature* defined as written work of various kinds, but this is just a reflection of our concentration with the written word that has briefly distracted us from awareness of the long-standing oral traditions in literature. Print has been the primary medium of artistic expression for only a fraction of human history and only in selected parts of the world. As we will find in Chapter 11, "Mass Communication," new media are re-establishing the preeminence of oral means in our country. As we become familiar with people of other cultures, such as the new arrivals from Vietnam or the traditions of Native Americans on reservations, it is apparent that people never strayed from the use of oral communication to disseminate their literatures.

It is true that the development of print did establish a new medium of artistic expression so that some materials are best communicated through reading. Some novels that have been adapted for performance on the stage or in the movies clearly show something can be lost through performance. Even some plays were written to be read rather than performed.

So much of our literature, however, is best communicated through performance. Written versions of what were originally oral materials obviously thrive on performance. Most dramatic materials such as plays are meant to be performed and are only stored between performances in print. Because poetry employs so much imagery and communicates so much through use of sound sense and meter, it usually is given full life only in the oral performance of it. For most of us, the greatest part of our literature is never put in print because it consists of the descriptions we give to others of our personal experiences, the stories we tell our friends, the jokes we share, the times we mimic some funny behavior, the times we relate our history to our children. The general rule to use in determining if some literature can be enhanced through oral performance is to perform it orally and ask whether it gains in meaning. Does the addition of a human being with voice and gesture and movement increase the satisfaction and understanding of the literature?

Literatures consist of the efforts of people to communicate their particular understandings and interpretations, actions and attitudes. Literatures may be original or traditional oral communications. Literatures consist of a speaker responding within a certain situation to an experience that is directed to herself, to another person, or to a generalized audience, with a view toward generating meaning and understanding through an imaginary experience in the mind of the listener. Literatures thus provide both an aesthetic experience and an interpretation.

Putting literatures into performance is *conceptually* seen as the act of communicating literature orally to others. It may be our own literature—our original expressions—or we may perform the literature of others, including the work of those few who are most gifted. Through our performance we achieve a fusion of the literature, our interpretation of it, and the responses of those who share our performance sometimes as co-performers and sometimes just as listeners. N. McCaslin[1] cites the view of Vera Mowry Roberts that the function of such performance is ". . . to increase understanding, to sharpen perceptions, to make active and operative the social nature of humanity, to bring the participants into active contact with the best that has been thought and said throughout human history, and to explore the nature of being human."

Operationally, we can define literatures in performance by describing the specific procedures people use. First, we must call attention to the work the children have already done with nonverbal communication for the movements, rhythms, symbolic behaviors, and pantomimes. Choric speaking or reading (it is sometimes called choral speaking) is the reciting of literature, typically poetry, in unison under the direction of a leader. Groups of children prepare to recite the material together, sometimes all saying the same thing at once and sometimes only part of the chorus speaks while the other part waits for its turn. The chorus, one of the oldest forms of performing literature, played a prominent role in Greek drama and in the religious rituals and ceremonies from ancient times to the present. It is recognized as an important educational tool in oral communication today.

Retelling stories is a common phenomenon in interpersonal and group communication. It involves nothing more than relating to others a story learned from some other source. So many of us have trouble even remembering stories that we would like to be able to share with others. Those who try to retell a story often fail to recall important elements, or they jumble the events, or they fail to pre-

---

[1] N. McCaslin, *Creative Drama in the Classroom* (New York: Longman, Inc., 1980), pp. xv–xvi.

sent the story with the same vigor and creativity with which it was originally told, and thus the story dies in the retelling of it.

Original storytelling involves the skills of retelling stories with the added opportunity to create the events and characters of the story. Freedom to make up the story allows the added creativity of content to accompany the performance of it.

Puppetry involves the personification of some symbol as the mechanism for the communicating of a story. The symbol is presented in such a way that the person doing the communication is not seen: hung from above by strings, or held from below with hands while the performers are hidden. The performer talks while the symbol is manipulated so as to be seen as the communicator. Through puppetry, children can tell stories and engage in dialog without having to develop the self-confidence and presence necessary to appear in person as the communicators. It is a good technique for introducing children to presentation of dialog, and it is also appropriate for children who for one reason or another are not physically able to stand or move or for children who are concerned about appearing in person.

Play making (it is sometimes called dramatic play) is an elementary form of improvisation in which two or more children engage in interaction spontaneously to tell a story with dialog. It is typically brief in nature and may relate a story in fragments. Even though it may be repeated by the same children or others, each instance is an original experience without development of story line or characters or dialog. It is basically doing the same kind of play that Amy and Laura were doing in private, but it may also be performed in the presence of others.

Improvisation carries play making into more careful development of complete stories and characterization. Children create or select a story they wish to relate through presentation of themselves as characters in the story who talk with one another. The improvisation may at first involve mostly pantomime. The next developmental stage uses dialog, but only sparingly. With practice and discussion, the performers may present more developed dialog and present a story in some detail. Still, dialog is not memorized and rehearsed as in more formal drama. Neither are the plot and characterization formally planned. Rather, children work at presenting their story with increasing familiarity and confidence in their knowledge of the characters and how the characters would speak to each other. Again, the object is not a polished dramatic performance but an opportunity for children to become comfortably familiar with characters and how they relate to one another. In so doing they live the story, experience the story, and bring the story to life.

Reading characters' parts aloud can be done with any prose or dramatic material. It involves assigning (or letting children select) roles and having them read the part of their character. In prose work, one child may take the part of the narrator or unnamed person and others will read the words assigned to named characters in the story. All this is done aloud just as professional actors will sit at a table for a reading of a play before starting the process of blocking movements and planning stage business. Dramatic material is easy to use because it is written with individual lines separated by character.

Oral interpretation is a prepared performance of some literary piece of any sort—prose, drama, or poetry—by a single person who communicates an interpretation of the literature to others orally. It is prepared in the sense that the performer studies the piece to be communicated in advance, determines the meaning and aesthetic qualities to be expressed, analyzes the characters so that they can be differentiated one from another, and decides how the totality of the literature can be communicated through words and minimal nonverbal elements. This is distinguished from dramatic presentations by the absence of costumes, stage movement, use of properties, and the fact that one person does the communication no matter how many different characters may be involved. Through oral interpretation, an interaction of the text, the performer, and the audience is achieved.

Oral interpretation through interaction with others, sometimes called readers' theater, carries the basic concept of oral interpretation into a situation in which two or more performers communicate a piece of literature by dividing the labor, sometimes by taking various roles, sometimes by dividing the oral presentation among different segments of the piece, and sometimes by combining artistic media such as music and speaking. There is still little or no use of costumes, movement or properties, although there may be use of different levels or locations on a stage and some use of lighting effects. It is the same as individual oral interpretation in the sense of preparation to determine the interpretation to be communicated and the goal of generating an interaction between literature, performers, and audience.

Skits and dramas constitute the familiar stage performance in which performers assume roles, work out relationships, story development, and characterizations. They employ costumes, properties, make-up, lighting, stage movement, and sets where appropriate. Lines are memorized and the performance is rehearsed so that interaction is well paced and spontaneous in appearance. The material for such dramas can be original with the children or they can use dramatic material written by others.

These specific operations do not necessarily constitute the only ways in which literatures can be put into performance. There are no limits, and people should feel free to be original in performance just as they are in the creation of literatures. The term *creative dramatics* has been commonly used in education to speak of these various behaviors. While we have not chosen to use the term here, what we are describing in each of the various elements of the oral performance of literatures can be described in common as creative dramatics.

THE TRADITION

The tradition of literatures communicated through oral performance is as old as literature itself and that seems to be as old as people's need to communicate. Our knowledge of the most ancient civilizations of Africa and the Orient is scanty, but the evidence suggests that literature was spread by dramatic performance. Homer writes in the *Odyssey* of events surrounding the Trojan War more than 1,100 years before the Christian Era, in which the minstrel Demodocus told again and again of the siege of Troy. The epics *Iliad* and *Odyssey* attributed to Homer were essentially the collecting of the tales of the minstrels who had carried the stories of the glories, valor, grief, and patriotism of the past. Although they were ultimately written for permanence, they continued to be disseminated orally. And that is the essence of the tradition: although literatures have come more and more to be written for storage and ready access, they come to life in the oral presentation of them. There is a continuous tradition of the oral communication of literature from the most ancient past to the present day, diverted but unbroken by our recent preoccupation with reading and writing. We may learn to love reading, but we never lose our love of being read to. We may be able to read the plays of Shakespeare, but we enjoy and understand them to the fullest by seeing them performed. The teacher of literature who reads to the students is an extremely important part of the oral tradition as well as one who recognizes the importance of oral presentation to the understanding of literature. We have not included the reading aloud by teachers in this chapter, but this is not because we deem it unimportant. Throughout the tradition of literature, the teacher's oral presentation of it has been critical. Even when reading poetry alone, people will often feel the need to read it aloud to enhance appreciation and understanding. The tradition of literature is the tradition of literatures in performance.

Common Ways of Thinking about the performance of literature in modern times can be traced to the work of elocutionists in the seventeenth and eighteenth centuries. Early advice called for the attempt at a natural presentation such as that demanded by Hamlet in his advice to the players:

> Speak the speech, I pray you, as I pronounced it to you, trippingly on the tongue; but if you mouth it, as many of your players do, I had as lief the town-crier spoke my lines. Nor do not saw the air too much with your hand, thus; but use all gently: for in the very torrent, tempest, and as I may say the whirlwind of passion, you must acquire and beget a temperance, that may give it smoothness.
>
> Suit the action to the word, the word to the action; with this special observance, that you o'erstep not the modesty of nature.
>
> (Hamlet, Act III, Sc. 2)

But the elocutionists were not content to leave nature alone. They devised more and more elaborate systems to guide the oral performer, moving from natural systems to mechanical ones that dictated virtually every aspect of performance.

The dictates of elocution led to contemporary teaching that can only be called artificial, such as we have described elsewhere in this book. Still, it is common to think of orotund voices, stage diction, archaic pronunciation, planned timing of sounds and pauses, and elaborate planned gestures in connection with the oral performance of literature.

Current Perspectives on putting literatures into performance in the classroom show a marked negative reaction to the elocutionistic traditions. Instead of focusing upon more formal performance with the objective of achieving a "professional" capability to please an audience, the goals now advanced center upon the personal development of the student. In fact, performance of literature is now claimed to be a vehicle for learning almost everything in the curriculum, including reading, writing, arithmetic, science, social studies, and art. Children can, it is claimed, develop their physical and mental health, improve thinking abilities, clarify values, and grow creatively through performing literature. There is emphasis upon independent thinking, group cooperation, social awareness, and release of emotion. Of course, current writers still perceive the performance process as an ideal way to build aesthetic understanding and knowledge of good literature. Although contemporary experts believe that some technical improvement in speech behaviors may be built through performance of literature, they do not put much emphasis upon growth of basic communication skills.

Finally, there is currently the tendency to suggest the avoidance of performance for audiences by elementary students. It is believed that presentations to an audience may inhibit the children and interfere with their self-expression. This seems to be a reaction against the stress generated by competitive performance atmospheres that pit children against one another, place demands upon them to develop a professional attitude, and drive them to perform with the elocutionistic precision of the past. These current perspectives seem dedicated at the very least to the avoidance of anything that would make the performance of literature take on the aspects of a Little League contest.

The View of This Book is that the movement away from the tradition of elocution is desirable, necessary, and inevitable in view of the extremism that school of thought reached. We agree that putting literatures in performance can contribute significantly to the personal growth of students and help them develop knowledge and understanding of many of the subjects in the curricula. We see severe problems with turning such performances into competitive challenges filled with stress.

We do not agree, however, that the total or even primary focus of literatures in performance should be on the individual student to the extent of avoiding

195

performance for others. On the contrary, we see the performance of literature to be one of the oral communication skills, necessarily concerned with sharing ideas and feelings with others. This includes an audience as well as other performers. Literature is meant to communicate, and the performer is part of the communication. So we will recommend performance for audiences, but we will still caution against performances that put excessive emphasis upon professional polish to the point of distracting children from the joy of communication.

COMPETENCIES TO BE DEVELOPED

Three *General Exit Competencies* call for children to

1. Communicate literatures of their own creation.
2. Communicate poetry written by others.
3. Communicate prose stories and dramas written by others.

Each of the three general exit competencies is headed by the verb *communicate* to call attention to the fact that the goal is just that: communication. This should be kept in mind so that work with students will not become aimed at stilted, artificial, arty manners of speech and action. The question to be asked in each case is whether the performance communicated the literature in the manner desired. As with all the other communication skills, the teacher is not expected to correct pronunciation or spend time calling attention to other aspects of formal correctness. Concentration should be upon positive reinforcement of communication outcomes.

In the first general competency, children are asked to participate in the creation of their own literature. This requires awareness of the meaning of literature, not as a written exhibition of unusual quality, but of people telling their own stories, communicating their own interpretations, and sharing their own feeling. Children should first identify themselves as participants in the creation of literature.

The second general competency brings children into contact with the poetry of others. Poetry is often seen as a complex, abstract, and even foreign medium of communication. Children may often feel disinterested in poetry, but as they participate in its performance, as they become part of the poetry by giving it life, they will come to understand it better, feel more familiar with it, and at the same time become knowledgeable with this aspect of great literature.

Finally, children are asked to perform the prose stories and dramas written by others. Here, again, they will come to view this part of literature as something more than a subject to be read and recalled for tests. They will see how this form of literature helps them understand and thereby express their own feelings and

196

helps them understand their own experiences. Of course, again they will become intimately familiar with some of the great literature that has been written.

Beginning Exit Competencies ask children to

1. Participate in choric speaking.
2. Retell stories.
3. Communicate with the use of puppets.
4. Participate in play making.

Choric speaking is a good place to begin because children work together. No single person is asked to perform alone and at the same time each one has the chance to hear a piece of literature performed and to be a part in it. All children are introduced to the process of thinking about the literature, what it means and who is talking to whom. They can experience the saying of the words, the pauses and points of emphasis, and the counterpoint that can be achieved by having part of the group take one segment while the other remains silent and then to be answered by the other part of the group. Putting actions to fit the words makes the poem more lively and exciting for the children and helps them communicate their joy and understanding.

Almost all of us have had the experience of having a child return from a movie or watch a television show and then try to tell us what it was about. They often become quite confusing by leaving out important details of story line or identity of characters. Our work in group communication reveals the strength of group recall over that of any individual. Several people will remember more details and the resultant story will be more clear and complete. So a good starting place for retelling stories is with a group. Again, they work together and thus provide mutual support. Each member of the group has the satisfaction of participating and they all will feel the satisfaction of a story well told. As students progress, they can add bits of dialog to make the telling of the story more communicative, and in doing this they will start their development in expressing characters more completely.

The addition of puppets in the telling of stories has several advantages. As we have already indicated, puppets allow greater freedom of expression by permitting the children to speak through a symbol rather than as themselves. They will thereby develop the confidence to take roles and use dialog in telling the story without having to assume all the role characteristics. Beyond that, working puppets is fun and is a delightful way to communicate.

By the last beginning exit competency, children will be ready to do some play making. Of course, they have been doing this for most of their lives, but they have not been aware of it as a perfectly acceptable and common form of communication. Their first efforts will be mostly a recreation of the kind of play they will probably do when they get home. With that start, they can move to more conscious efforts to act out a familiar situation so as to communicate its essence. They can then move to the telling of a story through play making, and that is the start of characterization through improvisation which they will move to next.

Intermediate Exit Competencies expect children to develop the ability to

1. Engage in original storytelling.
2. Participate in improvisation.
3. Read characters' parts aloud.

Telling an original story calls for skills in creation rather than just recall. So that the demands will grow with abilities, children can start by relating a story about events that are familiar to them. In this case, the basic thread of the story is already known and the only challenge is to put it together in a clear and interesting way. They will, however, quickly become aware of the needs of the listener to learn details that are so familiar to the speaker as to seem unnecessary to say. Perhaps we have all had the experience of meeting a stranger on a plane who wants to tell a story that begins, "I'm going to visit Fred and Danny out west. They've been worried about Vivian's problem and I'm going to offer my help." We presume that before the story ends we will know who Fred and Danny and Vivian are and what her problem is. We also hope to know where "out west" is and how this person can help. But, alas, the story just goes on and on with new characters and events added without further explanation. The speaker knows them all intimately and is insensitive to the fact that the listener does not. In telling stories, children will become aware of the listeners' needs and meet them.

The essence of improvisation, called for in the second intermediate competency, is already well explained. The children will assume gradually more difficult assignments to communicate by taking roles, performing actions, and talking among themselves. Simple fables are good beginnings as they provide easily identifiable characters, a well-focused story with a single point, and situations easy to improvise. A poem or historic event is a bit more demanding because the children will need to develop more of their own imagination to communicate characters, events, and the point of the story. At still a more advanced level, students can begin to do improvisations with no more stimulus than an abstract concept or image. Now their full range of creativity will be called into play, and they will essentially be creating both story and events as they do the improvisational communication.

With this background, moving to the reading of parts aloud will be a relatively easy transition. They will already have done the work of "getting into characters" through understanding and identification. They will have tried to make

198

themselves the other person so as to communicate more effectively what that person says and does. In reading the characters' parts, the students will be using another's words to portray characters and events, and they will be adding their voice to bring the story to life. It is easy in the sense of having the dialog already written. It is difficult in the sense that now there is the challenge of trying to understand what the writer had in mind when creating the characters and story. Now the students must think a bit about what is going on, what kind of person is this I am to play, why would people say these things. Now, the students will need to decide how they can assume those roles—become those characters living through those events—and do a good job of communicating the pre-established literature.

Advanced Exit Competencies have students demonstrate the ability to

1. Analyze a piece of literature for oral interpretation.
2. Engage in individual oral interpretation.
3. Participate in oral interpretation through interaction with others.
4. Perform in prepared dramas.

Analysis of literature for oral interpretation is necessary if the performance is to be communicative. A determination of the length of the reading governs whether or not some cutting will be required. Commonly, a reader will select only a portion of a complete story or poem because there is not time to read it in its entirety. Cutting will be done not just with an eye toward fitting the same length but toward selecting those portions that will make a complete idea. Sometimes this means taking parts of the story from various places, removing some unnecessary descriptions or narrations, and placing bits of dialog together. Of course, the whole piece must be read to determine the writer's intent—the essence of the story, the nature of the characters, and the flow of actions. Analysis will also work toward locating points of climax and resolution and becoming familiar with the age and personality of the characters. Then, one must practice reading the cutting to become familiar with what is said and how the characters speak. Although this is a reading, most oral interpreters should go over the cutting so many times that they have essentially memorized the piece. The book will still be held during the reading, but it will not be necessary to concentrate on the words. This will free the reader to look at the audience and work for communication.

The actual oral interpretation, mentioned in the second advanced competency, will ask a single person to stand in front of the class or audience. The interpreter holds a book or stiff-backed folder containing the reading in one hand with the small finger hooked underneath with the other hand placed on top of the open page. The reader will "locate" each character in the reading in a selected part of the room so that when George is speaking, for example, the reader will move her

199

head slightly to the right, when Isabell is speaking, the reader will look straight ahead, and when Irving is speaking, she will turn her head slightly to the left. By these subtle movements of the head in the chosen direction for each character, the reader will help the audience keep track of the person speaking. Obviously, oral interpreters typically choose selections that involve only a few characters so that these movements need not become exaggerated. The interpreter typically stands in front of the class without a lectern or desk between the audience and himself. His only prop is the book.

Oral interpretation providing interaction with others, or readers' theater, called for in the third advanced competency, is prepared in much the same way. The differences are that each person interprets a separate piece of literature on a common topic. Another variation is that instead of one person presenting each character, each member of the performing group takes one role, and there is opportunity for them to look at each other and even make some slight movements such as walking from one level to another as the scene changes. Sometimes changing lighting as performers move from scene to scene helps the audience follow the action. Background music or a musician on stage are sometimes used for added effect. A dancer may also be added.

Finally, students may perform in a drama, as suggested in the final advanced competency. The drama may be original or one written by another. The production may be quite informal, using little or no costuming, sets, lighting, or make-up. Or the drama may be one that is quite well produced and rehearsed. The important differences here are that the performers are now free to *become* their characters; they will assume what clothing, hairstyle, or make-up effects are necessary and possible to portray the character; they will move in response to the drama's action, using gestures and activities on stage; they will have the properties that are called for in the play, unless these are to be done through pantomime as in Thorton Wilder's *Our Town*. That is, if the character in the story has a hammer, the player will have a hammer. They will memorize their lines and present them as if it were spontaneous speech. The extent of the production and the nature of the audience are matters of choice for the teacher. But we caution once again to avoid making this such a challenge as to distract the students from the joy of participating in this form of communication.

Sample Exercises for Literatures in Performance

The following samples of lessons are planned in accordance with the general goals and the specific goals for each level. These lessons are designed to use communication skills for the enjoyment of studying and experiencing the literatures of the world. Through oral performances, the literatures become a reality—a living and meaningful force.

The word *literatures* has been used intentionally to include classical as well as transient writings. The most transient literatures will be those the children make up for the moment, and the least transient will be those that have already endured for generations. In the performance of these literatures the children will be working along the continuum.

The earliest stages of creative performances are movements, rhythms, and pantomimes. The children have already been quite familiar with these performances and should have met the prerequisite experience through the nonverbal competencies in Chapter 2. If the teacher senses any reluctance on the part of the children to perform, it may be wise to repeat some of the nonverbal exercises. However, these exercises require more experience than those for nonverbal competency. Consequently, these communication skills have been reserved as the culmination of the knowledge gained throughout all the previous lessons for each level.

The purpose of the performances in communication is primarily to develop the individual's enjoyment, experiences, and understanding. This philosophy should be foremost in the mind of the teacher and the children. However, in contrast to some current writers, we do not suggest that children should not put on a planned performance for an audience. At times children enjoy performing for an audience. When the time is right the children will indicate that it would be fun to do a certain thing for an audience. One of the authors put a class of educable mentally retarded (EMR) children on the stage before an audience of district principals to perform choric speaking with actions. The children took great pride in their work, and for many of them it was their only opportunity for such an experience. The performance was short but excellent. It would have been a shame to rob the children and the audience of this experience. In another situation a group of accelerated fifth- and sixth-graders wrote and produced an original play. Although the major learning occurred in the writing and learning to act the roles, the children wanted to use the stage to perform their production for their parents and friends. They saw this performance as the end result of all their efforts. So performance for an audience can be a worthwhile experience. In most of the following exercises, the students can perform privately or before an audience. The audience can be fellow classmates, another classroom, parents, PTA, or whatever seems desirable. However, such a performance at the elementary level should focus on the children and not on sets, costumes, lighting, or other such production aspects. On the other hand, if the children do not want an audience, it certainly isn't necessary. It should be remembered that literatures in performance are to develop the performer.

BEGINNING LEVEL EXERCISES

1. The class in unison speaks a repeated refrain in a poem. This repeated refrain can quickly be memorized. The teacher reads the poem and signals the class when it is time to do the refrain. Consider the refrain "diddle, diddle" in "Lavender's blue, diddle, diddle. . ." or the "pease porridge" refrain in that rhyme.

201

These are simple examples from Mother Goose poems, but the teacher can use any poem with repeated refrains or verses.

2. The entire class says a short poem in unison with associated actions. When children first memorize poems, associated actions help the memory process and also keep the poem in a more natural rhythm (away from sing-song reciting). The teacher may introduce the class to an appropriate available poem or adapt one to make it appropriate. We include an example here that was an adaptation of a Philippine folk rhyme written by one of the authors. This poem has been a success with the children:

Rope Jumping
Jumping rope is really fun.
Turn the rope. (move hands in action of turning a jump rope)
Three, two, one (hold hands up, ready enter, look at imaginary rope)
Jump. Jump. (jump on both feet for each word)
Clap. Clap. Clap. (clap hands on each word)
Jump. Jump. (jump on both feet for each word)
Tap. Tap. Tap. (tap right toe on each word)
Right foot hop. (hop on right foot)
Left foot hop. (hop on left foot)
Turn around like a top. (turn entire body)
Jump. Jump. (jump on both feet for each word)
Banana-peel slide (slide left foot forward, bring right foot up)
Jump. Jump. (jump on both feet for each word)
Horsie ride. (both hands on reins; move seat up and down as in a saddle)
Jump. Jump. (jump on both feet for each word)
Thorns prick. (index finger of left hand pokes palm of right hand)
Jump. Jump. (jump on both feet for each word)
A big sucker lick. (hold imaginary sucker in right hand and make large licking motion with tongue)

It is important for the teacher to remember that actions must be done simultaneously with words. Do *not* have the children say the words and then do the action because that breaks the chain of thought and the rhythm of the poem. All children say every word as they perform each action in unison.

3. The class says a poem with verses for different sections of the group to say. Any poem may be used. The teacher will need to assign the parts in advance. We have included a Mother Goose poem as it has been done by children in order to communicate the idea.

Sing a Song of Sixpence
Sing a song of sixpence, a pocket full of rye; (all)
Four and twenty blackbirds baked in a pie. (boys)
When the pie was opened, the birds began to sing; (all)
Wasn't that a dainty dish to set before the king? (girls)

The king was in the counting house, counting out his money (boys)
The queen was in the parlor, eating bread and honey; (girls)
The maid was in the garden, hanging up the clothes; (girls)
When down came a blackbird (boys)
And snipped off her nose. (all)

It may help to have all the boys stand together and all the girls stand together. The teacher can point in choir director fashion to each group to signal it's their turn to come in. A longer poem that is really excellent for such choric speaking is A. A. Milne's "Disobedience" (more commonly known as James James Morrison Morrison Weatherby George Dupree). This poem is in *When We Were Very Young*, (New York: E. P. Dutton & Co., Inc., 1961).

4. The class retells a story after the teacher has read it aloud. This is an exercise planned for repeated activity with both poetry and prose. The teacher may use any poem or prose and read it to the children when they are restless, for a break or near the end of the day. Reading aloud to children is too frequently left out in modern school programs. The children will enjoy hearing the story. Then the class works together to retell the story. There are many collections of retellable short stories in prose and poetry if the teacher needs assistance in finding a story (i.e. Gruenberg, S. M. *Let's Read A Story*. New York: Garden City, New York: Garden City Books, 1957).

5. A small group retells a story they have read the previous day. This exercise concentrates on the children reading and retelling. In this delayed recall, teachers should have the children read a story with pictures so the next day the small group looks at the pictures as a guide to retelling. This lesson is designed for reading groups, and the teacher may want to use a story from the reading books. However, another variation is to include stories from Beginner Books such as Dr. Seuss, *Green Eggs and Ham*, (New York: Beginner Books, Inc., 1960 (50 word vocabulary) or P. D. Eastman, *Are You My Mother?* (New York: Beginner Books, Inc., 1960 (100 word vocabulary). These stories are on a level the children can read, they provide interesting material, and the pictures are outstanding guides for delayed retelling. More delayed retelling with no picture guidelines is introduced in Chapter 11, "Mass Communication."

6. Small groups retell a story with brief dialog, using paper bag puppets. In this first introduction to roles, the children assuming the roles should not be visible. A platform can be devised by covering a table or desks with a sheet. This communication activity is designed to accompany art class. A book by L. Ross, *Hand Puppets*, New York: Lothrop Lee & Shepard Co., 1969, has a detailed guide for making paper bag puppets for "Rumpelstiltskin."

7. Small groups retell a story with brief dialog, using tongue depressor puppets. Small figures drawn and pasted on tongue depressors encourage more puppet movement. The teacher is planning this activity for more action and dialog. Again, a covered stage is used. Art class is excellent for this project. One

story we've seen children enjoy is "The Three Billy Goats Gruff." This story encourages different voices and dialog is easy.

8. Small groups engage in play making for a common, everyday activity. Tell the children to play pretend. One group can be a teacher and children at school, another a family at dinner, another a group at a tea party. The teacher may suggest any setting as long as the scene involves talking. This activity is good for a recess on a rainy day.

9. Small groups use play making to act out a familiar story. In this lesson, the teacher reads a story that the children have probably heard many times. For example, prose such as "The Gingerbread Boy" and poetry such as "Little Miss Muffet" are excellent choices. After the teacher reads it, he asks who would like to do this one for the class. It is best for children to volunteer, but reluctant participants can be encouraged. A child who is shy might enjoy being the spider for Miss Muffet. The teacher should expect minimal dialog, but whatever is done should be spontaneous and created at the time. This activity may need to be repeated, using different stories each time, for a brief period over several weeks until every child has had an opportunity to participate.

10. Small groups act out a story by play making. An appropriate place to begin this activity is to have a reading group act out a story they have just read. The dialog may be brief and it should be created on the spur of the moment. Each child should have a part. If a section of the story is left out, it can be discussed later, but the teacher should not interrupt the play making.

INTERMEDIATE LEVEL EXERCISES

1. Each child tells the class a story about herself when she was little. Most children know a familiar family story about them; however, children need at least one night to talk to parents about the story before telling the class. The teacher should encourage every child to bring a picture of herself at this age. Children delight in "baby" stories and the pictures.

2. Each child tells a story about some person in his family. This story might be about a brother, sister, or grandparent. Their stories could be current as well as past happenings. Again, advance preparation should be insisted upon. A good story takes advanced planning just as a good speech does.

3. Each child tells a new story about the story in reading. In reading groups, ask each child to change the story. One student may change the events, or another student, the ending. As soon as they have all changed the story, have each child tell the story with her variation. The entire story must be told, not just the change.

4. Each child tells an imaginary story about an animal. This lesson is designed to combine with science. The stories are imaginary but should reflect some real information. For example, one child may tell about Bob the bear who has a family preparing for winter hibernation; another may tell about the quail

families that have an apartment house in the evergreen tree; another may choose to tell about a bird family with new babies, and so on.

5. Small groups of children do improvisations about fables. The children in each reading group can read a fable. Then they do an improvisation to act it out. The dialog will not be in the fable (what dialog there is should not be required or memorized), so all dialog will be made up. The characters should be chosen and the children should practice their fable several times. Remember the lines are created and are not to be memorized, so each repeated practice will have different lines. As soon as the children are prepared, they can present it to the rest of the class. Fables that might be considered are "The Fox and the Crow," "The Tortoise and the Hare," "The Lion and the Mouse," or "Wolf, Wolf."

6. Small groups create improvisations about a poem. For this exercise several or all of the groups should do the same poem, so that children can see different groups improvise the same material differently. At Christmas time an excellent poem for improvisation is "The Night Before Christmas." At other times most of the A. A. Milne poems provide rich material. Suggestions include "Sneezles," "Forgiven," "Twice Times," "The Four Friends," or "Rice Pudding." These poems have little or no dialog and all suggest scenes to be improvised. The children will enjoy providing their dialog to retell the poem. Again, this may need to be practiced.

7. Small groups create improvisations of famous historic events. The event must be one the children have thoroughly studied. If a local event has been told many times, it is a good choice, but national happenings are equally satisfactory. The children in small groups assume character roles and improvise the scene as it may have occurred. The dialog must fit the characters portrayed and reflect the event. Of course, in any improvisation the children are free to create dialog and action as they imagine. Some viable topics are the trail of tears, the Mormons traveling from Nauvoo to the West, the Indians at Starved Rock, the Chicago fire, the arrival of the first 20 slaves at Jamestown, Molly Pitcher in the battle of Monmouth, or the signing of the Declaration of Independence. The object is to create what might have been said or done, and it should be practiced several times. This lesson combines with social studies.

8. Small groups improvise a scene for a lifestyle. In this assignment, we are suggesting moving children to improvisations about which little is known except how the people live. Examples are an Eskimo family, a pioneer family, a farm family, a rich city family, a ghetto family, and so on. This is designed for social studies and should be preceded by lessons on understanding various living conditions. If the teacher has a unit on Eskimos, she might want three or four groups to improvise a scene of an Eskimo family. Such an improvisation requires imagination. This can be done with no practice if the group plans the general scene ahead.

9. Each child reads a different part in a reading story. The teacher should make copies of a story for reading groups and then assign roles. One child will

be the narrator reading the script that appears between characters speaking. Other children have character roles. Each child should use a highlighter to mark everything he says on the reproduction copy. Then the story is read aloud by parts. This is an interesting variation for reading groups.

10. The class joins in reading a play. The purposes of this assignment are to understand the characters and to read the play. Students should be assigned parts. If there are not enough parts for everyone, then the readers are changed with every scene, or more frequently if necessary, for every child to participate. This is not to be acted, so characters remain seated. The concentration is on learning to read a script and assuming character roles. The children would probably enjoy L. Miller, *Heidi*, (Anchorage, Kentucky: The Anchorage Press, 1936) or other such plays. The play reading will doubtlessly extend over several days.

ADVANCED LEVEL EXERCISES

1. Each student analyzes the story in one selection of prose and one of poetry. The prose the student selects should be either a very short story or an excerpt from a story. The first part of this assignment is just retelling the story. The second part is to discuss the intent and the message of the author. This can be combined with a writing assignment, but the students should discuss their conclusions orally.

2. Each student analyzes every character in the prose cutting or on the poem he chose previously. Some selections may have one person, others several. Each person should be identified by age, by what the physical appearance might be, by feelings, thoughts, actions, and relationships. This assignment is best done when only one or two characters are presented, and careful monitoring of the previous lesson can help.

3. Each student presents to the class an oral interpretation of a prose reading. Such a reading must be preceded by analysis of the story and character. Prose readings should be kept fairly short (several pages or about five minutes). Children will find a number of excellent selections from books such as Mark Twain's *Tom Sawyer*. The prose selection is often preceded by a brief review of the story to set the scene for the passage.

4. Each student presents to the class an oral interpretation of a poem. The interpretation should be preceded by analyses of the story and, if necessary, the characters. Poems such as James Whitcomb Riley's "The Raggedy Man" have meaning for children. M. H. Arbuthnot also provides a good collection in *Time for Poetry* (Chicago: Scott, Foresman and Company, 1951).

5. Each student participates in a dual oral interpretation and pantomime. One student reads the poem in the oral interpretation manner and at the same time her partner pantomimes each line. Thus, two people are performing in front of the class for each reading. A favorite poem for this activity is "Casey at the Bat."

206

6. Each student participates in a dual oral interpretation and some other art form. As one student reads, the other dances or plays music. Rod McKuen created a number of poems that he read to background music. Without judging the quality of the poetry, the effect was impressive for much of the public. Students might enjoy some of his records before they try such a performance. Modern dance also expresses poetry in action beautifully. This creative project can combine with music class.

7. Students combine a program of a variety of oral interpretations. This is frequently referred to as readers' theater. The program may be around a theme such as Native Americans, caricatures of children, perspectives on nature, English literature, or American literature. The word *program* does not necessarily imply an outside audience. It refers to a coherently planned series of presentations, both prose and poetry.

8. The class performs a play that has been written. The Anchorage Press in Anchorage, Kentucky has a number of plays on various children's stories. In addition, M. R. Smith has combined a series of original plays written by children for children (*Plays*, published in New York by Henry Z. Walck, Incorporated, 1961). These are all appropriate for the advanced elementary student. Children who aren't acting can set the stage, manage the curtain, prompt, gather props and costumes. Costumes should be assembled from items children or families have on hand. Costumes made for the purpose or rented should be discouraged. The set should consist of available furniture. The stage may be the front of the room. The purposes are to memorize the parts, act the play, and get the experience in production.

9. The class participates in writing an original play. Original plays written at this age are more successful when based on a familiar story. The class should select a story they would like to act out from something they read. Careful decision making is required. As soon as the story is selected, the class jointly outlines the contents of each scene or act. Then groups can be assigned to each scene to write the script in play fashion. The final step is to put the scenes together and let the class make any changes in script that are necessary.

10. The class produces its original play. This production is done in the same manner as the available play used in Exercise 8, except now the play is what the class has written. This script must be memorized and followed. Any changes involve a return to the scriptwriters. In other words, once written, the play is performed as written and is not improvised. Children enjoy performing in their own play.

11

Mass Communication

OBJECTIVES

At the end of this chapter you should be able to

1. Explain how mass communication is essentially interpersonal communication on a global scale.
2. Discuss the variety of content of the media of mass communication.
3. Describe how people relate to mass media.
4. Discuss realistic expectations of receivership behavior.
5. Distinguish between production orientations and receiver orientations toward the mass media.
6. Discuss how the general and specific level competencies are designed to yield, by the time of exit, an elementary mastery of mass communication as currently conceived.
7. Explain how the general exit competencies represent broad goals that accompany each specific level competency.
8. Match each exercise to the general exit competency or competencies and the specific level exit competency or competencies that the exercise addresses.
9. Explain why the successful completion of one exercise does not fulfill the objectives of the competencies.
10. Design additional exercises for the fulfillment of the stated competencies.

"What time is it, Mom?"
"It's 6:30, Brian."
"Do you think we'll be finished and back home by 7 o'clock?"
"What comes on at 7 o'clock?"
"*Little House on the Prairie*."

This is not an uncommon conversation. A child's interest in being home at a certain time can reasonably be expected to signal an interest in a television show. Today if we ask someone, "What comes on at 7 o'clock?" it is not necessary to specify that television is the subject. Our lives are greatly influenced by the media of mass communication. In some ways, more than we realize. In other ways, our lives may not be so different from people in ancient times as we would like to believe. Consider, for a moment, those ancient people.

The people of the village are excited because of the arrival of a stranger from a distant city-state more than ten days' ride away. He must have traveled almost 100 miles through the countryside, stopping at villages along the way to tell them the news, recite tales from the history of the people, declaim on such subjects as politics, love, courage, and beauty, and to learn from them what news they had. He will leave in the morning to go on to still other villages to spread his words, but tonight we hear him inform and entertain us and thereby bring us closer to others in our culture and bring us up to date on important events. After his departure, the men will sit on the benches in the square, drink coffee or wine, and discuss what the man said. The women, too, will talk about the exciting tales learned from the stranger as they fill their water jugs at the fountain. It will be many weeks or months before another such opportunity for news and entertainment comes along, and we make the most of each. We will be happy to give the stranger a few coins in return for what he brings to us.

In the cities, they say there are many such men who alone or in groups go from place to place to put on plays, display marvelous feats of skill in singing, playing instruments, dancing, juggling, acrobatics, telling stories, giving declamations, reciting poetry, describing famous battles and heroes, and telling the people the news. City people are lucky to have such a variety of experiences available to them all the time. Wouldn't we all be lucky if we could look through a window and see all the world has to offer and everything that is happening?

Historians and archaeologists tell us that for thousands of years of human existence this brief and oversimplified description of the dissemination of news and entertainment was the standard pattern of mass communication. Most of the time, the news of the day and the discussions and performances that constituted entertainment took place in intimate, person-to-person or small group communication settings. Families would talk among themselves and tell about their experiences and sing, play instruments, do readings, or tell stories. They talked with their closest neighbors and sometimes got together for entertaining evenings. Gatherings on the town square or in the local coffeehouse or tavern provided opportunities for wider exchanges. So did church meetings and socials. The occasional visits from traveling performers, politicians, officials, or religious representatives were special opportunities for a wider exchange of cultural experiences. Such injections of new information or insights merely added to the storehouse of materials that would be talked about in families and village groups for a long time after the outsider had left. It was through such interpersonal communication that history was maintained and culture was rehearsed and preserved. The rare instances in which many people gathered together at one time for trading, observing a major sports or political event, or family reunions enhanced the quantity of material that could be discussed in the intimate group situations.

Technological advances such as the development of print and the ability to read books and newspapers have made a profound difference in the lives of almost everyone, but the basic pattern of communication is not so different as one might expect. People still read papers alone or in the presence of one or two other close acquaintances. They still discuss what they have read in small intimate groups. Access to a daily newspaper certainly increases the quantity and

211

sometimes the quality of material that can be talked about, but we still process it in interpersonal communication with the few people who are close to us.

The same can be said about radio, television, cable communication, and other technological possibilities that are now under development. In fact, it can be said that our new technologies that permit the transmission of voice and image over long distances have essentially restored our ancient traditions of oral communication. The electronic devices allow us to hear the news and be entertained by the "strangers" from afar in a manner much like the appearance of the strangers in the villages of the past. The comparatively brief time in which we relied almost totally upon print and the ability to read for our sources of news and entertainment can now be seen in perspective as a slight deviation in thousands of years of oral traditions. This is not to say that print is a thing of the past. Rather, it is to call attention to the fact that although modern developments have had an enormous impact on us, their ultimate effect has been to allow the establishment of what has been called a "global village" based upon various forms of interpersonal communication. We are still villagers processing what ideas are available to us within our small intimate groups. Our village, though, now encompasses the world.

THE CONCEPT

From this it can be seen that the label we have given to the media of modern communication—mass communication—can be quite misleading. It conjures an image of masses of people jointly responding to a single message as in thousands of voices shouting "sieg heil" in unison after a Hitler speech. There is something sinister and threatening about the image. But it is an inaccurate one.

The mass communication of which we speak here can be characterized *conceptually* as individuals or intimate small groups attending to and processing through interpersonal communication messages that come to them through channels which permit many other individuals and small groups to interact with the messages at more or less the same time.

To be sure, the marvelous technologies now available to us allow people in New York, Pittsburgh, Indianapolis, Chicago, Kansas City, Denver, Salt Lake City, San Francisco, Los Angeles, Honolulu, Tokyo, Rome, Paris, and Moscow to learn of an attempt on the life of the Pope almost simultaneously. In homes, markets, shops, and offices all over the world small groups of people could talk together about the meaning for them that someone would seek to assassinate a religious leader and man of peace. Thanks to mass communication, virtually all of us learned of the event and even watched the attempt on TV within about the same time. Thus we shared that common experience. For the next few hours or days, people all over the world added this topic to their interpersonal communication and processed it in terms of their own values, interests, politics, and culture. The same can be said of the Olympic Games or the latest trend in clothes or music.

But critical to the understanding of mass communication is its role as a *stimulus to interpersonal communication* rather than as a tool that coalesces masses into mobs. As long as people are not physically separated from one another or alienated from one another so that they cannot engage in interpersonal communication, mass communication is mediated by interpersonal communication. It provides grist for the mill of personal talk, and at times becomes part of personal talk as in audience participation or talk shows. In this sense, it must be contrasted with public speeches or other forms of communication in which large bodies of people attend to a message in the same place, at the same time, and with relatively little opportunity to engage in interpersonal communication before determining the meaning of the message or the behavioral response to it.

Operationally, there are two perspectives from which we could seek to characterize mass communication: the nature of the media, and the ways people relate to the media. Looking first at the nature of the media, it is useful to note that the particular technology employed is not critical to our purposes. Although broadcast specialists may be vitally concerned with the growth of cable connections which would make the role of typical radio and television stations different, the study of oral communication skills need not be concerned with such innovations. No matter what kind of instrumentation is used to bring programming into homes, offices, bars, and social halls, there will still be *content*, and that is what we are dealing with here. It may be useful to point out, however, that recent technological changes may well make citizen access to some forms of program content greater. Recent developments in cable, for example, allow many more channels to be used at the same time, and in the near future there will be the opportunity for two-way communication such that people in their homes will be able to communicate back to the point of origination rather than just receive the content being sent out. Both of these developments increase the importance of assuring that all citizens have the skills necessary to be a part of mass communication. The citizen access channels will mean that many more of us will be able to communicate with our fellow community members through some form of television than has ever been the case. Skill in mass communication thus is becoming as vital as the ability to speak up in a town meeting was 100 years ago.

So, we can characterize the nature of the media as involving a wide variety of content. The familiar programs can be noted: entertainment, news, and commercial messages. Entertainment can include dramas of varying kinds and qualities, game shows, variety shows, sports, music, and various specials. News involves not just the formal news, sports, and weather presentations we see several times a day but documentaries, morning shows, coverage of significant

213

events, analyses of important issues, interviews, and, increasingly, citizens talking about their concerns and decisions. Commercial messages are almost as complex and varied as any other type of program. They range from the usual brief breaks during other programs and in between them to more subtle attempts to promote business and sell products as are found on Public Television programs. Even cable systems for which subscribers pay a monthly fee in the hope of getting programs free from commercial breaks are increasingly finding ways to sell products. In the future, people may be able to use their cable connection to "call up" information on available products and businesses much the way we now use the telephone yellow pages, only with much more detail and up-to-date information. For example, before going to the grocery store we will be able to see items and prices from a variety of stores displayed on our TV set to help us decide on our shopping behavior.

Turning to the second way to characterize mass communication operationally, we can examine the ways people relate to the media. Specifically, we can review information on the ways children relate to the media. M. Ploghoft and J. Anderson report that children and adults do not view television in the same way. "Children in lower elementary grades are more likely to see a program as a series of quasi-independent events between which there may or may not be a connection."[1] Children often fail to see an entire story in perspective, they miss many of the subtleties of language and concentrate instead on action, and they fail to understand many of the nonverbal characteristics of television such as the effects of camera angle and change in shot size.

Children use the media in about as many different ways as there are children using the media. It is a mistake to picture children all over the country glued to the TV set watching the same programs in the same way with the same effect. Each child has a more or less special set of needs, values, and motives with which to approach the media. These characteristics may change from time to time, day to day, and year to year. At one time a child may use TV as a companion while eating and as a transition between school work and relating to family. At another time the program may be used as a background for play activity with other children; they will act out scenes and characters from their favorite show while watching it from time to time. Sometimes programs are an excuse to avoid work or go to bed, or they may serve as a distraction from problems and an aid to going to sleep. The same program may be viewed by many children for many different reasons and with many different effects.

Television viewing is a discontinuous experience. It is commonly done with some other activity such as eating. It is not viewed steadily, but instead we look away frequently with attention rising and falling throughout a single program

---

[1] M. Ploghoft and J. Anderson, *Teaching Critical Television Viewing Skills* (Springfield, IL: Charles C Thomas, Publisher, 1982), p. 16.

(commercials get the least attention and movies the greatest). E. Wartella,[2] summarizing various studies, says that children grow in their ability to deal cognitively with television in terms of drawing on broader sources for cues in perception, use of multiple dimensions of objects when assessing them, and in becoming less egocentric in understanding others' behavior. She also reports that by age five children begin to approximate adult styles of viewing and not viewing—short periods of close attention. Children are selective in what they view, she says, using the audio portion of the program to tell them when to look, and not looking when they cannot understand the program. Children as old as eight or ten have trouble remembering the essential scenes of a drama and how they relate to plot, and they have difficulty understanding characters' motivations. Younger children do not understand some aspects of production such as the use of flashbacks and slow motion, and they often fail to understand the role and purpose of advertising. By the third grade, children begin to understand that advertisers are trying to sell something, and they begin to recall commercials.

THE TRADITION

Mass communication as we are considering it here is a phenomenon of the present century. The technology of wireless communication became practical early in the 1900s, and for the first years it was limited to such specific uses as ship-to-ship and ship-to-shore communication—places where the wires of telegraph could not reach. By 1921 the country was ready for the first radio stations, and during that decade incredibly rapid growth occurred. Within about 30 years radio became an established medium, with a vast majority of families owning receivers, and within the same time television made its appearance and moved rapidly to almost total penetration of the United States. By the 1950s both radio and television were established parts of our culture and began to demand some attention from educators.

Early approaches toward teaching skill in performance on radio and television tended to be a last hurrah for the elocutionists. Concentration was on "correctness" in voice, pronunciation, language, and scripting. Men with deep, mellow voices were sought out (women's voices were considered too shrill and unpleasant). Pronunciations from the general American dialect were demanded, and handbooks of words and their proper pronunciations were published for broadcasters. Language was carefully monitored to avoid vulgarisms, colloquial-

---

[2] E. Wartella, "Children and Television: The Development of the Child's Understanding of the Medium," in G. Wilhoit and H. deBock, *Mass Communication Review Yearbook*, Vol. 1 (Beverly Hills, CA: Sage Publications, Inc., 1980).

isms, or any hint of obscenity. And everything was scripted, even apparently spontaneous interviews. It was believed that no surprises were acceptable over the airwaves, so both questions and answers were written in advance. It was a structured and rather stilted form of communication. Of course, great stress was put on articulation so that /s/ sounds would not cause unpleasant whistles on the receivers, and words were formed with great precision so that they could be understood on radios subject to considerable static interference.

Early performers were drawn from the stage, mostly vaudeville. They carried their training in stage diction with them to broadcasting along with their burlesque routines. Early training in mass communication skills tended to reflect this carryover of stage performance techniques.

Common Ways of Thinking about mass communication skills have been oriented toward the peculiarities of the medium rather than the communication possibilities. Professional schools and colleges have given much attention to the technical demands for sound-tight studios, elaborate equipment, and imitations of professional broadcasters' mannerisms and programs. The suggestion has been made that schools are preparing students to be professional broadcasters, and often they do. Professional broadcasting schools, separate from formal schools and colleges, exist to teach the professional skills for entry into broadcasting. But the implication has been that only professionally trained people have the skill to communicate by radio and television and that professional training must be special to the peculiarities of the media.

At the same time, orientation of skills training has been almost totally on the production of programs. What attention there has been to audience analysis has been on discovering ways to get people to listen to particular programs and buy certain products. There has not commonly been much interest in examining mass communication as an opportunity to participate in the wide range of human communicative transactions.

Current Perspectives show some marked changes in orientation. Over the past few years there has been a growing interest in discovering the effects broadcasting has on the people who watch and listen. Research has examined the ways in which people use the media, the gratifications they expect and receive from their use, and the ways in which their experience with the media changes their lives for good or ill. There is much concern for the possibility that mass communication may cause such undersirable effects an antisocial behavior, loss of interest in reading, loss of interest in more physically active lives, and reduction in interpersonal communication. Some have feared that radio and television may increase violent behavior, lower moral standards, encourage bad habits, and cause unwise consumer practices. There is also fear that the persuasive involvement of the media in the political process may reduce democracy to an act of selling candidates.

216

Most recently, there is interest in teaching children how to be more *competent receivers* of the media programs. Looking away from attempts to control content in order to achieve socially desired ends, these scholars are more interested in helping young people learn to use their *critical faculties* in approaching the media so that they can serve as their own judges of quality and moral and social acceptability, and can regulate their own consumer behavior.

The View of This Book is that elementary children should experience two kinds of skill training. First, we support the current trends toward receivership training. In a nation strongly committed to a system of freedom of expression there does not seem to be much fruit to be gained by continued efforts to control the effects of the media by various forms of censorship, either voluntary or government enforced. As has been so of most censorship, it is repugnant to our sense of freedom and it is not a very successful way to regulate effects. The more desirable approach, in our view, is to help children become more aware of themselves and their values in relation to the media and to apply that sense to a critical evaluation of what they see and hear on the media. This is accomplished through early training in receivership, which we consider to be part of oral communication skills.

Second, recognizing that future developments in mass communication will make it increasingly likely that ordinary citizens—not just broadcast professionals—will have regular opportunity to do their communicating by means of one of the media, we believe that all students should become comfortable in expressing themselves on radio and television. We believe that current trends toward the rejection of the elocutionistic, stilted, formal manners of speech in broadcast situations should be encouraged. Children should learn that anyone with ordinary oral communication skills can participate in mass communication.

COMPETENCIES TO BE DEVELOPED

Three *General Exit Competencies* ask students to

1. Recognize and report on the purpose and the audience of entertainment, news, and commercial messages in the mass media.
2. Recognize and report on the various elements in the content of entertainment, news, and commercial messages in the mass media.
3. Create and perform mass media messages in news, entertainment, and commercials.

The first two general exit competencies address receivership skills and the third deals with performance skills. Combined, they work toward a child who is

217

sensitive to the media process and is capable of using it for communication when appropriate.

Programs on radio and television hardly occur by happenstance. Commercial broadcasts in particular are devised to research particular audiences at particular times with an intended effect. This is done in relation to competing broadcasters and potential and actual advertisers. Even programs on cable and noncommercial stations are devised with an audience and purpose in mind. For example, we are sometimes impressed by an unusually attractive schedule of movies, programs, and specials on all stations during one week without realizing that this is done during the time that major ratings are taken, from which estimates of audience size and characteristics will be made. From these ratings, schedules of rates that can be charged to advertisers will be established. All competitors are working to establish the most favorable audience profiles so that they can increase profits. The alert receiver is aware of this.

Again, it is no accident that programs appealing to children are presented in the afternoon during the after-school periods and on the weekends. Nor is it coincidental that the advertisers who buy time on these programs are typically trying to sell products that are appealing to children. Daytime programs are aimed at homemakers who are most likely to be watching, and the commercials stress products for women. Sports programs are scheduled for weekend afternoons to attract a largely male audience, and they tend to be sponsored by companies marketing beer, automobile accessories, and shaving preparations.

As students are asked, under the first general exit competency, to notice the audiences sought for various programs and the kinds of sponsoring agencies connected with them, they will become more capable and critical receivers of the mass media. This is not done to change their viewing habits. They will, however, be able to exercise personal choices and obtain their own maximum benefits from the media.

The second general exit competency calls attention to content variables of the mass media. Here the students should notice the ways in which stories are selected and presented, how characters are developed, how choices are made in what will constitute "news" of the day, and the ways in which commercial messages are structured to achieve a desired persuasive effect. In this competency, students can call upon their already established skills in listening, nonverbal communication, persuasion, and reasoning. They can talk about the ways in which media communication makes use of the kinds of skills discussed in those chapters. They can notice the adjustments that are made to suit the particular medium being considered. They can observe their own reactions as receivers.

Finally, the third general exit competency brings children into participation as media communicators. Two points need to be stressed here. First, students should become aware of the extent to which they have already developed the basic skills necessary to perform in mass communication. They have learned to present a public speech, to develop a persuasive message, to engage in an interview, to advance reasons for a point of view, to read aloud, to do a creative performance, to listen carefully to what others say, and to employ the wide range of nonverbal communication necessary to television in particular.

Second, they will become sensitive to the ways in which these communication skills must be adapted for use in the mass media. The importance of time will quickly become clear: how to tell a story, make a persuasive appeal, or report on an event within a highly limited time span. They will learn that the medium shapes and, in the view of some, becomes the message. One of the authors was interviewing a famous champion in professional bowling one time on the radio when he got up in the studio to "show" the listeners how to make an approach. Of course, those listening on the radio only heard the sounds of movement and the frantic effort of the interviewer to describe what the champ was doing. The bowler was insensitive to the limitations of radio. Another time a geologist was being interviewed on television when he unexpectedly brought a map out of his case and began talking about it. The director tried in vain to get him to hold it up toward a camera long enough for the viewers to see it. But instead, he held it for a second or two, and just as the camera began to get into focus, he moved it to point out some detail. The viewers never saw it. These are some performance skills children can readily learn.

Beginning Exit Competencies expect students to

1. Identify the purpose and bits of content of different segments of productions in mass media including programs and commercials.
2. Identify real and fantasy characters in mass media productions.
3. Identify real and fantasy stories in the mass media.
4. Record and listen to their own and others' voices on audiotape.

By the time they reach school, children have become quite familiar with the mass media, particularly television. However, they may not have done much thinking about what they like and why. Nor have they had the need to think at any length about what they like and why. Nor have they had the need to think at any length about the things on TV they do not like and why. In the first exit competency, the students should begin a sensitization process by noting and reporting on their reaction to commercials and programs. Having already studied persuasion at an elementary level, the children should be able to talk about their favorite commercials and why they might be persuasive. Having studied creative performance, they should be able to talk about their favorite entertainment programs and why they find them appealing. In so doing, children will become more aware of the variety of events that occur even within a half hour of television viewing.

The second and third beginning exit competencies address a problem that seems to bother adults as well as children: separating reality and fantasy. We are aware that adults bombard actors who portray doctors on television with requests for medical advice, that those who act as lawyers are even invited to address meetings of bar associations, and those who perform as villains are often booed when they make a public appearance as themselves. If adults have such confusion, imagine how children perceive the people and events they see on television.

In the second competency at the beginning level, children talk about real and fantasy characters with whom they are familiar. First, we must caution you that we are not so naive as to believe there is a clear line separating reality and fantasy. Think instead of a continuum with "almost real" at one end and "almost fantasy" at the other. We say "almost" intentionally because we would be hard put to say what is absolutely real and we will approach fantasy with the same conservatism. For example, is the public official who walks out of a meeting, is stopped by a reporter with a minicamera, asked a question and given seconds to answer "real" in an absolute sense? Is the official still real when presented on the evening news but with the answer now cut to five seconds? Are people who engage in a riot, knowing that they will be covered by the news organizations, being "real?" On the other hand, imaginary characters such as dog, cats, mice, and lions in cartoon shows, who talk and act like adults but not really like adults, do not seem so fantastic to children who talk to their pets and love their stuffed animals. So it is not our intention to ask children to make a strict division of the world of characters into real and fantasy. Neither do we seek to disabuse children of their delightful capacity to be creative. Instead, we seek at this stage to begin alerting children to the range of characters they meet on the media and to start the development of a mature but not stodgy approach to representations of reality.

The third competency carries this development into the examination of stories. As we did with characters, we do not wish to make a strict division between stories that are "true" and those that are make-believe. We again see a range. Children will benefit, we believe, by talking about the stories they are familiar with in terms of what happens and what seems real to them and why. Even a show that is studiously realistic such as "Wild Kingdom" necessarily contains scenes that are re-enactments of what actually happened when the cameras were not present. They tell the viewer that fact, and to that extent some of this program might be considered unreal, but is it?

Finally, the fourth beginning exit competency introduces children to the process of sound recording. Tape recorders are now so common that they are rapidly becoming as essential an instrument as a pencil. Just as young people should certainly learn some basic principles of using pencils and crayons, they should learn the rudiments of sound recording. Furthermore, we are all familiar with our own feelings the first time we heard ourselves talking on a recorder: there was nervous laughter and loud claims that "it doesn't sound like me."

Children can hear themselves and others in a variety of settings and will gradually outgrow embarrassment attached to the sound of the recorded voice. This will establish a foundation for further skill development.

Intermediate Exit Competencies anticipate the development of the ability of children to

1. Note and report on their uses of the mass media and the gratifications derived from them.
2. Identify the audiences of programs on the media.
3. Report on the story line, characters, and informative content of media programs.
4. Prepare and deliver an individual recorded 30- to 60-second program.

There has been a good deal of research into what is called the uses and gratifications of the mass media. The findings show that different people make widely different uses of the programs watched and obtain various benefits from them. Some of these findings are surprising because they do not support some of our stereotyped assumptions about people using TV as a form of hypnosis. In the first intermediate exit competency, students can do some of that research for themselves. They can discover what they watch, when they watch, how frequently they watch, and how steadily they watch. They can take some time to think together about what they do with the media and why. This is the start of making use of the media a more conscious process with more choice involved.

It is easy to move from this type of self-examination to a broader understanding of the intentions of those who produce the programs. That is, students can begin to see more clearly that certain programs are aimed at selected audiences who are most likely to be watching at the time of the broadcast. Work previoulsy done with thinking about audience analysis in connection with persuasion might be helpful here. Children begin to see that they are part of several different audiences such as families, groups of peers, and alone.

Research mentioned early in this chapter noted that during the first three grades children have great difficulty understanding the flow of a story from event to event. They do not do a very good job of identifying characters and their motivations, and they may not appreciate the information provided. This development should be taking place at the intermediate level, and class discussion of stories, characters, and information content will help make that development more certain.

Again, the final competency at the intermediate level allows students to build performance skills. In this case they are asked to prepare and deliver an individual recorded program of no more than a minute's length. Having outgrown their self-consciousness about hearing their recorded voice, students can now move to the process of trying to do some communicating as they would in a mass communication setting. This means that they must have something to communicate, they must consider how it can be best expressed in sound alone, and how they must prepare both what is to be said and how it is to be said within the confines of a recording. Remember, we do not expect children to try to "sound like radio announcers." They should not work for stilted and artificial speech or affect an artificial voice. Instead, they should work for communication of an idea so that those who hear the program will understand.

Advanced Exit Competencies call for the ability to

1. Survey media audiences and analyze preferences.
2. Identify and note differences in what is communicated by the audio and video elements of segments.
3. Review critically and compare the personnel, content, and production elements of media messages.
4. Participate as a member of a group to create and produce a mass media program and commercials.

Now children can fully draw upon their understanding of audience analysis begun in the persuasion exercises. They can talk to other people to gain some general understanding about who uses what media for what purpose. They can now move from egocentric understanding of their own uses and gratifications of the media to a grasp of what various types of people find of value. This will help students generalize their own experience, to see the extent to which they are like and unlike other people, and, perhaps most important, to see that there are many differences among people and groups. They can talk with understanding about the differences among people and draw some value in thinking about how they might do their own communication through the mass media as well as how they serve as different audience members.

In the second advanced competency, children can become more effective critical receivers by noticing with greater care and understanding all the elements that go into any production. They will begin to notice production techniques such as flashbacks, flashforwards, rapid sequencing of many events in the form of a preview of what is to come. They can examine the contribution of the video and audio elements to total communication. They can become sensitive to the choices made by the director in various shots—close-ups, panorama, zooms. The artistic choices made regarding scene, composition, color, and action can be discussed. We know from research that children use the audio portion of a program to cue them to look at what is happening after they have ceased watching. They can now ask themselves what it is about the sound that would make them look back at the set. They can employ some of their study of the process of listening to recall that listening is enhanced by the novel or unexpected and

222

apply that to what is done with music, sound effects, rising and falling volume, or even silence.

The third advanced competency calls on students to become sensitive to all the components of a finished production. They can observe the use of children in programs and commercials designed to appeal to children. They can talk about why they like or dislike programs involving animals, cartoon characters, or other personalities. They can discuss why some commercials hold their attention and lead to recall and others do not—what were the production techniques, what about music or jingles, what about little dramas? They can watch carefully for ways in which programs are put together to hold viewers, such as blending a commercial into the entertainment content so that the viewer is hardly aware at first that a commercial is on. They can notice that at the start of some programs a series of previews is provided to draw them into watching; they can see that often a crisis is left unsolved or a character is put into a dangerous situation just before cutting to a commercial so that attention will not wane during the commercial. They can talk about the sequencing of shows one after another to keep viewers tuned into the same channel for long periods. They can look at news shows to discover why some are more attractive and pleasant to hear than others. They can notice how stories are told and resolved within limited time spans. They can, in other words, become rather sophisticated viewers.

With these experiences, students should be ready to become part of their own production team as called for in the final advanced exit competency. Now they can truly work to become practical communicators on radio and television. They can draw upon all their previous oral communication skills to do this work. They will need to employ their skills in group communication to discover roles that must be performed and divide the labor. They can use their experiences in creative performance, public speaking, and persuasion to put together a program that does the desired communication. They can use their newly developed knowledge of the role of audio and video to use the capacities of mass communication to the fullest. They can have the satisfaction of doing a rather polished job of mass communication.

Sample Exercises for Mass Communication

The following exercises provide samples of lessons for teaching mass communication at three levels of elementary instruction. The lessons are planned to help students meet the general exit competencies as well as the specific ones at each level.

Learning about mass media as a communication skill involves considerable time on receivership skills at the elementary level. It is quite evident that children devote a large portion of their time to receiving information and entertainment from television. Although newspapers and magazines are also forms of mass media, the concentration of this book is on oral communication. The majority of oral communication exposure to mass media is television. The radio is another type of mass oral communication, but with large portions of radio time devoted to the disc jockey, the radio does not provide the broad range of exposure that television does. Also, before children are teen-agers they have little interest in the radio. Thus, this chapter is designed primarily to develop receivership skills in television.

In addition, some attention is given to the performance aspects of television. Children will learn to hear and see themselves as others would through audio and video tape. This experience can lead to improvement in clarity of expressing oneself in terms of speech production as well as message communication. At the same time experience in various levels of performance helps students appreciate that which they are observing. At each level there is one performance competency. The sample lessons on performance to meet that competency may seem to be slighted. But the students have built many of the prerequisite skills in preceding chapters. These performance aspects seem so obvious that the teacher can readily expand the sample lessons to a variety of subjects in order to meet the performance competency.

Many of the lessons have been suggested to include with other academic subjects and some lessons are designed to stand alone. However, it will be obvious to any teacher that most lessons can be designed for a specific subject matter and that any lesson that involves production will also include writing and reading skills. These lessons build upon the oral communication skills in all the preceding chapters, and to attempt most of these lessons without children having developed the previous skills is likely to be much more difficult.

In addition to the following lessons, teachers who want to cover the topic more extensively will find the book by M. E. Ploghoft and J. A. Anderson, *Teaching Critical Television Viewing Skills* (Charles C Thomas, 1982) useful. They have devoted an entire book to the topic that is included here as just one chapter.

BEGINNING LEVEL EXERCISES

1. Each child describes her favorite commercial and identifies the purpose of that commercial. Because the children are already acquainted with the persuasion element of commercials in the beginning level of persuasion, this is a logical place to start having children see the purpose of this element of the mass media. The teacher needs to precede the assignment by a discussion of commercials as one part of mass media productions. It is also wise to explain that commercials help pay for program production. For the media, the purpose is to pay for programming, but as a receiver, the child needs to state that the purpose is to sell a product, to have the viewer purchase the item. After having studied persuasion, a child should be able to see that she enjoys a certain commercial

and that the purpose is to sell X product. In addition, she can see whether she would be persuaded to buy.

2. Each child writes the name of his favorite television show for entertainment. The teacher should precede this assignment with a class discussion that the purpose of some parts of the mass media is to entertain. Then each child thinks about a television show that entertains him. This lesson is designed to combine with a writing assignment. Depending on the abilities of the children in the class, the teacher may want the children to write a brief description of the program as well.

3. Small groups of children talk about the phonics segments presented on the "Electric Company" show the preceding day. This lesson is planned for reading groups, although other groups could be used. The teacher has a group discussion that talks about the purpose of some programs being information. Such a program is usually planned to entertain as well as to inform so that learning is done by an entertainment. Then he asks all the children to see the "Electric Company" and watch for the segment on sounds. If this program is not available, "Sesame Street" has some phonics sections, but they are not as detailed or as lengthy. The "Electric Company" provides excellent segments on consonants and consonant clusters. The following day in reading group, the children talk about the program and the sound they learned about during the program.

4. The class discusses the information presented on "Wild Kingdom." This will coordinate well with a science lesson. It must be planned in advance so that the teacher and the students can discuss the program after it has occurred.

5. Each child reports one item she learned from a news broadcast. Although news programs are not as an appealing type of information for children as the ones mentioned in the previous lessons, the program can be more appealing by having a news time each day in combination with social studies. Each day two children are assigned to watch the news. The following day both children report on something of interest to them during news time. This is continued until every child has reported.

6. The class discusses real people versus fantasy characters on a television program. The teacher may want to use "Sesame Street" for the first discussion. The children can discuss that Bob and Susan are real people and that Big Bird and Oscar are fantasy characters. There are many other real and fantasy roles in that program. If the class is advanced enough, the teacher can also discuss that Bob and Susan are actors who are playing a role and that they don't really live there either. This lesson combines readily with reading lessons and discussion of reality versus fantasy in reading.

7. Each child draws a fantasy character she enjoys on television. This lesson is, of course, planned for art class. The children should be warned in advance so they can be watching their favorite programs for a fantasy character they want to draw. In this lesson, the teacher is working for the obvious fantasy of

puppets, cartoons, animal characters such as Big Bird, and so on. The children's shows provide numerous examples.

8. The class discusses a real story versus a fantasy story in a television production. A good program to use for this is "3-2-1, Contact." This program uses teenagers who discuss actual information in some segments, and in other segments of the same program they present a short play of the Bloodhound Gang. Again, the children should be asked in advance of the discussion to watch the program.

9. The class discusses the audio recording of people talking, environmental sounds, music, and so on. The purpose of this lesson is to introduce students primarily to tape recorders. The lesson can be combined with science class so the children can learn some of the details of sound reproduction. At the same time every child should learn how to use a tape recorder.

10. Each child hears himself and his classmates on a tape recorder. The tape recorder should be present in various activities until all children are at ease with the tape recorder, both during the recording and listening to it afterwards. It is wise to begin recording groups such as a reading group, a math group, and the whole class singing. Then the children can listen. They will, of course, learn that their own voices sound different over the tape recorder. Then children can use it one at a time so they can just hear themselves. Each may record a lesson he did alone, a speech, a news report, or anything he is saying for any class. This is an excellent time to call attention to the need to speak clearly, both in terms of production and in terms of ideas presented.

INTERMEDIATE LEVEL EXERCISES

1. Each child keeps a television viewing diary for a week. The teacher explains that children should keep a careful record of everything they watch for a week and note the time period (by the clock) in which they watched. Such a record means recording each program, whether it is part or all of the program. It also means recording what commercials are watched. Such a diary demands a lot of writing and thus can provide a writing lesson with a purpose.

2. Each child outlines his TV diary according to the type of program. Now children have a list of information programs, entertainment programs, and commercial segments. This is a good method to begin teaching functional outlining in conjunction with English. At the same time the children reinforce recognition of different purposes for television production and their uses of these choices.

3. Each child computes the hours she watched television for a week. This lesson is designed to be used in combination with arithmetic, and thus is can be as complicated as the abilities of the children allow. Each child can add her total hours of watching each day and subtract that from the hours in a day. Each child may also add her hours for the week and subtract that from the hours in

a week. Then the hours spent in each type of program can be figured. Many combinations are possible.

4. Each child reads the TV schedule for the week (from after school to bed-time and Saturday, and notes what audience each program is designed for. The teacher may want to reproduce a weekly TV schedule, or if each child has a newspaper, he can use his own. The child may have to take the sheet home and quickly turn channels in order to decide whether this program is for young children, older children, adults, teenagers, or mixed ages. This assignment is an interesting variation for reading as well as mass media.

5. Small groups of children name commercials aimed at a child audience and those for an audience. Each small group could be assigned different hours to view commercials. Then each small group makes a list of commercials during that time period that are for children and for adults. The groups should share their information with the class. It will be interesting to note how many commercials are repeated in time slots throughout the day as well as how many are at certain hours. It is expected that hours of presentation will predict anticipated audience.

6. Small groups retell a story line of a program on TV. Each small group in the class should agree on a television program they want to see. The next day, after watching the program, the group meets together and retells the exact story line. Then after this planning, they retell the story to the class. It will be more interesting if the teacher sees that each group selects a different program. Each group can retell the story following the program, which will schedule the retelling on different days.

7. Each child selects a favorite character on a TV show and describes that character in a short speech to the class. The children will find it easy to name and physically describe the person, but this assignment is designed to go beyond that. They must describe the character that is developed—for example, kind, considerate, thoughtful, caring, macho, mean, mischievous, and so on. The typical actions or thoughts of that character should be explored so children can describe expectations and predictable character roles. Each child may pick his own person to describe, but roles in a series are easier to understand; and the teacher may need to provide guidance. For instance, the varied and carefully built characters in "Little House on the Prairie" provide excellent subject matter. Because the children will have been through the public speaking chapter, this assignment will depend on the intermediate skills developed there as well as investigating characters in the media.

8. Small groups of children retell information conveyed in a media program. This assignment is easily coordinated with science. Shows such as "Wild King-dom" and "3-2-1, Contact" provide science information that can be retold. The accuracy of information is an important element. As mentioned before, the group should share the retelling with the class.

9. Each child writes a 30- to 60-second segment of a program. The segment

227

may be a commercial, news, weather, sports, or a brief dialog between characters. This assignment should be original, *not* a reproduction of a show. For example, a child may want to sell sand or a rock. The sports report may be for a kickball game during recess. This is a writing assignment that has meaning. Each child should do the assignment even if it involves a number of people. The children are writing a script.

10. Each child participates in the actual taping of some of the previously written scripts. The class may select the scripts they would most like to do from those written in the previous assignment. Careful decision-making skills are involved. Each child volunteers or is assigned a role in one of the scripts. The performances should be put on videotape and replayed for the class to see. The videotaping is an important part of understanding mass media. If no video is available, an audiotape recorder is a second choice, but some of the lesson will be lost.

ADVANCED LEVEL EXERCISES

1. Each student surveys three young children, three peers, three teen-agers, and three adults to find what television programs each watches regularly. A record must be kept of persons contacted and the answers. The survey can be made as complicated as the teacher desires.

2. The class works as a group to combine the results of the previous survey. Now it is possible to analyze the resulting preferences in terms of the media audience. A discussion should follow.

3. Small groups select programs to analyze the audio portions. Each group should select a different program. Before the groups begin the independent analysis, the class should discuss the messages of music, of the various sounds of cars or motorcycles, of the sounds of planes, bombs, gunfire, and so on. In addition, the students need to be aware of variations of the human voice. In other words, any portion of the audiotape that draws attention should be discussed. The attention should be on those audio portions rather than the verbal script. Each group reports to the others on their observation. This lesson can combine with science or with a music class.

4. Each student gives a speech on the visual elements of a program. Each student should select a program, turn off the sound, and watch the visual elements. They may note scenery, colors, abstract designs, as well as facial expressions and actions. This is an excellent assignment to combine with art class. Students can learn how visual elements set a mood, convey a feeling, send a message and so on. Some shows are better done visually than others, and lack of sound will help students distinguish this element.

5. Each student writes a comparison of the audio and video elements of a television segment. The script should be included here. Commercials often provide good material for this assignment. For example, a term such as *luxury car*

may not be supported by the visual display, or an advertisement for a beverage may provide talk about the beverage but the visual display may concentrate on people having fun. Children may note the beautiful teeth of the people who advertise toothpaste or the typical doctor's coat on a person talking about a headache remedy. This can produce a thoughtful writing assignment.

6. Each student compares two programs prepared for young children in terms of personnel, content, and production. The assignment to ask them to look at programs that they believe they have outgrown may give students the detachment needed to make comparisons. For example, reading groups at the advanced level can be asked to compare the phonics presentations on "Electric Company" with those on "Sesame Street." Such a comparison provides a good review of phonics that students might otherwise resist, as well as a mass media lesson.

7. Each student gives a short speech comparing two news programs in terms of personnel, content, and production. The student may turn from channel to channel or may watch one channel at six o'clock and one at ten o'clock. Students should consider information delivered, video and audio aspects, and the personnel. This lesson combines readily with social studies.

8. Each student compares two programs he watches. This may be an oral or a written comparison, but the class should discuss it. These two programs may be quite different in nature. They must be compared in terms of content, personnel, and production.

9. Small groups prepare a brief weekly program of news and commercials for the school intercom. Each week the teacher assigns about three students to write about a five-minute segment to be delivered on news and commercials for the school. This should be real material that the children in the school are concerned with. For example, the news could be about what some class is doing, new equipment for the playground, signing up for school patrol, the car traffic after school, a student who has broken a leg, a teacher's wedding, and so on. The commercials should also be real—an upcoming assembly, a play or musical group coming to town, Girl Scout cookies, and so on. After the script is written, a day should be chosen in the week when these student can use the school intercom to produce their broadcast. If this is done every week or every two weeks, each student will have the opportunity to participate. If carefully done, the students and the school will benefit.

10. The class writes and produces a 30-minute program on videotape. This project will take an extended period of time. The class may be divided into groups with one group that writes, one that produces, and one that acts for each segment. In a 30-minute program, students can have a factual segment (news, a science experiment, or a cooking demonstration), several short skits, and a number of commercials. In addition, the production may center around any academic area. In other words, such a production can be a lesson for any subject as well as a mass media lesson. This project should be put on videotape and viewed by the class. Invited guests can be included in the viewing.

12

Intercultural
Communication

OBJECTIVES

At the end of this chapter you should be able to

1. Define culture.
2. Define intercultural communication.
3. Describe various people and situations in intercultural communication both within and among cultures.
4. Discuss how respect of both our own and other cultures is necessary to intercultural communication.
5. Explain how communication can facilitate human functioning in our intercultural world.
6. Discuss how the general and specific level competencies are designed to yield, by the time of exit, an elementary mastery of intercultural communication as currently conceived.
7. Explain how the general exit competencies represent broad goals that accompany each specific level competency.
8. Match each exercise to the general exit competency or competencies and the specific level exit competency or competencies that the exercise addresses.
9. Explain why the successful completion of one exercise does not fulfill the objectives of the competencies.
10. Design additional exercises for the fulfillment of the stated competencies.

"Mom, there was a new kid in class today, and he's really weird."

"What was strange about him?"

"Well, in the first place he didn't say a word. I tried to talk to him and he acted as if he didn't understand. And he looks funny. He has a little nose and thin lips and his hair is really ugly. And you ought to see him, his skin looks like paper."

"That does sound odd."

"Oh, and he was chewing all the time. I guess he was chewing betel nut, but everyone knows kids don't chew betel nut. At least they sure don't do it in school."

"What was his name?"

"Some silly name I can't pronounce. It sounds like jon-es-soon."

"My goodness, that must be the son of that new family that just came to work here. Their name is Johnson. They're from the United States. They're sure different from us."

We know now that communication is no simple process even under the best of circumstances. In this chapter we shall examine communication operating within a most difficult situation: among people of different cultures. In this dialog the initial problem of overcoming overt differences is revealed along with the fact that we are all different to somebody. Look at another example which exposes a problem in initiating communication from different cultural expectations.

The professor was at his desk, busily grading papers, when he heard a voice say, "May I have some time to talk with you?"

He looked up to see Susie Iyamba, a student from Nigeria, who had been in his communication course last quarter. "Of course, Susie, come on in."

He came out from behind his desk, motioned her to a chair, and then seated himself opposite her on another chair. He leaned toward her with a businesslike posture and said, "What can I do for you today?"

There was a pause. Susie began to speak, stopped, and then went on, hesitantly, "Can we . . . is it possible . . .to . . . just talk . . . make small talk before we turn to the purpose of my visit?" Her ebony face communicated nonverbally both friendly courtesy and concern that she might upset the professor by her request.

She relaxed as he smiled in apparent understanding. He said, "You mentioned last quarter that your husband is studying in chemistry. Do you have children?"

Her joy was now obvious and her tension seemed to melt away. "Oh yes! I have two beautiful children. Do you have children?"

Ten minutes later, after a discussion of families and some unusual experiences involved in coming to another country to study, the talk gradually moved toward her program of study, how she was responding to other professors, and finally a request that the professor accept her for an independent study course of readings in decision making for the following quarter. That was, it finally turned out, the purpose of her visit.

The professor had, indeed, understood. In his culture, common to many North Americans, when someone comes to a business office to ask for a conference, the approach is to get down to business immediately. The attitude is let's get to the task. Don't beat around the bush, state your business, and let's go to work. Time is important.

But in other cultures, Susie's for example, such a brusk manner is considered rude and can be quite disconcerting. They would prefer to take some time establishing human contact, talk of trivial things or topics unrelated to the reason for coming together, and then let the conversation gradually come around to the specific subject of the interview. The central purpose may then seem to come up almost casually. Without this warm-up period, people in some cultures may simply be unable to talk business at all. Many American negotiators have discovered this to their dismay. Contracts have been lost and agreements have never been reached simply because the abrupt, hard-charging manner of one side has left the other totally unhappy with the interaction.

THE CONCEPT

In Chapter 1 we discussed some aspects of differences of which teachers of communication skills should be aware. Now we need to characterize culture and then relate that to intercultural communication.

Culture exists wherever human beings exist because it is the rationale of their ways of thinking and behaving. Culture defines us in contrast to others in that it is something that we have that other groups do not have, but that does not say that the other groups do not have culture as well. We have a tendency to be culturally chauvinistic by believing what *we* have is culture and others who are not like us are uncultured. There was the poet, for example, who objected to career-oriented students who fail to major in the humanities, "These people have no interest in art or literature; they are only concerned with making money," he said. "If this trend continues, art and literature may soon die, and if they die, culture dies." What he was saying was that culture as he knew it would die, and he had no respect for what other people held to be culture. He was being culturally chauvinistic. Poets and writers have for years labeled those without similar literacy as uncultured. They have insisted that everyone should learn to appreciate "good" literature, art, music, and manners so that they, too, can be cultured. In this, they are being culturally imperialistic: trying to spread their idea of culture to others. This can lead some groups to feel as if their culture is threatened. Black Americans, for example, have felt a strong need to protect their culture from the imperialistic encroachments of others. The same can be said for Native Americans and other ethnic groups living in the United States. Cultural imperialism presents problems to many people and stands as an impediment to intercultural communication.

Our cultural imperialism works two ways: we confidently, sometimes arrogantly, expect others to see the superiority of our culture; we confidently and sometimes arrogantly seek to diminish the culture of others. Those who do not share our religion may be called pagan or heathen, those who do not look as we do may be called ugly, those who do not share our socioeconomic system may be called uncivilized or backward, those who do not think and talk like us may be called ignorant, those who do not share our conventions in art or literature may be called primitive, those who have different political practices may be called barbaric, those who do not eat as we do may be labeled crude or tasteless, people with different forms of music and dance may be thought of as simple or unrefined. In doing this, we do not perceive ourselves as trying to win acceptance of our ways over others; we believe we are superior. It might be helpful to go back and read this paragraph again, only this time putting yourself on the other side and understand that those of other cultures make about the same judgments of you.

As long as human beings lived in a highly segmented world with little contact with outsiders, culture presented few problems. After all, culture is vitally necessary to humans. The newborn infant has the genetic, biological capacity to be any one of thousands of different kinds of people, and the culture into which she is born provides the decision-making criteria which guide her to become the one person she ultimately will be. It provides the traditions, customs, norms, beliefs, values, thought patterns, language, and self-image necessary to functioning. It helps us control our behaviors and relate to our environment. We all have the same abilities and needs to eat, sleep, act, and eliminate, and our culture helps us work out satisfactory ways of doing these things. The very expression, "go to the bathroom," to communicate elimination is cultural to the extent that some North Americans just cannot spend any time in the woods without carrying along their porta-potty. The British imperialists in Africa could not spend a night in the jungle without putting on their dinner jackets, drinking a gin and tonic, and sitting down to a meal set on a table with white linen. The Africans thought they were absurd and the British thought the Africans were barbaric. But both groups had their ways of functioning and did quite well with them. The problem comes only when two or more cultures are brought into contact. Then come the problems in understanding and ultimately, communication.

For millennia the way people dealt with those of another culture who might come in contact with them was to suppress, enslave, or kill them. We read that the common punishment in ancient cultures for various crimes was banishment, and in our modern view that may not sound so bad. It might be compared with forcing war protesters in the 1960s to exile themselves to Canada. But in the olden times banishment was tantamount to a death penalty. The stranger of another culture who wandered into our village might hope at best to be made a slave and at worst to be put in a cage, fattened up, and then eaten. Christians were thrown to the lions or forced into fatal gladitorial combat. Jews were forced into ghettos or put to death. Native Americans were driven from place to place, slaughtered in mass, and finally placed on reservations. Sometimes strangers were seen as witches and burned at the stake. Japanese Americans were forced into concentration camps. Of course, starting early in the seventeenth century, black Africans were kidnapped and taken to other places as subhuman slaves very much the way prisoners of war in ancient times were brought back to Rome as slaves. Today, we speak easily of black ghettos and Hispanic ghettos as if it is quite natural that some people must be segregated.

Living as we are today in a global village as described in Chapter 11, it is not possible to behave toward other cultures as we have in the past. With instant worldwide communication we are constantly in touch with people of many different cultures. Greater awareness through communication of conditions in the United States has put the lie to the "melting pot" ideal we once held. It is now apparent through nationwide communication that after generations of close proximity within one country, the people who came to North America have not become a single culture. We cannot even say we have a single language, even though English predominates. There are, for example more than 15 million people in the United States for whom Spanish is a significant, if not primary, language. That number is predicted to exceed 27 million by 1990. There are many other language groups in this country, as well as some significant dialectical variations among those who can be said to speak English. With world peace hinging upon people's ability to work out differences among widely disparate cultures, we must learn effective intercultural communication.

Conceptually, we will characterize intercultural communication as a process of human symbolic transactions involving the sharing of beliefs, attitudes, values, perceptions, intentions, ideas, and information among people representing different traditions, customs, norms, beliefs, values, thought patterns, or languages. Because anthropologists typically suggest that of all the elements that characterize culture, tools and speech are the most fundamental, and because the use of tools is largely dependent upon the availability of communication, we conclude that communciation behaviors are virtually indistinguishable from culture. In that sense, intercultural communication can be described as that which occurs whenever two or more cultures come in contact. Of course, the outcome of such contact can run along a continuum from disastrous to successful, depending upon the interpretations placed upon it and the communication abilities of those involved.

Our definition of intercultural communication is quite broad. A purist in the study of culture would probably say the definition encompasses transactions among those within a culture, representing some subcultural differences. In other words, they might say we have included *intracultural* communication as well, and that is our intention. The operational definition will make this clear.

Operationally, we will characterize intercultural communication by describing briefly some of the various situations in which we suggest it occurs. These situations will range along a continuum embracing communication among people with relatively few cultural differences at one end to those with profound cultural differences at the other.

Families develop some of their own traditions, customs, beliefs, norms, values, or thought patterns. When those of different families communicate, some elements of intercultural communication occur. Think of the problems of the little boy whose mother was a student of Greek and always referred to the bathroom as the "Beta Rho." The first time he asked his teacher if he could go to the Beta Rho, some intercultural communication was needed. For some, the family is an extraordinarily important group, and decisions outside the home may be influenced by the tradition that family always comes first. Those without such a tradition may need sensitivity to understand the other person.

For good or ill, most people in the world establish significant differences between boys and girls. Our traditions and norms are often clearly distinguished according to sex so that communication between the sexes is often a problem in intercultural communication. Women are becoming increasingly self-assertive and less inclined to accept a subordinate position to men. This is leading to significant changes in the cultural dialog between the sexes and thus it is more clearly an instance of intercultural communication than ever before.

Even within families, there sometimes develops what has been called the generation gap. The children cannot communicate effectively with parents because of the emergence of some culturelike differences. Failure to work out these communication problems often results in serious consequences.

Geographic proximity tends often to create commonalities of a cultural nature. Thus, persons from various locations often find that communication is difficult with those of other places. This can be found within cities as one moves from one neighborhood to another. It can be encountered as people move from place to place within the country. It is clearly faced as people go from nation to nation.

Religion is in many respects the embodiment of culture. So many traditions, customs, norms, beliefs, values, and thought patterns are bound up in the religion to which one subscribes. Thus, communication among those of different religions can be seen as a form of intercultural communication.

Social and economic factors can be found at the base of many subcultures. Although it is difficult to face such issues in a classroom where some children are from groups with high amounts of education, social status, and wealth whereas other children come from families with little education, status, or money, it cannot be overlooked as a problem in intercultural communication. As we have observed in Chapter 1, such differences have been documented as the basis of significant differences in language and communication behavior.

Ethnic differences, by definition, suggest that groups of people have maintained cultural characteristics derived rather directly from a heritage born in another place. Problems between French and English Canadians, or ongoing tensions between Moslem and Jewish citizens of Israel provide dramatic illustrations of cultural differences that go beyond religious distinctions. In the United States the examples are easy to find. Since the earliest settlement of our continent there have been problems in transactions between people of largely white European background and those Native Americans who had settled the area earlier or those from parts of Africa who came as black slaves. As soon as immigrants from the Orient arrived, there were problems of communication between them and those of European, African, or Native American background. And the problems were not solely a function of language differences. Among settlers from Europe there have been difficulties in communication, for example, between those from the British Empire and those from the continent. Strongly held cultural differences among people from France, Germany, Italy, Poland, Russia, and Scandinavia have caused challenges to intercultural communication. And again from the very first settlements, those people who either arrived from

Spain or those who developed Hispanic cultural characteristics by virtue of being occupied by the Spanish have confronted communication problems with peoples from other parts of Europe who moved more easily toward adoption of English influence.

Finally, we can operationally identify intercultural communication as occurring in contacts between people of different nations who maintain not only the various cultural differences already described, but also continue to occupy a different locality and language. Our continued difficulties in diplomatic communication not just with potential enemies but allies as well illustrates this point.

THE TRADITION

Significantly, there is virtually no tradition in the study of intercultural communication. As we look back over the thousands of years of scholarly study of communication, we notice the universal tendency to focus on transactions among people of the same or similar culture. Even in the rhetorical theories that have been so influential on our current thinking, we notice the habit of searching back through theory along cultural lines. For example, we trace theoretical development from ancient Greeks, through ancient Romans, into medieval Europe, renaissance Europe and England where Greek and Roman thought was rediscovered, and finally into modern England and contemporary American thought.

To the ordinary communication historian, the only serious study of our discipline has taken place in locations that have also provided the main lines of our culture: Western and Christian. One might conclude that nothing is to be found in the history of communication theory by examining the work of ancient China, Japan, or Africa, but that would be dead wrong. Little by little, as people have looked, they have learned that before the ancient Greeks built their own scholarly institutions, they studied under African teachers who were well advanced in various scholarly pursuits long before the Greeks. And when scholars have taken the time to do the research, they have found that China and Japan and other nations of the Orient gave attention to the study of communication and developed theories we have simply ignored. The same is true of scholars in various parts of the Middle East.

The conclusion cannot be escaped: even our search for knowledge of communication reflects a cultural bias. Is it any wonder that contemporary theories and research in communication have little to say about communicating from culture to culture? Should we be surprised to learn, for example, that principles of reasoning, persuasion, and decision making that we believed to be universally true turn out to be relevant to our culture and virtually inoperative when we try to reason with, persuade, or make joint decisions with people representing other cultures?

238

Political and anthropological research into interactions among different cultures can be found as early as the 1930s, but work focused directly on intercultural communication did not begin to surface until the 1960s. As with any line of study that sets substantially new directions, there has been slow progress as people have worked to gain the necessary skills to do the work and as resistance to anything new is gradually overcome. Enormous advances in mass communication, explained in Chapter 11, have given a boost to intercultural communication studies. Significant advances can be expected in the next few decades, but at this time we have a thin research base on which to build intercultural communication skills in elementary children. We know only that by the time the children who are now starting their elementary education reach their maturity, they will move into a world intimately involving communication with people of different cultures. They must be made ready for that world.

Common Ways of Thinking about intercultural communication have largely focused on international transactions. A reasonable first step in study was to notice some of the gross differences in communication behavior that could be found by comparing behaviors in different countries. Work was done in Hawaii where populations that still quite closely identified with an origin in another country could be observed. Language differences were a natural point of attention. Nonverbal behaviors, which offer noticeable differences from culture to culture, were a focus of research. We discovered, for example, that people of some cultures stand quite close to one another while talking, whereas Americans maintain greater distance. When talking across cultures, the close talkers moved closer and closer but the distance talkers kept moving away. Some conversations covered the entire width of a room as the conversationalists advanced and retreated from one another. The essence, then, of common ways of thinking about intercultural communication can be explained by the effort to learn the ways in which people of different cultures communicate differently. Acknowledgement of differences served the purpose of providing a basis for us to respect our own cultural communication characteristics.

Learning to respect our own cultural communication characteristics has been important as a contrast to the more traditional view that anyone who deviated from mainstream American English communication behavior was somehow deficient. Black Americans, for example, had been taught that their use of Black English or Ebonics was ignorant and improper. They had been led to believe that their nonverbal communication was strange and inappropriate. They had been taught that their only recourse was to learn to communicate in the same way as white Americans. We now view black-white communication as an instance of intercultural communication and allow children to choose whether or not they wish to learn white communication patterns. We see that white Americans bear an equal burden in learning to communicate with black citizens. Recognition of differences has had a similar impact on people representing Hispanic or Native

American communication patterns, and it has helped people who have only recently come to the United States from other countries.

Current Perspectives show a continued interest in refining our understanding of differences in communication among various cultures, and additionally we have turned to what is called the cultural dialog approach. The cultural dialog perspective is aimed at using our understanding of intercultural communication to develop mutually satisfying ways of transacting among diverse people. Here the focus is more on ways people can overcome differences to achieve effective communication rather than to note the differences per se.

Furthermore, current perspectives reveal an interest in pulling together the emerging body of research in intercultural communication so that more coherent understanding can result and so that future research can be firmly based upon what is known. An example of this effort is the work of M. Asante, E. Newmark, and C. Blake in their edited *Handbook of Intercultural Communication* (Beverly Hills, CA: Sage Publications, 1979).

The View of This Book is that research into intercultural communication is too undeveloped to provide a sound basis for generalization either about communication differences or approaches to a cultural dialog. Although we believe that the research should and will continue to grow, we do not believe that at this time there are grounds for reliable assertion of theory or principle. There is without question, however, a need to alert students to the variety of cultural patterns of communication that exist in this nation and in the world. There is no doubt that with every year that passes the need to communicate effectively with people of other cultures is growing and that the need has indeed existed from the very start of this country. It cannot and should not be ignored further. To that end, we believe that while research continues children should be sensitized to communication differences among cultures and introduced to an understanding of the many different cultures they meet or will meet. They should learn to respect their own and others' cultural communication behaviors and start to develop on their own and with others' help ways of engaging in a cultural dialog.

COMPETENCIES TO BE DEVELOPED

Two *General Exit Competencies* can be identified for skills in intercultural communication. Children should be able to

1. Identify and communicate the essential features of their own culture.
2. Demonstrate sensitivity to and knowledge of other cultures' self-concept.

The start of intercultural communication learning is the recognition that we are all members of a culture. It is easy to talk about culture in terms of other people while holding to the belief that the traditions, norms, customs, values, and thought patterns we engage in are the correct or normal ways all people should behave. We may find it comfortable to read *National Geographic* and notice the quaint behaviors of people in other parts of the world, knowing all the time that if they only had the chance they would readily see that living in the United States, speaking English, making lots of money, and watching television is the way any sensible person would choose to go. But the fact is that people of other cultures find us rather quaint. Sometimes our practices of cultural imperialism lose their quaintness and become downright objectionable. The image of the "ugly American" comes from our efforts to impose our culture on others against their will. The tourist in another country who becomes irate over the fact that "these idiots can't speak English," or complains about the lack of television or hamburgers is much like the diplomat who cannot understand why all countries do not have a political system just like ours. These are the results of the failure to understand that our values are characteristic of our culture and not necessarily the best for all people.

So the first general exit competency aims at helping children recognize their culture as a culture and nothing more. They need to hold themselves up to a mirror and try to see themselves as people from other cultures see them. They need to become sensitive to the essential features of their own culture. They need not be ashamed of their culture; they need not apologize for what they are. On the contrary, they should be proud of their culture and at the same time know that what is appropriate for them may not be for others, and that is just fine.

Turning to the second general competency, the children can become sensitive and knowledgeable of the self-concepts characteristic of other cultures. Remember, "other" means a culture to which a student does not belong. Only when children know their own culture can they successfully look at others. But with that personal knowledge, they can study the ways other cultures are similar or different from an analytical perspective. That is, they can notice differences without feeling either threatened or arrogant. They can, instead, develop appreciation. This can be fun. For example, while dining at the home of an East Indian in Washington, D.C., a left-handed guest started to reach into the bowl of chicken curry with a piece of fried bread, using his left hand. A look of horror crossed his host's face as he said, "I know you are left-handed and your hand is clean, but please use your right hand. Keeping the left hand away from food is too deeply a part of my culture." This led to a discussion of why Indians do not use a left hand for eating (it was traditionally used as toilet paper), and brought up a similarly quaint custom among Americans, the raising of an open right hand in greeting, which was traditionally done to show that a person was not carrying a weapon. Both practices have lost their original purpose, but the culture retains them nevertheless.

241

Beginning Exit Competencies look for children to be able to

1. Talk about how people are different.
2. Observe people of other cultures communicating.
3. Engage in some typical communication forms of other cultures.

The objective of the beginning level is to develop an appreciative awareness of the wonderful ways in which people are different. How boring it would be if we were all alike. The first beginning competency allows children to look at themselves and others more carefully than they have probably done before. Some people go through life almost totally unaware of differences. If you ask some people to describe someone else, they may fail to recall color of eyes, hair, size and shape of head, location of ears, skin coloring, height, weight, and so forth. People differ in appearance, speech, family structure, mannerisms, likes and dislikes, dress, and so on. Now the children can start this sensitivity early in life, and they will build both an appreciation for differences and an ability to perceive them. To notice differences is to realize how very different we all are and how little such differences mean in our relationships.

The second beginning exit competency alerts children to the ways others communicate. They will see differences in languages and build an understanding of the dignity and power of all languages. They will notice the nonverbal communication characteristic of other cultures and become comfortable with such differences.

Finally, at the beginning level, children can try their hand at doing things in the way those from other cultures would do them. They can in this way become at least momentarily a part of another culture. Walking in the shoes of other children can build sensitivity and appreciation.

Intermediate Exit Competencies include the ability to

1. Talk about one's own cultural traditions.
2. Perform literatures of other cultures.
3. Interview people from other cultures.

In the first intermediate exit competency, children move from noticing obvious differences among themselves to concentrating on some of the cultural backgrounds they carry with them. With the popularity of "Roots" the study of genealogy has expanded and many families have traced their ancestors back through many generations. This will help students talk about their cultural heritage. Different cultures have defined sex roles more or less strictly. For example, in the home of the East Indian mentioned earlier, a guest was present for a full week without ever meeting the man's wife and only saw her once. She stayed in other parts of the home, cooked the meals but stayed in the kitchen while the

242

men ate and the daughter served them. This is in contrast with other cultures where men and women share the cooking and other domestic work equally.

Holidays are a particularly easy place to locate some cultural traditions. Although many Americans have put aside some of their more obvious cultural characteristics to adopt those of modern America, they will often retain them during special days. Here the cultures of other countries and various religions may be continued. Be careful here to remember that there is no correct way to celebrate a holiday. The goal is for children to report on how they and their families celebrate, even though they may have made some changes from the strict practices of the culture from which they come. Families representing two or more cultural backgrounds may have combined their traditions for adaptation to their family.

Like holidays, literature is a medium for the retention and display of cultural traditions, norms, and ways of thinking. By performing the literatures of various cultures, children can become more familiar in a pleasant and instructional way with the differences they represent. Sometimes we are surprised to learn that a story or poem so familiar to us in the United States was originated long ago in another country. By calling attention to this fact, teachers can alert children to notice the ways in which the literature is typical of another culture. As with walking in another's shoes, assuming the roles of other people in other cultures is an excellent way to build understanding.

Now, the intermediate students are ready to try their hand at some intercultural communication through a series of interviews. They will have learned in their study of person-to-person communication that one needs to know a good deal about the person to be interviewed well in advance of the interview. A balance must be struck between being so cautious about offending the person as to ask virtually nothing and being so curious as to ask insensitive and hurtful questions. By talking about the culture of the person to be interviewed in advance, children can develop a pretty good sense of what can be discussed. Healthy and honest curiosity should be encouraged. We recall the day a little blonde, blue-eyed white girl who had never met a black person was introduced to a brown-eyed, black-haired black girl who had never met a white person. They were hesitant at first, then they played together some, and finally they were touching each other's skin and hair, asking about favorite toys, and learning the marvelous ways in which they were alike and different. With these preliminaries over, they could really begin to communicate and did so for the entire summer.

Advanced Exit Competencies ask children to develop the ability to

1. Present an oral report on significant people from their own and other cultures.
2. Present an oral report on significant artifacts of their own and other cultures.
3. Present a reasoned statement on the importance of another culture.

4. Talk about the ways they as individuals respect or appreciate their own culture and the ways they do not.

The United States and the Soviet Union carry on a humorous contest to claim credit for major discoveries and innovations. It would seem as if it is a part of cultural imperialism to boast that all the great contributions to the world have been made by a person from one's own culture. Of course, close examination reveals that there have been significant people doing important things in every culture. Cultural chauvinism spawns mean jokes about the stupidity or uselessness of people from other cultures. We sometimes disregard or discredit the contributions of people from cultures other than our own. If we come from a position of believing the person we are talking with is part of a culture of stupid, lazy, and useless people, we are unlikely to carry on fruitful communication. Such a posture has caused havoc in diplomatic, military, business, educational, and religious conferences.

Thus, the objective of the first advanced exit competency is to have the students engage in communication centered around the significant people of another culture as well as their own. From this experience, children should learn to take a balanced view of intercultural communication. They will build pride in their own culture by noticing how many important people have come from it. They will develop respect for other cultures as they learn of the important people representing them.

Important to this assignment is the fact that students are not to compare and contrast the people discussed. They should not get into a contest on the basis of, "Our important people are more significant than yours." Rather, they should come to the conclusion that it is amazing to find significant people everywhere, throughout the cultures.

In the second advanced competency, awareness is continued into a study of artifacts from various cultures. By artifact we mean any object or work of human beings, including tools, works of art, architecture, music, clothing, means of transportation, food, and the like. Again, the purpose is not to compare and contrast. Rather, students should broaden their knowledge of the works of different cultures and in so doing increase their appreciation and understanding of the ways in which cultures and artifacts are related. Recall that two fundamental elements of culture identified by anthropologists are tools and speech. In this competency, we broaden the concept of tools to include characteristic artifacts.

With a good background of understanding of cultures and a recognition of the nature of their own culture, students can move to the third advanced competency and prepare and present a reasoned statement on the importance of another culture. They will need to review the work they have done on reasoning. Moving beyond identification and appreciation, they will need to develop lines of reasoning and find supporting materials for their claims about the importance of a culture. As they do this reasoning, a number of communication skills will be developed. Of course, they will obtain practice in doing reasoning. Beyond that, they will become an advocate for a culture and in that way identify themselves with it and build a knowledge of how one might communicate with people of that culture. And they will need to grow in their appreciation of the ways of thinking typical of that culture, which will lead to a more sophisticated knowledge of the variations of reasoning patterns from culture to culture. Only through such understanding of different ways of thinking and valuing can children advance in their ability for intercultural communication.

The fourth advanced exit competency is particularly important. Students will take time to think critically about their own culture and focus on its strengths and weaknesses. Talking in this analytical way will help children overcome the widespread tendency to engage in cultural chauvinism and imperialism. If they have a reasonable sense of the ways in which they appreciate their own culture, they will have the self-confidence and pride similar to that we observed as necessary to person-to-person communication. But if they take time as well to call attention to the ways in which they are not so appreciative of their culture, they will have the humility needed to deal effectively with someone who is different without trying to denigrate or evangelize him. They can, in other words, engage in meaningful interpersonal communication.

Because so much of the school experience is devoted to teaching cultural pride and patriotism in a rather unthinking or jingoistic way, a period of thoughtful criticism of our own culture is important. This does not demand constant negativism. It merely suggests a look at our own culture with a constructively critical eye. There will be pressure to do this cautiously lest someone seem unpatriotic, but antipatriotism is not our goal. Indeed, the best patriotism is that which is thoughtful and well founded and not that which is unthinking acceptance of our country, right or wrong. Until children can think critically of their own culture they cannot openly communicate with people of other cultures. This means awareness of both good and bad, and as adults these students may take the lead in making positive changes in their culture.

Sample Exericses for Intercultural Communication

The following lessons are suggestions for exercises in intercultural communication. They are planned to provide ideas for teaching the general and each specific level competencies.

The purpose of this chapter is to help children learn about and respect cultural differences. The United States continues to be a polyglot of people from various cultures. Being able to communicate with and about other cultures can be developed effectively when such instruction is begun in elementary schools. The legislation to encourage bilingual education is desirable and has provided definite steps in recognition of other cultures, but the concepts in this chapter extend beyond that paradigm. Intercultural communication is not accomplished by separating those who are different to communicate only among themselves. We are planning communicative interaction within every classroom. The perspective of mutual supportiveness has been encouraged throughout the book and has been particularly emphasized in person-to-person and group communication. This view of mutual supportiveness is the essence of the theoretical basis of this chapter.

The concept of cultural differences includes those living in other countries, those who have newly arrived, those who retain cultural identification and have been an integral part of the United States for many years. However, the concept is further expanded to include differences not often considered such as women as a cultural group, migrant workers, or persons from a different section of the United States. The cultural considerations should be broad. Some schools will provide a considerable mixture in the population of the school. Other school populations may seem culturally homogeneous, but that does not preclude the possibility or the necessity of intercultural study. The problems of intercultural cooperation and understanding are readily recognized in culturally mixed schools so these lessons become immediately viable. The danger is that a school that seems culturally homogeneous remains uninterested in such a study. Nearly every school will have male and female students and that is a cultural difference. Furthermore, the schools that seem culturally isolated are probably in a greater need for broad intercultural exposure. Those students may well be the ones to become adults with the least knowledge of any other culture and consequently may remain judgmental and bigoted in this isolation. The expression that ignorance builds contempt seems appropriate to this situation.

Likewise many children and adults have little real understanding and appreciation of their own culture. Although it is assumed that the children have been inundated in their own culture and the previous lessons in this book will probably be mainly oriented toward the communication culture of that group, now is the time to have children recognize cultural specific differences. So as the teacher approaches these lessons, the concern for understanding and accepting differences is, of course, interwoven with a development of pride in one's own culture. The essence of the mutual supportiveness proposed is a respect for one's own culture and a respect for those who are different. Supportiveness means knowing about others. Supportiveness means avoiding judgments of right and wrong or good and bad.

The following lessons are suggestions and in order to offer a variety, one cultural group or another may be mentioned. The teacher should not feel bound by the plan for a certain cultural group. The lessons can be modified to fit the students in the class. The teacher can take advantage of lessons concentrating on differences that children in the class can really communicate because they are living them. However, it is intended that a wide exposure to cultural differences should be offered, whether or not the class provides a representation of those differences. The lessons suggest a range. The teacher should be free to expand cultural experiences as far as possible. Some of the lessons can be repeated many times with a variation in culture each time. Other lessons demonstrate such variation in one assignment.

BEGINNING LEVEL EXERCISES

1. The class participates as a group to discuss how families are different. This lesson is designed to emphasize differences in family structure including traditional families, single-parent family, single child, various siblings, adopted children, other relatives. The teacher might find a book by N. Simon, *All Kinds of Families* (Chicago: Albert Whitman and Company, 1979) useful to read aloud to the children preceeding this discussion. This lesson accompanies social studies.

2. The class talks about different colors that are a part of people. Different colors of skin, hair, and eyes are the most apparent. This lesson accompanies art and may be augmented by having each child draw her face with colors and the face of someone else with different colors.

3. This class learns to sing "Black and White." This lesson is for music and is a natural follow-up to the preceeding lesson. A book by D. Arkin, *Black and White* (Los Angeles: The Ward Ritchie Press, 1968) illustrates and explains the song. In the back of this book are the words and music to "Black and White" (words by D. Arkin; music by E. Robinson). This song, sold by Shawnee Press, Inc., Delaware Water Gap, Pa., was popular a few years ago.

4. The class listens to and discusses stories about people from other cultures. The lesson is planned for the teacher to read aloud to the students. Libraries have numerous books of this nature, and several are suggested here as examples. L. Bannon, *The Gift of Hawaii* (Chicago: Albert Whitman and Company, 1961) is a story children enjoy about a child from a state that many children know little about. J. Fraser, *Las Posadas* (Flagstaff, AZ: Northland Press, 1963) is a Christmas story about children in a Hispanic culture with delightful pictures and a simple explanation of some Christmas traditions.

5. The class listens to and discusses stories about people communicating across cultures. A book by Bettina, *Cocolo Comes to America* (New York: Harper & Row, Publishers, 1949) tells a fantasy story about a little boy and his donkey who leave a war-torn country to come to America. A book by L. Bannon, *Manuela's Birthday* (New York: Albert Whitman and Company, 1939) is a Junior Literary Guild publication about a Mexican child, her culture, and her American friends. Another type of cross-culture communication is that between those of cultural differences in the United States. Differences in language interpretation that are possible are cleverly told in the Amelia Bedelia stories such as P. Parish, *Thank you, Amelia Bedelia* (Pleasantville, NY: Reader's Digest Services, Inc., 1974).

6. The class listens to a short story in another language. For example, if most of the students speak American English, the collection of stories translated in Spanish as a part of Pequeños Libros De Oro series provides a contrast to the

247

same story in American English. For example, Walt Disney's Donald Duck's Toy Sailboat, "Chips Ahoy" is translated by A. N. Bedord, *El Pato Donald Y Su Barquito De Vela* (Mexico 1, D. F.: Organizacíon Editorial Navaro, S. A., 1967). For these little Golden Books that are reproductions of Disney stories, the rights are reserved by Walt Disney Productions, so if the teacher is having trouble locating the books, that is a likely source. Any of the Pequeños Libros De Oro provide the same pictures and story as those originally told in American English. Familiar stories are *Bambi, Mary Poppins,* and *Pollyanna.* The children can hear the story first in English and then follow the same story pictures as they listen to the Spanish. The idea is to help children hear another language and to understand that different languages can communicate the same message. If any children are Spanish speaking, they will delight in the sharing of the language.

7. The class listens to people from different cultures communicate the same message. In this lesson, the teacher needs to locate as many speakers of another language as possible. These people come to the class or are students in the class. Each person is given the same role to play. For example, tell a child it's time to go to bed, get a child to eat dinner, and so on. The class listens to the different languages. Don't forget that Black English should also be included.

8. The class sings songs from other cultures. Christmas is an excellent time for this. The lesson provides an interesting variation for music class. There are Spanish songs and Japanese songs. There are some records available that have songs specifically for children. For example, a record presented by Webley Edwards with Nina Kealiwahamana's Chorus and Haunani called *Merry Hawaiian Christmas* (Los Angeles: Capitol Records) has such songs as Kani Kani Pele (Jingle Bells) in Hawaiian and Mele Kalikimaka (Merry Christmas) with the title phrase in Hawaiian and the remainder in English, and the Hawaiian version of the Twelve Days of Christmas in English. This time of year coincides with the Jewish celebration of Hanukkah. Delightful songs compiled or written by a teacher, Jackie Cytrynbaum, and sung by Fran Avni for Hanukkah and other times is *Latkes and Hamentashen* (Cote St. Luc., Quebec: Lemonstone Records). We have observed children enjoying both of these records and wanting to learn the songs.

9. The class plays games from different cultures. For example, dreidel games in M. Drucker, *Hanukkah* (New York: Holiday House, 1980), or nut games in M. Drucker, *Passover* (New York: Holiday House, 1981) are a fun way for children to become acquainted with the Jewish culture. Another favorite is the piñata, a traditional game of Mexican people. Children love to wear a blindfold and take turns trying to break the piñata with a stick.

10. Each child completes a craft project that represents another culture. Children can make African masks, Eskimo masks, Shaman (Native American) medicine sticks, Japanese fish kites, Philippine wind chimes, and many others. This lesson is designed to combine with art class. The teacher can make his own designs, or S & S Arts and Crafts, Colchester, Connecticut, 06415 produces a vari-

ety of kits for such projects. Any such project should be accompanied by a discussion of the item and its place in the culture.

INTERMEDIATE LEVEL EXERCISES

1. Each child presents a speech on his family origins. The teacher needs to have a class discussion before the speech so that students can consider what countries their ancestors came from as well as where the family has lived. Then each child should have time to discuss these factors with his parents before he gives the speech. In line with the intermediate exit competencies in public speaking, the speech will be a minute or two long.

2. Each child presents a speech on the roles of men and women in her family. Before this speech, the class should discuss traditional role perceptions and changing or shifting role images. It is creative for children to consider roles of the female and male in grandparents, in parents, and in young children. In some families, roles will be traditional and clearly defined for all generations, in some roles will be changing, and in others roles will not be clearly defined. The broader the differences, the more cultural learning will occur. This lesson accompanies social studies.

3. Small groups discuss how holidays are celebrated in their families. The teacher may want to give groups different times of the year such as fall, winter, and spring. It's possible to have a range of students who can discuss Thanksgiving, Christmas, Hanukkah, Chinese New Year, Valentine's, St. Patrick's Day, Easter, Passover, May Day festivals, and so on. If such a range does not occur, the teacher can expand the cultural experience by having the class discuss other holidays after the group discussions.

4. The class presents poems from other countries by choric speaking. Poems from around the world that are excellent for choric speaking are available in M. McGuire, *Finger and Action Rhymes*, The Instructor Handbook Series (Dansville, NY: F. A. Owen Publishing Company, 1959).

5. The class retells stories from another culture. A book by P. Nabokov, Ed., *Native American Testimony* (New York: Thomas Y. Crowell Company, 1978) contains stories from the various Native American tribes about Indian and white relations. These stories will have to be read aloud by the teacher because the reading is too difficult for the level, but the children will enjoy retelling the stories. They provide additional understanding about the period through many perspectives of Native Americans that will be a valuable adjunct to history classes.

6. Small groups use puppets to retell stories from various countries. The children have had experience with this exercise in performances of literature (Chapter 10). Now the concept will be expanded to include recognition of the country of origin. Examples are any of the *Grimm's Fairy Tales* from Germany, sections of *Heidi* from Switzerland, any of the Hans Christian Anderson fairy tales from

249

Denmark, *Pinocchio* from Italy, Beatrix Potter's Peter Rabbit series from England, and so on.

7. Small groups read character parts in a play representing a specific culture. This lesson is planned for reading groups. The important aspect of this assignment is to broaden cultural experiences by play reading. Stewart has written short plays for children based on oral stories from widely diverse African folklore. These plays are in original cultural context that provide a basis for current Black history. See J. T. Stewart, "Five Plays for Children," *Black Lines*, **2**, 1: 42-68, 1971). *Black Lines* has been produced quarterly by the Department of Black Studies at the University of Pittsburgh.

8. The class performs a dance from another country. It is important to discuss the cultural meaning and place for this dance before learning it. A short dance and song for children is "La Fiesta" written about the Santa Fe fiesta, that is a three-day traditional celebration of old New Mexico. This dance and song are explained in detail in M. Martínez Raizizun, *Niños Allegres* (Dallas: Banks Upshaw and Company, 1942), p. 74-77.

9. The class interviews adults from various countries. The teacher should invite a variety of adults from other countries to come talk to the class about their customs. The children should be prepared in advance to ask questions in interview fashion. They have learned these skills in Chapter 4, but some review before the person comes will be helpful.

10. Small groups interview small groups of young persons from another culture within the United States. The teacher will need to take care that this is done with the respect for self-definition learned in person-to-person communication and with courteous group interaction learned in group communication. Frequently, this classroom or other classes in the school will provide a variety of cultural backgrounds. The important aspect to remember is that the small groups talking with each other are not from the same cultural background. Thus, the teacher might have three Black children talk to three white children, or three Native Americans talk to three Black children, or two white children talk to two Puerto Ricans, or four city children talk to four children from rural areas. Each of these groups should interview each other. Similarities are as important to note as differences.

ADVANCE LEVEL EXERCISES

1. Each student presents a speech about a person from his own culture who has made an important contribution. Most students will know about someone they'd like to report on immediately. To help students who are searching for a person or a source, a book by J. Silverman, *An Index to Young Reader's Collective Biographies* (New York: R. R. Bowker Company, 1970) provides an alphabetical listing of professions such as acting, medicine, or science, and by areas such as peace, skating, or women. Under each heading is a grouping by ethnic

origin such as Puerto Rican, South African, or Japanese. Under each of these headings is a list of people and a reference as to where the biographies are contained.

2. Each student presents a speech on a person from another culture who has made an important contribution. The speech must be researched and information based on some outside authority. Such a speech can be combined with a written report, but the information must be shared orally.

3. Small groups present an oral report to the class on foods of their own culture. This activity is suggested for small groups because it is hoped that each student will bring a food for the class to sample. If a small group combines efforts, the class would have an interesting array of food to taste. However, if a single child represents a cultural group, that child should be able to present alone. This activity combines with a health or a social studies class, and it would be wise to pick a different day for each group report. Children need to understand that everyday foods are as culturally important as special holiday foods. Thus, grits for a southern child, matzah ball dumplings for a Jewish child, anise cookies for a child with German ancestry, and bread from an adobe oven for a Pueblo child are all important cultural foods to experience.

4. Each student gives a speech on art of a different culture than her own. This speech is intended to cover art from ceramics to paintings to wood carving. Students should use outside authority—encyclopedias—if necessary. This assignment accompanies art class, of course.

5. Each student gives a speech on the current way of life in another culture. The *National Geographic* is an excellent source for such material. This lesson is planned to combine with social studies.

6. Small groups compare the music of two cultures. This lesson accompanies music. The lesson will be more effective if children from different cultures can be combined in one group so that the music of the culture the children represent can be covered. The cultural comparisons may be across countries or within a country.

7. Each student gives a speech about a number of people in a culture different from her own to support a reasoned statement about the contributions of the people of that culture. This lesson will take careful research and planning and may accompany a writing assignment.

8. Each student gives a speech about the influence of a certain culture on the American way of life. These speeches should include a broad range of topics such as words in the language, art, music, foods, and sex role identification.

9. Each student gives a speech about things he likes about his own culture. This is the time for each student to think about pride and good feelings. Such a speech is based strictly on individual opinion. There is no right or wrong and all opinions should be supported.

10. Small groups make an outline of things they do not like about their own culture. The outline should be organized by listing the items under the categories

251

of things that have shown little or no change and things that are changing. Then the group decides which of these items they think can be changed and which they think can not. If the group varies in opinion on the last two decisions, differences of opinion should be indicated. Students should understand that listing things you do not like about a culture does not mean rejection of a culture anymore than stating things you do not like about yourself means rejection of self. After the groups have completed the outlines, the group should give an oral report to the class.

Bibliography

Andersen, H. C. *His Classic Fairy Tales.* (E. Haugaard, trans.). London: Victor Gollancz Ltd., 1976.

Arbuthnot, M. H. *Time for Poetry.* Glenview, IL: Scott, Foresman and Company, 1951.

Arkin, D. *Black and White.* Los Angeles: The Ward Ritchie Press, 1968.

Asante, M., E. Newmark, and C. Balke. *Handbook of intercultural communication.* (3rd ed.). Beverly Hills, CA: Sage Publications, 1979.

Bannon, L. *Manuela's Birthday.* Chicago: Albert Whitman and Company, 1939.

Bannon, L. *The Gift of Hawaii.* Chicago: Albert Whitman and Company, 1961.

Barker, L. *Listening Behavior.* Englewood Cliffs, NJ: Prentice-Hall, Inc., 1971.

Bentley, R. H., and S. D. Crawford. *Black Language Reader.* Glenview, IL: Scott, Foresman and Company, 1973.

Berenstain, S., and J. Berenstain. *The Bike Lesson.* New York: Random House, Inc., 1964.

Berenstain, S., and J. Berenstain. *The Bears' Vacation.* New York: Random House, Inc., 1968.

Bettina. *Cocolo Comes to America.* New York: Harper & Row, Publishers, 1949.

Bormann, E., and N. Bormann. *Effective Small Group Communication.* Minneapolis: Burgess Publishing Company, 1972.

Boyer, E. L., and A. Levine. *A Quest for Common Learning.* Washington, D.C.: The Carnegie Foundation for the Advancement of Teaching, 1981.

Bryant, J., and D. Anderson. (Eds.). *Watching TV, Understanding TV.: Research on Children's Attention and Comprehension.* New York: Academic Press, Inc., 1983.

Chomsky, N. *Syntactic Structures.* Netherlands: Mouton and Company, 1957.

Clark, H. H., and E. V. Clark. *Psychology and Language.* New York: Harcourt Brace Jovanovich, Inc., 1977.

Cronkhite, G. *Communication and Awareness.* Menlo Park, CA: Cummings Publishing Company, 1976.

Cytrynbaum, J. *Latkes and Hamentashen.* Cote St. Luc., Quebec, Canada: Lemonstone Records.

Dahl, R. *Charlie and the Great Glass Elevator.* New York: Alfred A. Knopf, Inc., 1972.

Dale, P. S. *Language Development.* New York: Holt, Rinehart and Winston, 1976.

DeVito, J. *The Interpersonal Communication Book.* New York: Harper & Row, Publishers, 1980.

Denes, P., and E. Pinson. *The Speech Chain.* Bell Telephone Laboratories, 1963.

Disney, W. *Chips ahoy.* (A. N. Bedord, trans.). "El Pato Donald Y Su Barquito De Vela." Mexico l, D. F.: Organizacion Editorial Navaro, S. A., 1967.

Drucker, M. *Hannukkah.* New York: Holiday House, 1980.

Drucker, M. *Passover.* New York: Holiday House, 1981.

Dublinske, S. "New opportunity for speech-language pathologists and audiologists." *Asha* (1979), **21**, 12: 998–1002.

Eastman, P. D. *Are You My Mother?* New York: Beginner Books, Inc., 1960.

Edwards, E., N. Kealiwahamana (Chorus), and Haunani. *Merry Hawaiian Christmas.* Los Angeles: Capitol Records.

Elementary and Secondary Education Act of 1965, Title II. Public Law 95–561 (20 USC), November 1, 1978.

Fernandez, T. L. (Ed.). *Oral Interpretation and the Teaching of English.* Champaign, IL: National Council of Teachers of English, 1969.

Fishbein, M., and I. Ajzen. *Belief, Attitude, Intention and Behavior.* Reading, MA: Addison-Wesley Publishing Co., Inc., 1975.

Fisher, B. A. *Small Group Decision Making* (2nd ed.). New York: McGraw-Hill Book Company, 1980.

Fraser, J. *Las Posadas.* Flagstaff, AZ: Northland Press, 1963.

Galvin, K. M., and B. J. Brommel. *Family Communication.* Glenview, IL: Scott, Foresman and Company, 1982.

Gersoni-Stavn, D. *Sexism and Youth.* New York: R. R. Bowker Company, 1974.

Gouran, D. *Making Decisions in Groups.* Glenview, IL: Scott, Foresman and Company, 1982.

Gruenberg, S. M. *Let's Read a Story.* Garden City, NY: Garden City Books, 1957.

Hinde, R. A. (Ed.). *Non-verbal Communication.* London: Cambridge University Press, 1975.

Janis, I. L., and L. Mann. *Decision Making.* New York: The Free Press, 1977.

Johnson, W. and D. Moeller (Eds.) *Speech Handicapped School Children* (3rd ed.). New York: Harper & Row, Publishers, 1967.

Knapp, M. L. *Nonverbal Communication in Human Interaction.* New York: Holt, Rinehart and Winston, 1978.

Lair, J. *I Ain't Much, Baby – But I'm All I've Got.* New York: Doubleday & Company, Inc., 1972.

Lair, J. *I Ain't Well – But I Sure Am Better.* New York: Doubleday & Company, Inc., 1975.

Lakoff, R. *Language and Woman's Place.* New York: Harper & Row, Publishers, 1975.

Larson, C. *Persuasion, Reception and Responsibility.* Belmont, CA: Wadsworth Publishing Co., Inc., 1979.

Lindfors, J. W. *Children's Language and Learning.* Englewood Cliffs, NJ: Prentice-Hall, Inc., 1980.

McCandless, G. A., and D. E. Rose. "Evoked cortical responses to stimulus change." *Journal of Speech and Hearing Research* (1970), **13**, 3:624–634.

McCaslin, N. *Creative Drama in the Classroom.* New York: Longman, Inc., 1980.

McCroskey, J., and V. Richmond. *The Quiet Ones: Shyness and Communication Apprehension.* Dubuque, Iowa: Gorsuch Scarisbrick Publishers, 1980.

McGuire, M. *Finger and Action Rhymes.* Dansville, NY: F. A. Owen Publishing Company, 1959.

McKuen, R. *Listen to the Warm.* New York: Random House, Inc., 1967.

Mecham, M. J., and M. L. Willbrand. *Language Disorders in Children.* Springfield, IL: Charles C Thomas, Publishers, 1979.

Menyuk, P. *The Acquisition and Development of Language.* Englewood Cliffs, NJ: Prentice-Hall, Inc., 1971.

Milne, A. A. *Now We Are Six.* New York: E. P. Dutton & Co., Inc., 1961.

Milne, A. A. *When We Were Very Young.* New York: E. P. Dutton & Co. Inc., 1961.

Miller, G., and M. Steinberg. *Between People.* Chicago: Science Research Associates, Inc., 1975.

Mudd, C., and M. Sillars. *Speech Content and Communication* (4th ed.). New York: Harper & Row, Publishers, 1979.

Nabokov, P. (Ed.). *Native American Testimony.* New York: Thomas Y. Crowell Company, 1978.

Nix, G. W. *Mainstream Education for Hearing Impaired Children and Youth.* New York: Grune & Stratton, Inc., 1976.

Odum, E. P. *Ecology: The Link Between the Natural and the Social Sciences.* New York: Holt, Rinehart and Winston, 1975.

Pace, R. W., B. Peterson, and T. Radcliffe. *Communicating Interpersonally.* Columbus, Ohio: Charles E. Merrill Publishing Company, 1973.

Parish, P. *Thank you, Amelia Bedelia.* Pleasantville, NY: Reader's Digest Services, Inc., 1974.

Pellowski, A. *The World of Storytelling.* New York: R. R. Bowker Company, 1977.

Ploghoft, M., and J. Anderson. *Education for the Television Age.* Springfield, IL: Charles C Thomas, Publisher, 1981.

Ploghoft, M., and J. Anderson. *Teaching Critical Television Viewing Skills.* Springfield, IL: Charles C Thomas, Publisher 1982.

Raizizun, M. R. *Niños Allegres.* Dallas, Texas: Banks Upshaw and Company, 1942.

Rees, N. S. "Breaking Out of the Centrifuge." *Asha* (1979), **21**, 12: 992–997.

Rieke, R., and M. Sillars. *Argumentation and the Decision-making Process.* New York: John Wiley & Sons, Inc., 1975.

Rieke, R. "Adult reasons in supplication: Nondebaters vs. debaters; nontraditional vs. traditional." In G. Ziegelmueller and J. Rhodes (Eds.). *Dimension of Argument.* Annandale, VA: Speech Communication Association, 1981, 579–594.

Rosenfeld, L., and J. Civikly. *With Words Unspoken: The Nonverbal Experience.* New York: Holt, Rinehart and Winston, 1976.

Ross, L. *Hand puppets.* New York: Lothrop, Lee & Shepard Company, 1969.

Seeger, P. *Birds, Beasts, Bugs and Little Fishes.* New York: Folkways Records and Service Corporation, 1958; distributed by Folkways/Scholastic Records, Englewood Cliffs, NJ.

Silverman, J. *An Index to Young Reader's Collective Biographies.* New York: R. R. Bowker Company, 1970.

Simon, N. *All Kinds of Families.* Chicago: Albert Whitman and Company, 1979.

Smith, M. R. *Plays.* New York: Henry Z. Walck, Incorporated, 1961.

Smith, M. *Persuasion and Human Action.* Belmont, CA: Wadsworth Publishing Co., Inc., 1982.

Steinfatt, T. *Human Communication: An Interpersonal Introduction.* Indianapolis, IN: The Bobbs-Merrill Co., Inc., 1977.

Stewart, J. T. "Five Plays for Children." *Black lines.* Department of Black Studies: University of Pittsburgh (1971), **2**, 1: 42–68.

Stoller, P. (Ed.). *Black American English.* New York: Dell Publishing, Co., Inc., 1975.

Suess, Dr. *Green Eggs and Ham.* New York: Beginner Books, Inc., 1960.

Toulmin, S., R. Rieke, and A. Janik. *An Introduction to Reasoning.* New York: Macmillan Publishing Co., Inc., 1979.

Travis, L. E. (Ed.). *Handbook of Speech Pathology and Audiology.* New York: Appleton-Century-Crofts, 1971.

Wagner, G., M. Hosier, and M. Blackman. *Listening Games.* Darien, CT: Teachers Publishing Corporation, 1970.

Wartella, E. "Children and television: The development of the child's understanding of the medium." In **G. Wilhoit and H. DeBock,** *Mass Communication Review Yearbook* (Vol. 1). Beverly Hills, CA: Sage Publications, Inc., 1980.

Willbrand, M. L. "Language acquisition: The continuing development from nine to ten years." In **F. Ingemann (Ed.),** *Mid-American Linguistics Papers.* Lawrence, Kansas: Linguistics Department, University of Kansas, 1976, 555–576.

Willbrand, M. L. "Child reason in supplicatory discourse: Rules to be refined." In **C. Ziegelmueller and J. Rhodes (Eds.),** *Dimensions of Argument.* Annandale, VA: Speech Communication Association, 1981.

Williams, R., and W. Wolfram. *Differences vs. Social Dialects.* Rockville, MD: American Speech-Language-Hearing Association, 1977.

Woods, B. S. *Children and Communication* (2nd ed.). Englewood Cliffs, NJ: Prentice-Hall, Inc., 1981.

Index

Index

Index